ENGLISH / ARABIC

انجليزي / عربي

OXFORD PICTURE DICTIONARY

THIRD EDITION

Jayme Adelson-Goldstein
Norma Shapiro

ACKNOWLEDGMENTS

Translated by: Techno-Graphics & Translations, Inc.
Illustrations by: Lori Anzalone: 13, 70-71, 76-77; Joe "Fearless" Arenella/Will
Sumpter: 196; Argosy Publishing: 66-67 (call-outs), 108-109, 114-115
(call-outs), 156, 196, 205, 206-207, 215; Barbara Bastian: 4, 15, 208; Philip
Batini/AA Reps: 50; Thomas Bayley/Sparks Literary Agency: 162; Sally Bensusen:
217, 220; Peter Bollinger/Shannon Associates: 14-15; Higgens Bond/Anita Grien:
232; Molly Borman-Pullman: 118, 119; Mark Duffin: 7, 37, 61, 94, 238, 239, 240,
241; Jim Fanning/Ravenhill Represents: 80-81; Mike Gardner: 10, 12, 17, 22, 134,
116-117, 145-146, 179, 225, 234-235; Garth Glazier/AA Reps: 106, 111, 120; Dennis
Godfrey/Mike Wepplo: 214; Steve Graham: 126-127, 230; Julia Green/Mendola Art:
231; Glenn Gustafson: 9, 27, 48, 76, 100, 101, 119, 134-135, 138, 159, 165, 197;
Barbara Harmon: 218-219, 221; Ben Hasler/NB Illustration: 94-95, 101, 174, 188,
198-199; Betsy Hayes: 136, 140, 143; Matthew Holmes: 75; Stewart Holmes/
Illustration Ltd.: 204; Janos Jantner/Beehive Illustration: 5, 13, 82-83, 124-125,
132-133, 152-153, 166-167, 168, 169, 174, 175, 182-183, 192, 193; Ken Joudrey/
Munro Campagna: 52, 68-69, 187; Bob Kaganich/Deborah Wolfe: 40-41, 123;
Steve Karp: 237, 238; Mike Kasun/Munro Campagna: 224; Graham Kennedy: 27;
Marcel Laverdet/AA Reps: 23; Jeffrey Lindberg: 33, 42-43, 92-93, 135, 164-165,
176-177, 186; Dennis Lyall/Artworks: 208; Chris Lyons/Lindgren & Smith: 203;
Alan Male/Artworks: 216, 217; Jeff Mangiat/Mendola Art: 53, 54, 55, 56, 57, 58, 59,
66-67; Adrian Mateescu/The Studio: 200-201, 238-239; Karen Minot: 28-29; Paul
Mirocha/The Wiley Group: 206, 222-223; Peter Miserendino/P.T. Pie Illustrations:
208; Lee Montgomery/Illustration Ltd.: 4; OUP Design: 20-21; Roger Motzkus: 235;
Laurie O'Keefe: 112, 222-223; Daniel O'Leary/Illustration Ltd.: 8-9, 26, 34-35, 78, 137,
138-139, 244; Vilma Ortiz-Dillon: 16, 20-21, 60, 98-99, 100, 217; Terry Pazcko: 46-47,
148-149, 156, 194, 233; David Preiss/Munro Campagna: 5; Pronk & Associates: 204-
205; Tony Randazzo/AA Reps: 160, 240-241; Mike Renwick/Creative Eye: 128-129;
Mark Riedy/Scott Hull Associates: 48-49, 79, 142, 157; Jon Rogers/AA Reps: 114; Jeff
Sanson/Schumann & Co.: 84-85, 246-247; Ben Shannon/Magnet Reps: 11, 64-65, 90,
91, 96, 97, 121, 147, 170-171, 172-173, 180-181, 245; Reed Sprunger/Jae Wagoner
Artists Rep.: 18-19, 238-239; Studio Liddell/AA Reps: 27; Angelo Tillary: 108-109;
Samuel Velasco/5W Infographics: 10, 11, 12, 13, 15, 48, 49, 80-81 (design), 110, 112,
113, 138, 143, 146, 156, 159, 210, 211, 212-213; Ralph Voltz/Deborah Wolfe: 50-51,
130-131, 144, 158, 163, 185, 190, 191, 207 (top left), 215 (bot. left), 242-243; Jeff Wack/
Mendola Art: 24, 25, 86-87, 102-103, 136-137, 237; Brad Walker: 104-105, 154-155,
161, 226-227; Wendy Wassink: 112-113; John White/The Neis Group: 209;
Eric Wilkerson: 32, 140; Simon Williams/Illustration Ltd.: 2-3, 6-7, 30-31, 36, 38-39,
44-45, 72-73, 141, 178, 184; Lee Woodgate/Eye Candy Illustration: 228-229; Andy Zito:
62-23; Craig Zuckerman: 14, 88-89, 114-115, 122-123, 206-207.

Cover Design: Studio Montage
Chapter icons designed by Anna Sereda

Commissioned studio photography for Oxford University Press done by Dennis
Kitchen Studio: 37, 61, 72, 73, 74, 75, 95, 96, 100, 189, 194, 195, 232.

*The publishers would like to thank the following for their kind permission to reproduce
photographs:* 20-21 (calender) dikobraziy/Shutterstock; 26 (penny) rsooll/
Shutterstock, (nickel) B.A.E. Inc./Alamy Stock Photo, (dime) Brandon Laufenberg/
istockphoto, (quarter) magicoven/Shutterstock, (half dollar) mattesimages/
Shutterstock, (Sacagawea dollar) Ted Foxx/Alamy Stock Photo; 31 (flowers photo)
Digital Vision/OUP; 48 (apartment interior) Sindre Ellingsen/Alamy Stock Photo;
61 (oven) gerenme/Getty Images, (table) Stefano Mattia/Getty Images, (window)
nexus 7/Shutterstock, (shower) FOTOGRAFIA INC./Getty Images, (dishes) Nika Art/
Shutterstock, (kitchen counter/sink) zstock/Shutterstock; 94 (watch) WM_idea/
Shutterstock; 98 (cotton texture) Saksan Maneechay/123RF, (linen texture)
daizuoxin/Shutterstock, (wool texture) riekephotos/Shutterstock, (cashmere texture)
ovb64/Shutterstock, (silk texture) Anteromite/Shutterstock, (leather texture) Victor
Newman/Shutterstock; 99 (denim) Jaroslaw Grudzinski/123RF, (suede) KPG Payless2/
Shutterstock, (lace) Nataliia Melnychuk/Shutterstock, (velvet) Neirfy/Shutterstock,
(corduroy) Eldad Carin/Shutterstock, (nylon) B Calkins/Shutterstock; 141 (Pentagon)
Don S. Montgomery/Corbis; 208 (civil rights) PhotoQuest/Contributor/Getty
Images, (Civil War) Philip Gould/Corbis, (Great Depression) Rolls Press/Popperfoto/
Contributor/Getty Images, (Industrial Revolution) Mary Evans Picture Library/
Alamy Stock Photo, (Jazz Age) Underwood & Underwood/Underwood & Underwood/
Corbis, (Progressivism) AS400 DB/Corbis, (Reconstruction) MPI/Stringer/Getty
Images, (Spage Age) AFP/Stringer/Getty Images, (Western Expansion) AS400 DB/
Corbis, (WWI) ASSOCIATED PRESS, (WWII) Joe Rosenthal/Associated Press; 212
(thoughtful woman) Di Studio/Shutterstock; 213 (people in uniform) Rawpixel.com/
Shutterstock; 232 (tent) Hurst Photo/Shutterstock, (campfire) wolv/Getty Images;
244 (flute) cowardlion/Shutterstock, (clarinet) Vereshchagin Dmitry/Shutterstock,
(oboe) Matthias G. Ziegler/Shutterstock, (bassoon) Rodrigo Blanco/Getty Images,
(saxophone) Ocean/OUP, (violin) Ocean/OUP, (cello) Stockbyte/Getty Images, (bass)
the palms/Shutterstock, (guitar) Photodisc/OUP, (trombone) seen/Shutterstock,
(trumpet) Photodisc/OUP, (tuba) Ingram/OUP, (French horn) Venus Angel/
Shutterstock, (piano) liangpv/Getty Images, (xylophone) Yuri Kevhiev/Alamy Stock
Photo, (drums) lem/Shutterstock, (tambourine) Vereshchagin Dmitry/Shutterstock,
(keyboard) George Peters/Getty Images, (accordion) Stockbyte/Getty Images, (organ)
C Squared Studios/Getty Images, (harmonica) Goran Bogicevic/Alamy Stock Photo.

*The publisher would like to thank the following for their permission to reproduce
copyrighted material:*
127, 136–137: USPS Corporate Signature, Priority Mail, Express Mail, Media Mail,
Certified Mail, Ready Post, Airmail, Parcel Post, Letter Carrier Uniform, Postal Clerk
Uniform, Flag and Statue of Liberty, Postmark, Post Office Box, Automated Postal
Center, Parcel Drop Box, Round Top Collection Mailbox are trademarks of the United
States Postal Service and are used with permission. Flag and Statue of Liberty © 2006
United States Postal Service. All Rights Reserved. Used with Permission. 156:
MetroCard and the logo "MTA" are registered trademarks of the Metropolitan
Transportation Authority. Used with permission. 156: Metro token image courtesy of
LA Metro ©2016 LACMTA. 156: Amtrak ticket image courtesy of Amtrak. 174: National
Center for O*NET Development. O*NET OnLine. Retrieved November 23, 2015, from
https://www.onetonline.org/. 191: Microsoft Word® is a registered trademark of
Microsoft Corporation. Screen shot reprinted with permission from Microsoft
Corporation. 191: Microsoft Excel® is a registered trademark of Microsoft Corporation.
Screen shot reprinted with permission from Microsoft Corporation. 191: Microsoft
PowerPoint® is a registered trademark of Microsoft Corporation. Screen shot reprinted
with permission from Microsoft Corporation. 210: Microsoft icons reprinted by
permission of Microsoft.

This third edition of the Oxford Picture
Dictionary is lovingly dedicated to the
memory of Norma Shapiro.

Her ideas, her pictures, and her stories
continue to teach, inspire, and delight.

Acknowledgments

The publisher and authors would like to acknowledge the following individuals for their invaluable feedback during the development of this program:

Nawal Abbas, Lawrence Tech University, MI; **Dr. Macarena Aguilar**, Cy-Fair College, TX; **Penny Aldrich**, Durham Technical Community College, NC; **Deanna Allen**, Round Rock ISD, TX; **Angela Andrade-Holt**, Western Nevada College, NV; **Joseph F. Anselme**, Atlantic Technical Center, FL; **Stacy Antonopoulos**, Monterey Trail High School, CA; **Carol Antunano**, The English Center, FL; **Irma Arencibia**, Thomas A. Edison School, NJ; **Stephanie Austin**, CBET Program Moreland School District, CA; **Suzi Austin**, Alexandria City Public School Adult Program, FL; **Carol Beebe**, Niagara University, NY; **Patricia S. Bell**, Lake Technical Center, FL; **Derick Bonewitz**, College of Lake County, IL; **Emily Box**, Granite Peaks Learning Center, UT; **Diana Brady-Herndon**, Western Nevada College, NV; **Jim Brice**, San Diego Community College District, CA; **Theresa Bries**, Black Hawk College, IL; **Diane Brody**, St. John's Lutheran Church; **Mindy Bruton**, Abilene ISD, TX; **Caralyn Bushey**, Montgomery College TESOL Certificate Program, MD; **Phil Cackley**, Arlington Education and Employment Program (REEP), VA; **Frieda Caldwell**, Metropolitan Adult Education Program, CA; **Anne Marie Caney**, Chula Vista Adult School, CA; **Lynda Cannon**, Ashland Community and Technical College, KY; **Lenore Cardoza**, Brockton Public Schools Adult Learning Center, MA; **Victor Castellanos**, Covina Public Library, CA; **Marjorie Castillo-Farquhar**, Community Action/Austin Community College, TX; **Patricia Castro**, Harvest English Institute, NJ; **Paohui Lola Chen**, Milpitas Adult School, CA; **Alicia Chicas**, The Hayward Center for Education & Careers (Adult School), CA; **Michelle Chuang**, East Side Adult Education, CA; **Lori Cisneros**, Atlantic Vo-Tech, FL; **Joyce Clapp**, Hayward Adult School, CA; **Stacy Clark**, Arlington Education and Employment Program (REEP), VA; **Melissa Cohen**, Literacy New Jersey - Middlesex Programs, NJ; **Dave Coleman**, LAUSD District, CA; **Edith Cowper**, Wake Technical Community College, NC; **Leslie Crawley**, The Literacy Center; **Kelli Crow**, City College San Francisco Civic Center, CA; **Nancy B. Crowell**, Southside Programs for Adults in Continuing Education, VA; **Doroti da Cunha**, Hialeah-Miami Lakes Adult Education Center, FL; **Brenda Custodio**, Ohio State University, OH; **Dory Dannettell**, Community Educational Outreach, CO; **Paula Da Silva-Michelin**, La Guardia Community College, NY; **Peggy Datz**, Berkeley Adult School, CA; **Cynthia L. Davies**, Humble I.S.D., TX; **Christopher Davis**, Overfelt Adult Center, CA; **Laura De Anda**, Margaret Aylward Center, CA; **Tyler Degener**, Drexel University College of Medicine, PA; **Jacquelyn Delaney**; **Mariana De Luca**, Charlotte-Mecklenburg Public Schools, NC; **Georgia Deming**, Johnson County Community College (JCAE), KS; **Beverly De Nicola**, Capistrano Unified School District, CA; **Irena Dewey**, US Conversation; **Frances Tornabene De Sousa**, Pittsburg Adult Education Center, CA; **Matthew Diamond**, The University of Texas at Austin, TX; **Beatriz Diaz**, Miami-Dade County Public Schools, FL; **Druci Diaz**, Program Advisor, Adult & Career Services Center Hillsborough County Public Schools, FL; **Natalya Dollar**, North Orange County Community College District, CA; **Marion Donahue**, San Dieguito Adult School, CA; **Nick Doorn**, International Education Services, MI; **Mercedes Douglass**, Seminole Community College, FL; **Joan Dundas**, Brock University, ON (Canada); **Jennifer Eick-Magán**, Prairie State College, IL; **Jenny Elliott**, Montgomery College, MD; **Paige Endo**, Mt. Diablo Adult Education, CA; **Megan Ernst**, Glendale Community College, CA; **Elizabeth Escobar**, Robert Waters School, NJ; **Joanne Everett**, Dave Thomas Education Center, FL; **Jennifer Fadden**, Arlington Education and Employment Program (REEP), VA; **Cinzia Fagan**, East Side Adult Education, CA; **Jacqui Farrell**, Literacy Volunteers on the Green, CT; **Ross Feldberg**, Tufts University, MA; **Sharyl Ferguson**, Montwood High School, TX; **Emily Finch**, FCI Englewood, CO; **Dr. Robert Finkelstein**, Willammette Dental, OR; **Janet Fischer**, Lawrence Public Schools - Adult Learning Center, MA; **Dr. Monica Fishkin**, University of Central Florida, FL; **Jan Foley**, Wilbur Wright College - City Colleges of Chicago, IL; **Tim Foster**, Silver Valley Adult Education Center, CA; **Nancy Frampton**, Reedley College, CA; **Lynn A. Freeland**, San Dieguito Union High School District, CA; **Sally A. Fox**, East Side Adult Education, CA; **Cathy Gample**, San Leandro Adult School, CA; **Hillary Gardner**, Center for Immigrant Education and Training, NY; **Elizabeth Gibb**, Castro Valley Adult and Career Education, CA; **Martha C. Giffen**, Alhambra Unified School District, CA; **Elgy Gillespie**, City College San Francisco, CA; **Lisa Marcelle Gimbel**, Community Learning Center, MA; **Jill Gluck**, Hollywood Community Adult School, CA; **Richard Goldberg**, Asian American Civic Association, MA; **Carolyn Grebe**, The Hayward Center for Education & Careers (Adult School), CA; **Carolyn Grimaldi**, LaGuardia Community College, NY; **Cassell Gross**, Intercambio, CO; **William Gruenholz**, USD Adult School, CA; **Sandra G. Gutierrez**, Hialeah-Miami Lakes Adult Education Center, FL; **Conte Gúzman-Hoffman**, Triton College, IL; **William J. Hall**, M.D. FACP/FRSM (UK); **Amanda Harllee**, Palmetto High School, FL; **Kathy Harris**, Portland State University, OR; **Kay Hartley**, Fairfield-Suisun Adult School, CA; **Melissa Hassmanm**, Northwest Iowa Community College, IA; **Mercedes Hearn**, Tampa Bay Technical Center, FL; **Christyann Helm**, Carlos Rosario International Public Charter School, WA; **Suzanne Hibbs**, East Side Adult Education, CA; **Lindsey Himanga**, Hiawatha Valley ABE, MN; **Marvina Hooper**, Lake Technical College, FL; **Jill A. Horohoe**, Arizona State University, AZ; **Roxana Hurtado**, Miami Dade Adult, FL; **Rachel Johnson**, MORE Multicultural School for Empowerment, MN; **Randy Johnson**, Hartford Public Library, CT; **Sherry Joseph**, Miami Dade College, FL; **Elaine Kanakis**, The Hayward Center for Education and Careers, CA; **Phoebe Kang**, Brock University, ON (Canada); **Mary Kaufman**, Brewster Technical Center, FL; **Jeanne Kearsley**, City College San Francisco Chinatown, CA; **Sallyann Kovacs**, The Hayward Center for Education & Careers (Adult School), CA; **Jennifer Latzgo**, Lehigh Carbon Community College, PA; **Sandy Lawler**, East Side Adult Education, CA; **Xinhua Li**, City College of San Francisco, CA; **Renata Lima**, TALK International School of Languages, FL; **Luz M. Lopez**, Sweetwater Union High School District, CA; **Osmara Lopez**, Bronx Community College, NY; **Heather Lozano**, North Lake College, TX; **Marcia Luptak**, Elgin Community College, IL; **Betty Lynch**, Arlington Education and Employment Program (REEP), VA; **Matthew Lyter**, Tri-County OIC, PA; **Meera Madan**, REID Park Elementary School, NC; **Julia Maffei**, Texas State IEP, TX; **Ivanna Mann Thrower**, Charlotte Mecklenburg Schools, NC; **Anna Mariani**, The English Center (TLC Online), FL; **Michael R. Mason**, Loma Vista Adult Center, CA; **Terry Masters**, American Schools of Water for Ishmael, OH; **Debbie Matsumura**, CBET Program Moreland School District, CA; **Holley Mayville**, Charlotte Mecklenburg Schools, NC; **Margaret McCabe**, United Methodist Cooperative Ministries, FL; **David McCarthy**, Stony Brook University, NY; **Todd McDonald**, Hillsborough Adult Education, FL; **Nancy A. McKeand**, ESL Consultant, LA; **Rebecca L. McLain**, Gaston College, NC; **John M. Mendoza**, Redlands Adult School, CA; **Nancy Meredith**, Austin Community College, TX; **Marcia Merriman**, Community College of Baltimore County, MD; **Bet Messmer**, Santa Clara Adult Education Center, CA; **Holly Milkowart**, Johnson County Community College, KS; **Jose Montes**, The English Center M-DCPS, FL; **Elaine Moore**, Escondido Adult School, CA; **Lisa Munoz**, Metropolitan Education District, CA; **Mary Murphy-Clagett**, Sweetwater Union High School District, CA; **Jonetta Myles**, Rockdale County High School, GA; **Marwan Nabi**, Troy High School, CA; **Dale Nave**, San Marcos Academy, TX; **Dr. Christine L. Nelsen**, Salvation Army Community Center, FL; **Michael W. Newman**, Arlington Education and Employment Program (REEP), VA; **Virginia Nicolai**, Colorado Mountain College, CO; **Phoebe Nip**, East Side Adult Education, CA; **Rehana Nusrat**, Huntington Beach Adult School, CA; **Cindy Oakley-Paulik**, Embry-Riddle Aeronautical University, FL; **Judy O'Louglin**, CATESOL, CA; **Brigitte Oltmanns**, Triton College, IL; **Nora Onayemi**, Montgomery College, MD; **Lorena Orozco**, Catholic Charities, NM; **Allison Pickering**, Escondido Adult School, CA; **Odette Petrini**, Huron High School, MI; **Eileen Purcell**, Clatsop Community College, OR; **Teresa Reen**, East Side Adult Education, CA; **Jean Renoll**, Fairfax County Public Schools – ACE, VA; **Carmen Rivera-Diaz**, Calvary Church; **Fatiana Roganova**, The Hayward Center for Education & Careers (Adult School), CA; **Rosa Rojo**, Escondido Adult School, CA; **Lorraine Romero**, Houston Community College, TX; **Phoebe B. Rouse**, Louisiana State University, LA; **Dr. Susan Rouse**, Southern Wesleyan University, SC; **Blair Roy**, Chapman Education Center, CA; **Sharon Saylors**, The Hayward Center for Education & Careers (Adult School), CA; **Margret Schaefer**, Round Rock ISD, TX; **Arlene R. Schwartz**, Broward Community Schools, FL; **Geraldyne Blake Scott**, Truman College, IL; **Sharada Sekar**, Antioch High School Freshman Academy, TN; **Denise Selleck**, City College San Francisco Civic Center, CA; **Dr. Cheryl J. Serrano**, Lynn University, FL; **Janet Setzekorn**, United Methodist Cooperative Ministries, FL; **Terry Shearer**, EDUCALL Learning Services, TX; **Rob Sheppard**, Quincy Asian Resources, Inc., MA; **Dr. Ira M. Sheskin**, University of Miami, FL; **Glenda Sinks**, Community College of Denver, CO; **Elisabeth Sklar**, Township High School District 113, IL; **Jacqueline Sport**, LBWCC Luverne Center, AL; **Kathryn Spyksma**, The Hayward Center for Education & Careers (Adult School), CA; **Linda Steele**, Black Hawk College, IL; **Robert Stein**, BEGIN Managed Programs, NY; **Martin Steinman**, Canal Alliance, CA; **Ruth Sutton**, Township High School District 113, IL; **Alisa Takeuchi**, Chapman Education Center, CA; **Grace Tanaka**, Santa Ana College School of Continuing Education, CA; **Annalisa Te**, East Side Adult Education, CA; **Oscar Tellez**, Daley College, IL; **Fotini Terzi**, University of Texas at Austin, TX; **Geneva Tesh**, Houston Community College, TX; **Maiko Tomizawa**, D.D.S., NY; **Don Torluemke**, South Bay Adult School, CA; **Francisco Torres**, Olive-Harvey College, IL; **Shawn Tran**, East Side Adult Education, CA; **Serife Turkol**, Literacy Council of Northern Virginia, VA; **Cristina Urena**, CC/Tech Center, FL; **Maliheh Vafai**, East Side Adult Education, CA; **Charlotte van Londen**, MCAEL, MD; **Tara Vasquez**, Robert Waters School, NJ; **Nina Velasco**, Naples Language Center, FL; **Colin Ward**, Lone Star College-North Harris, TX; **Theresa Warren**, East Side Adult Center, CA; **Lucie Gates Watel**, Truman College, IL; **Wendy Weil**, Arnold Middle School, TX; **Patricia Weist**, TALK International School of Languages, FL; **Dr. Carole Lynn Weisz**, Lehman College, NY; **Desiree Wesner**, Robert Waters School, NJ; **David Wexler**, Napa Valley Adult School, CA; **Kathy Wierseman**, Black Hawk College, IL; **Cynthia Wiseman**, Borough of Manhattan Community College, NY; **Nancy Whitmire**, University of Arkansas Community College at Batesville, AR; **Debbie Cullinane Wood**, Lincoln Education Center, CA; **Banu Yaylali**, Miami Dade College, FL; **Hongyan Zheng**, Milpitas Adult Education, Milpitas, CA; **Yelena Zimon**, Fremont Adult and Continuing Education, CA; **Arlene Zivitz**, ESOL Teacher, FL

Table of Contents قائمة المحتويات

4. Food الطعام

5. Clothing الملابس

6. Health الصحة

7. Community المجتمع

Contents المحتويات

Welcome to the OPD THIRD EDITION

The Oxford Picture Dictionary Third Edition provides unparalleled support for vocabulary teaching and language development.

- Illustrations present over 4,000 English words and phrases within **meaningful, real-life contexts**.
- **New and expanded topics** including job search, career planning, and digital literacy prepare students to meet the requirements of their daily lives.
- Updated activities prepare students for **work, academic study, and citizenship**.
- **Oxford 3000 vocabulary** ensures students learn the most useful and important words.

Color coding and icons make it easy to navigate through *OPD*.

Vibrant illustrations and rich contexts improve vocabulary acquisition.

Subtopics present the words in easy-to-learn "chunks."

Revised practice activities help students develop academic and workforce skills.

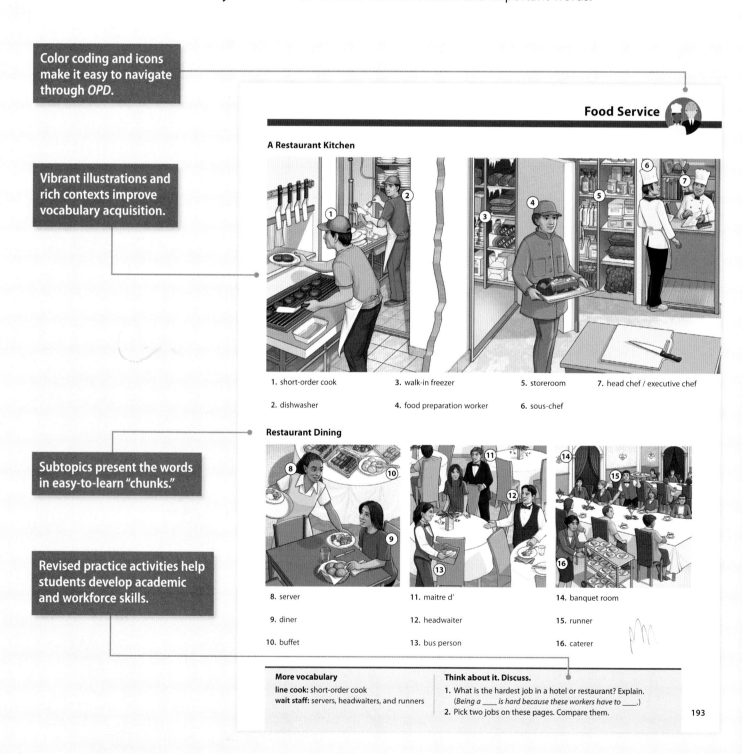

Food Service

A Restaurant Kitchen

1. short-order cook
2. dishwasher
3. walk-in freezer
4. food preparation worker
5. storeroom
6. sous-chef
7. head chef / executive chef

Restaurant Dining

8. server
9. diner
10. buffet
11. maitre d'
12. headwaiter
13. bus person
14. banquet room
15. runner
16. caterer

More vocabulary

line cook: short-order cook
wait staff: servers, headwaiters, and runners

Think about it. Discuss.

1. What is the hardest job in a hotel or restaurant? Explain.
   (*Being a _____ is hard because these workers have to _____.*)
2. Pick two jobs on these pages. Compare them.

193

Intro pages open each unit with key vocabulary related to the unit theme. Clear, engaging artwork promotes questions, conversations, and writing practice for all levels.

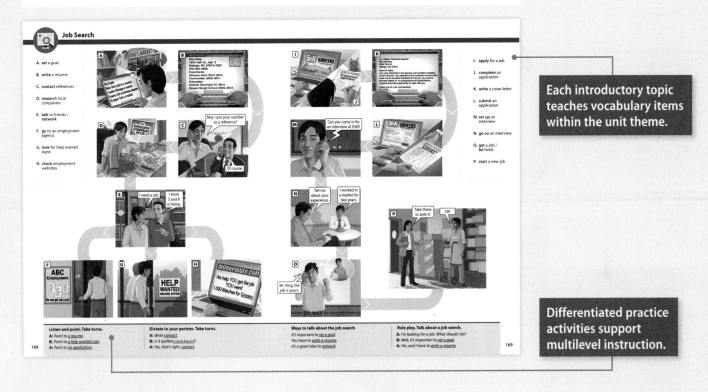

Each introductory topic teaches vocabulary items within the unit theme.

Differentiated practice activities support multilevel instruction.

Story pages close each unit with a lively scene for reviewing vocabulary and teaching additional language. Meanwhile, rich visual contexts recycle words from the unit.

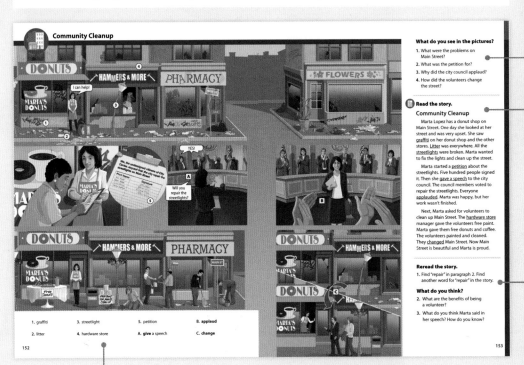

Pre-reading questions build students' previewing and predicting skills.

End-of-unit readings promote literacy skills.

Post-reading questions support critical thinking and textual analysis skills.

The word list previews key vocabulary that students will encounter in the story.

Meeting and Greeting اللقاء والتحية

A. **Say**, "Hello."
قل، "أهلا وسهلا."

B. **Ask**, "How are you?"
اسأل، "كيف حالك؟"

C. **Respond**, "Fine, thanks."
جاوب، "بخير، شكرا."

D. **Introduce** yourself.
عرّف / قدّم نفسك.

E. **Smile**.
ابتسم.

F. **Hug**.
احضني.

G. **Wave**.
سلّمي وودعي ملوّحة بيدك.

Hello.

How are you?

Fine, thanks.

Hi.

Hi. I'm Tom.

Hi, Tom. I'm Ana.

Tell your partner what to do. Take turns.

1. *Say, "Hello."*   4. *Shake hands.*
2. *Bow.*   5. *Wave.*
3. *Smile.*   6. *Say, "Goodbye."*

Dictate to your partner. Take turns.

A: *Write smile.*
B: *Is it spelled s-m-i-l-e?*
A: *Yes, that's right.*

2

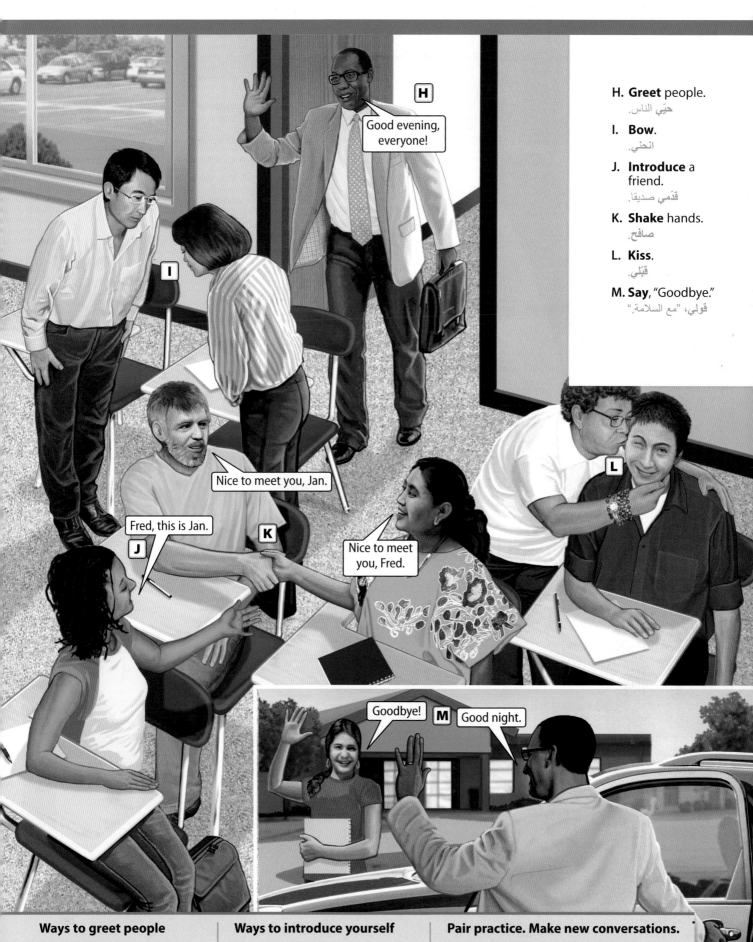

A. **Say** your name.
قل اسمك.

B. **Spell** your name.
تهجّ اسمك.

C. **Print** your name.
اكتب اسمك.

D. **Type** your name.
اكتب اسمك باستخدام لوحة المفاتيح.

E. **Sign** your name.
وقع اسمك.

Filling Out a Form ملء استمارة

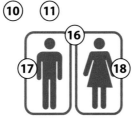

(813) 555-1234
(813) 555-5005
(813) 555-8976

COSTA RICA
San Jose

SOCIAL SECURITY
262-00-0000
CARLOS R. SOTO
Carlos R. Soto

Carlos R. Soto

---

https://www.registrationformOPD.com

1. name الاسم:

2. first name
الاسم الأول

3. middle initial
الحرف الأول من اسمك الأوسط

4. last name
اسم العائلة

address العنوان

5. street address
عنوان المنزل

6. apartment number
رقم الشقة

7. city
المدينة

8. state
الولاية

9. ZIP code
الرمز البريدي

work phone هاتف العمل   **additional numbers** أرقام إضافية

10. area code
رمز / مفتاح المنطقة

11. phone number
رقم الهاتف / التليفون

12. home phone
هاتف المنزل

13. cell phone
الهاتف المحمول (النقال)

14. date of birth (DOB)
تاريخ الميلاد

15. place of birth (POB)
مكان الميلاد

16. gender
الجنس / النوع

17. male
ذكر

18. female
أنثى

19. Social Security number
رقم بطاقة الضمان الاجتماعي

20. signature
التوقيع

Pair practice. Make new conversations.

A: *My first name is* <u>Carlos</u>.
B: *Please spell* <u>Carlos</u> *for me.*
A: <u>C-a-r-l-o-s</u>.

Internet Research: popular names

Type "SSA, top names 100 years" in the search bar.
Report: *According to the SSA list,* <u>James</u> *is the number* <u>1</u> *male name.*

Campus حرم المدرسة

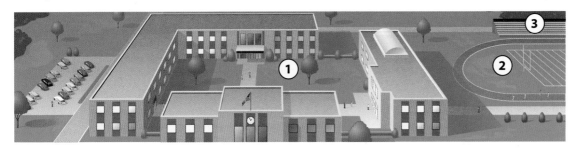

1. **quad**
   فناء مربع
2. **field**
   أرض الملعب
3. **bleachers**
   مدرجات
4. **principal**
   ناظر المدرسة / مدير المدرسة
5. **assistant principal**
   مساعد الناظر
6. **counselor**
   مشرف
7. **classroom**
   حجرة صف / فصل دراسي
8. **teacher**
   معلّم
9. **restrooms**
   دورات مياه
10. **hallway**
    رواق
11. **locker**
    خزانة
12. **main office**
    مكتب الإدارة
13. **clerk**
    موظف / ة ك
14. **cafeteria**
    كافتيريا
15. **computer lab**
    مختبر حواسيب
16. **teacher's aide**
    معاون معلّم
17. **library**
    مكتبة
18. **auditorium**
    قاعة محاضرات
19. **gym**
    جمنازيوم (قاعة الجمباز)
20. **coach**
    مدرِّب
21. **track**
    مضمار الجزئي / السباق

Administrators الإداريون

Around Campus حول الحرم

More vocabulary

Students do not pay to attend a **public school**.

Students pay to attend a **private school**.

A church, mosque, or temple school is a **parochial school**.

Use contractions and talk about the pictures.

He **is** = He**'s** She **is** = She**'s**

It **is** = It**'s** They **are** = They**'re**

He's a teacher. *They're* students.

1. whiteboard
سبورة بيضاء

2. screen
شاشة للعرض

3. chalkboard
سبورة

4. teacher / instructor
معلمة / مدرّسة

5. LCD projector
آلة عرض على شاشة بيلور سائل
(ال سي دي)

6. student
طالبة

7. desk
مكتب

8. headphones
سماعات رأس

A. Raise your hand.
ارفع يدك.

B. Talk to the teacher.
تكلّم مع المعلم.

C. Listen to a recording.
استمع إلى تسجيل.

D. Stand up.
قف.

E. Write on the board.
اكتب على السبورة.

F. Sit down. / Take a seat.
اجلس. / اقعد على مقعد.

G. Open your book.
افتح كتابك.

H. Close your book.
أغلق كتابك.

I. Pick up the pencil.
التقط القلم الرصاص.

J. Put down the pencil.
أنزل القلم الرصاص.

6

9. clock	**11.** chair	**13.** alphabet	**15.** computer
ساعة	كرسي	حروف الهجاء	حاسوب
10. bookcase	**12.** map	**14.** bulletin board	**16.** document camera
رف للكتب	خريطة	لوحة منشورات	مصورة (كاميرا) وثائق

17. dry erase marker	**21.** (pencil) eraser	**25.** highlighter	**29.** notebook paper
قلم جاف للتخطيط قابل للمحو	ممحاة (القلم الرصاص)	قلم تمييز / قلم فسفوري	ورق الدوسيه
18. chalk	**22.** pen	**26.** textbook	**30.** spiral notebook
طباشير	قلم حبر	كتاب مدرسي	كراسة بسلك
19. eraser	**23.** pencil sharpener	**27.** workbook	**31.** learner's dictionary
ممحاة	مبراة الأقلام الرصاص	كراسة تمارين	معجم المتعلم
20. pencil	**24.** permanent marker	**28.** 3-ring binder / notebook	**32.** picture dictionary
قلم رصاص	قلم تخطيط غير قابل للمحو	دوسيه ذو 3 حلقات / كراسة	معجم مصوَّر

Grammar Point: *there is / there are*

There **is a** map.   There **are 15** students.

Describe your classroom. Take turns.

A: *There's a clock.*   B: *There are 20 cha___*

Survey your class. Record the responses.

Learning New Words تعلّم كلمات جديدة

A. Look up the word.
ابحثي عن كلمة في المعجم.

B. Read the definition.
اقرني التعريف.

group
組

C. Translate the word.
ترجمي الكلمة.

D. Check the pronunciation.
راجعي النطق.

E. Copy the word.
انسخي الكلمة.

F. Draw a picture.
ارسمي صورة.

Working with Your Classmates العمل مع زملائك في الصف

Are cell phones a problem in class?

Yes, they are.

G. Discuss a problem.
ناقشي مشكلة.

Put them away.

Turn them off.

Silence them.

H. Brainstorm solutions / answers.
تبادلوا الأفكار للوصول إلى حلول / أجوبة.

I. Work in a group.
اعمل في مجموعة.

Here.

J. Help a classmate.
ساعدي أحد زملائك في الصف.

Working with a Partner العمل مع رفيق

Can I share your book?

Sure.

K. A

They are students.

N. Dictate a sentence.
قومي بإملاء جملة.

Following Directions إتباع الإرشادات

O. **Fill in** the blank.
املأ الخانة (الفراغ).

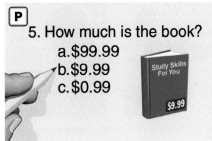

P. **Choose** the correct answer.
اختر الجواب الصحيح.

Q. **Circle** the answer.
ضع دائرة حول الجواب.

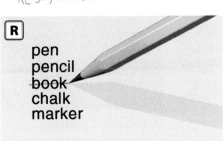

R. **Cross out** the word.
اشطب الكلمة.

S. **Underline** the word.
ضع خطا تحت الكلمة.

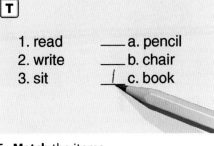

T. **Match** the items.
طابق الكلمات مع بعضها.

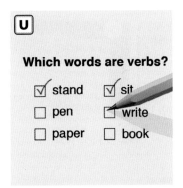

U. **Check** the correct boxes.
ضع علامة صح في المربعات الصحيحة.

V. **Label** the picture.
سمِّ الصورة.

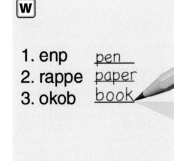

W. **Unscramble** the words.
حل الكلمات.

X. **Put** the sentences in order.
ضع الجمل في ترتيبها الصحيح.

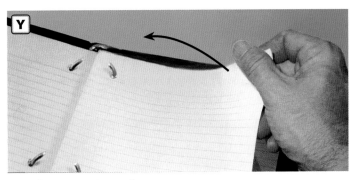

Y. **Take out** a piece of paper.
أخرج قطعة ورق.

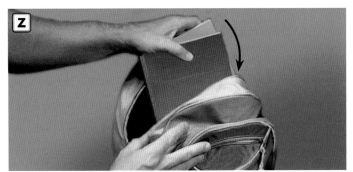

Z. **Put away** your books.
ضع كتبك في مكانها المعتاد.

Survey your class. Record the responses.

1. Do you prefer to study in a group or with a partner?
2. Do you prefer to translate or draw new words?
Report: *Most of us… Some of us…*

Identify Tom's problem. Brainstorm solutions.

Tom wants to study English with a group.
He wants to ask his classmates, "Do you want to study together?" but he's embarrassed.

Ways to Succeed وسائل النجاح

A. **Set** goals.
حدد أهدافا.

B. **Participate** in class.
شارك في الصف.

C. **Take** notes.
دوّن مذكرات.

D. **Study** at home.
ذاكر في المنزل.

E. **Pass** a test.
انجح في امتحان.

F. **Ask** for help. / **Request** help.
اسأل عن المساعدة. / اطلب المساعدة.

G. **Make** progress.
حقق تقدما.

H. **Get** good grades.
أحرز درجات جيدة.

Taking a Test التقدم لامتحان

 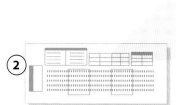

1. test booklet
كتيب الامتحان

2. answer sheet
ورقة الإجابات

3. score
النتيجة

Numeric Grade	Standard Grade	Grade Point Average
90%-100%	A	4.0
80%-89%	B	3.0
70%-79%	C	2.0
60%-69%	D	1.0
Less than 60%	F (Fail)	0.0

4. grades
علامات مدرسية

5. online test
امتحان على الإنترنت

I. **Clear off** your desk.
أزل كل شيء من على مكتبك.

J. **Work** on your own.
اعمل بمفردك.

K. **Bubble in** the answer.
أدخل جوابك بتسويد الدائرة الصحيحة.

L. **Check** your work.
راجع عملك.

M. **Erase** the mistake.
امحُ الخطأ.

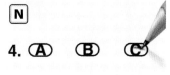

N. **Correct** the mistake.
صحّح الخطأ.

O. **Hand in** your test.
سلِم ورقة امتحانك.

P. **Submit** your test.
قدّم ورقة امتحانك.

A Day at School

A. **Walk** to class.
تمشِ إلى الصف.

B. **Run** to class.
اركض إلى الصف.

C. **Enter** the room.
ادخل الحجرة.

D. **Turn on** the lights.
أشعل الأنوار.

E. **Lift / Pick up** the books.
ارفع / التقط الكتب.

F. **Carry** the books.
احمل الكتب.

G. **Deliver** the books.
سلّم الكتب.

H. **Take** a break.
خذ استراحة.

I. **Eat**.
كُلي.

J. **Drink**.
اشرب.

K. **Buy** a snack.
اشترِ وجبة خفيفة.

L. **Have** a conversation.
اجرِ محادثة.

M. **Go back** to class.
ارجعوا إلى الصف.

N. **Throw away** trash.
ألقِ القمامة.

O. **Leave** the room.
اتركوا الحجرة.

P. **Turn off** the lights.
أطفئ الأنوار.

Grammar Point: present continuous

Use **be** + <u>verb</u> + **ing** (What **are** they **do**ing?)
He **is walk**ing. They **are talk**ing.
Note: run—run**n**ing leave—leav**ing** [e]

Look at the pictures. Describe what is happening.

A: They are <u>entering the room</u>.
B: He is <u>walking</u>.
C: She's <u>eating</u>.

A. **start** a conversation
ابدئي الحديث

B. **make** small talk
دردش

A — Tell me about your job. — It's great. I fix computers.

B — It's a nice day. — Yes, it is.
BUS STOP

C. **compliment** someone
جاملي شخصا

D. **thank** someone
اشكر شخصا

E. **offer** something
اعرض شيئا

F. **refuse** an offer
ارفض عرضا

C — That's a great sweater!
D — Thank you.

E — Here. Use my pen. F — No, thanks. I have one.

G. **apologize**
اعتذر

H. **accept** an apology
تقبّل الاعتذار

I. **invite** someone
ادعي أحدا

J. **accept** an invitation
اقبلي دعوة

K. **decline** an invitation
ارفض دعوة

G — I'm sorry. H — That's OK.

I — Please come to my party. J — OK! I'll be there. K — Sorry. I can't.

L. **agree**
وافق

M. **disagree**
اختلف

N. **explain** something
اشرح شيئا

O. **check** your understanding
تأكدي من فهمك للكلام

L — This is a great book! — Yes, it is.
M — This book is great, too. — No, it isn't.

N — The air filter is there. O — Here?

More vocabulary

accept a compliment: to thank someone for a compliment

make a request: to ask for something

Pair practice. Follow the directions.

1. Start a conversation with your partner.
2. Make small talk with your partner.
3. Compliment each other.

12

Temperature درجة الحرارة

1. Fahrenheit
   درجة فهرنهايت
2. Celsius
   درجة مئوية
3. hot
   حار
4. warm
   دافئ
5. cool
   معتدل
6. cold
   بارد
7. freezing
   بارد جدا
8. degrees
   درجات

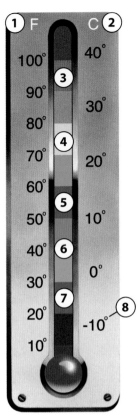

A Weather Map خريطة أحوال الطقس

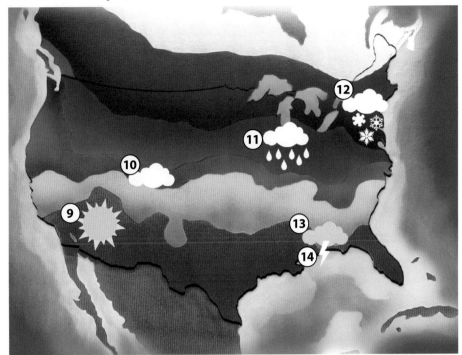

9. sunny / clear
   مشمس / صافي
10. cloudy
    غائم
11. rain
    مطر / أمطار
12. snow
    ثلج / ثلوج
13. thunderstorm
    عاصفة رعدية
14. lightning
    برق

Weather Conditions أحوال الطقس

15. heat wave
    موجة حارة
16. smoggy
    ضباب محمّل بدخان
17. humid
    رطب
18. hurricane
    إعصار
19. windy
    شديد الرياح

20. dust storm
    عاصفة ترابية
21. foggy
    ضبابي
22. hail
    عاصفة بَرَدية
23. icy
    جليدي
24. snowstorm / blizzard
    عاصفة ثلجية / عاصفة ثلجية شديدة

Ways to talk about the weather

It's _sunny_ and _hot_ in _Dallas_.
It's _raining_ in _Chicago_.
Rome is having _thunderstorms_.

Internet Research: weather

Type any city and "weather" in the search bar.
Report: It's _cloudy_ in _L.A._ It's _70 degrees_.

11 Hi!

12 I can't hear you. Can you hear me?

1. **phone line**
   خط الهاتف / التليفون

2. **phone jack**
   مقبس الهاتف / التليفون

3. **base**
   قاعدة

4. **handset / receiver**
   سماعة الهاتف / سماعة التليفون

5. **keypad**
   لوحة المفاتيح

6. **star key**
   مفتاح النجمة

7. **pound key**
   مفتاح الباوند

8. **cell phone**
   هاتف محمول أو خلوي

9. **charger cord**
   سلك الشاحن

10. **charger plug**
    قابس الشاحن

11. **strong signal**
    إشارة قوية

12. **weak signal**
    إشارة ضعيفة

Hi, Bob. I'll text.

Hi. It's Bob. Call me.

Hi Bob! Text me!

13. **headset**
    سماعة رأس بميكروفون

14. **Bluetooth headset**
    سماعة رأس بنظام بلوتوث

15. **contact list**
    قائمة جهات الاتصال

16. **missed call**
    مكالمة فائتة

17. **voice mail**
    بريد صوتي

18. **text message**
    رسالة نصية

Hi, Grandpa.

Hello, Jun.

Operator.

City and state, please.

411

For customer service, please press the star key.

19. **Internet phone call**
    مكالمة هاتفية / تليفونية على الإنترنت

20. **operator**
    البدالة / السنترال

21. **directory assistance**
    الاستعلامات

22. **automated phone system**
    نظام الهاتف / التليفون الآلي

23. phone card
بطاقة هاتفية (بطاقة مكالمات)

24. access number
رقم الوصول / الدخول

25. smartphone
هاتف (تليفون) ذكي

26. TDD*
جهاز هاتف / تليفون للمعوقين سمعيا

Reading a Phone Bill قراءة فاتورة الهاتف / التليفون

27. carrier
شركة الاتصالات

28. area code
رمز / مفتاح المنطقة

29. phone number
رقم الهاتف / التليفون

30. billing period
فترة الفوترة

31. monthly charges
تكاليف شهرية

32. additional charges
تكاليف إضافية

HORIZON

BILL SUMMARY

For 823-555-1357

From May 15, 2018 to June 14, 2018

5/15 - 6/14 charges	$40.00
Other charges	$5.34
Tax	$9.84
TOTAL CHARGES	**$55.18**

Types of Charges أنواع التكاليف

33. local call
مكالمة محلية

34. long-distance call
مكالمة خارجية

35. international call
مكالمة دولية

36. data
بيانات

Making a Phone Call إجراء مكالمة هاتفية / تليفونية

A. Dial the phone number.
اطلب (اضرب) رقم الهاتف / التليفون.

B. Press "talk".
اكبس على مفتاح "تكلم" "talk".

C. Talk on the phone.
تحدث في الهاتف / التليفون.

Hi!
Hi!

D. Hang up. / End the call.
اقفل السماعة. / انه المكالمة.

Making an Emergency Call إجراء مكالمة في حالة طارئة

E. Dial 911.
اضرب (اطلب) رقم ٩١١.

This is Roy Chu.
F. Give your name.
أعطِ / اذكر اسمك.

There's a fire on 5th and Oak.
G. State the emergency.
اذكر الحالة الطارئة.

Please stay on the line.
H. Stay on the line.
انتظر على الخط.

*telecommunication device for the deaf

Cardinal Numbers الأعداد الأصلية

0	zero صفر	20	twenty عشرون
1	one واحد	21	twenty-one واحد وعشرون
2	two اثنان	22	twenty-two اثنان وعشرون
3	three ثلاثة	23	twenty-three ثلاثة وعشرون
4	four أربعة	24	twenty-four أربعة وعشرون
5	five خمسة	25	twenty-five خمسة وعشرون
6	six ستة	30	thirty ثلاثون
7	seven سبعة	40	forty أربعون
8	eight ثمانية	50	fifty خمسون
9	nine تسعة	60	sixty ستون
10	ten عشرة	70	seventy سبعون
11	eleven أحد عشر	80	eighty ثمانون
12	twelve اثنا عشر	90	ninety تسعون
13	thirteen ثلاثة عشر	100	one hundred مائة
14	fourteen أربعة عشر	101	one hundred one مائة وواحد
15	fifteen خمسة عشر	1,000	one thousand ألف
16	sixteen ستة عشر	10,000	ten thousand عشرة آلاف
17	seventeen سبعة عشر	100,000	one hundred thousand مائة ألف
18	eighteen ثمانية عشر	1,000,000	one million مليون
19	nineteen تسعة عشر	1,000,000,000	one billion بليون (مليار)

Ordinal Numbers الأعداد الترتيبية

1st	first الأول	16th	sixteenth السادس عشر
2nd	second الثاني	17th	seventeenth السابع عشر
3rd	third الثالث	18th	eighteenth الثامن عشر
4th	fourth الرابع	19th	nineteenth التاسع عشر
5th	fifth الخامس	20th	twentieth العشرون
6th	sixth السادس	21st	twenty-first الواحد والعشرون
7th	seventh السابع	30th	thirtieth الثلاثون
8th	eighth الثامن	40th	fortieth الأربعون
9th	ninth التاسع	50th	fiftieth الخمسون
10th	tenth العاشر	60th	sixtieth الستون
11th	eleventh الحادي عشر	70th	seventieth السبعون
12th	twelfth الثاني عشر	80th	eightieth الثمانون
13th	thirteenth الثالث عشر	90th	ninetieth التسعون
14th	fourteenth الرابع عشر	100th	one hundredth المئوي
15th	fifteenth الخامس عشر	1,000th	one thousandth الألفي

Roman Numerals الأعداد الرومانية

I = 1	VII = 7	XXX = 30
II = 2	VIII = 8	XL = 40
III = 3	IX = 9	L = 50
IV = 4	X = 10	C = 100
V = 5	XV = 15	D = 500
VI = 6	XX = 20	M = 1,000

A. divide
اقسم

75% of 10 = 7.5

B. calculate
احسبي

3 inches

C. measure
قِسْ

1 mi. = 1.6 km

1 MILE TO LAKE

D. convert
حوِّلي

Fractions and Decimals الكسور والكسور العشرية

1. one whole
1 = 1.00
واحد كامل

2. one half
1/2 = .5
نصف

3. one third
1/3 = .333
ثلث

4. one fourth
1/4 = .25
ربع

5. one eighth
1/8 = .125
ثمن

Percents النسب المئوية

.75

8. 100 percent — 100%
9. 75 percent — 75%
10. 50 percent — 50%
11. 25 percent — 25%
12. 10 percent — 10%

0% 10% 20% 30% 40% 50% 60% 70% 80% 90% 100%

6. calculator
آلة حاسبة

7. decimal point
فاصلة عشرية

8. 100 percent
١٠٠ بالمائة

9. 75 percent
٧٥ بالمائة

10. 50 percent
٥٠ بالمائة

11. 25 percent
٢٥ بالمائة

12. 10 percent
١٠ بالمائة

Measurement قياسات

13. ruler
مسطرة

14. centimeter [cm]
سنتيمتر [سم]

15. inch [in.]
بوصة

Dimensions أبعاد

16. height
ارتفاع

17. length
طول

18. depth
عمق

19. width
عرض

Equivalencies

12 inches = 1 foot

3 feet = 1 yard

1,760 yards = 1 mile

1 inch = 2.54 centimeters

1 yard = .91 meter

1 mile = 1.6 kilometers

Telling Time قراءة الوقت بالنظر إلى الساعة

1. hour
ساعة

2. minutes
دقائق

3. seconds
ثوان

4. a.m.
ق.ظ. (قبل الظهر)

5. p.m.
ب.ظ. (بعد الظهر)

6. 1:00
one o'clock
الساعة الواحدة

7. 1:05
one-oh-five
five after one
الواحدة وخمس دقائق

8. 1:10
one-ten
ten after one
الواحدة وعشر دقائق

9. 1:15
one-fifteen
a quarter after one
الواحدة وخمسة عشر دقيقة
الواحدة والربع

10. 1:20
one-twenty
twenty after one
الواحد وعشرون دقيقة
الواحدة والثلث

11. 1:30
one-thirty
half past one
الواحدة وثلاثون دقيقة
الواحدة والنصف

12. 1:40
one-forty
twenty to two
الواحدة وأربعون دقيقة
الثانية إلا ثلث

13. 1:45
one-forty-five
a quarter to two
الواحدة وخمسة وأربعون دقيقة
الثانية إلا ربع

Times of Day أوقات النهار

   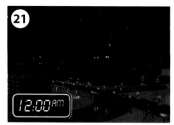

14. sunrise
شروق الشمس

15. morning
الصباح

16. noon
الظهر

17. afternoon
بعد الظهر (العصر)

18. sunset
غروب الشمس

19. evening
المساء

20. night
الليل

21. midnight
منتصف الليل

Ways to talk about time

I wake up at 6:30 a.m.
I wake up at 6:30 in the morning.
I wake up at 6:30.

Pair practice. Make new conversations.

A: *What time do you wake up on weekdays?*
B: *At 6:30 a.m. How about you?*
A: *I wake up at 7:00.*

22. early
مبكرا

23. on time
في الموعد المحدد

24. late
متأخرا

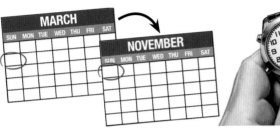

25. daylight saving time
التوقيت الصيفي

26. standard time
التوقيت القياسي (الشتوي)

Time Zones مناطق التوقيت

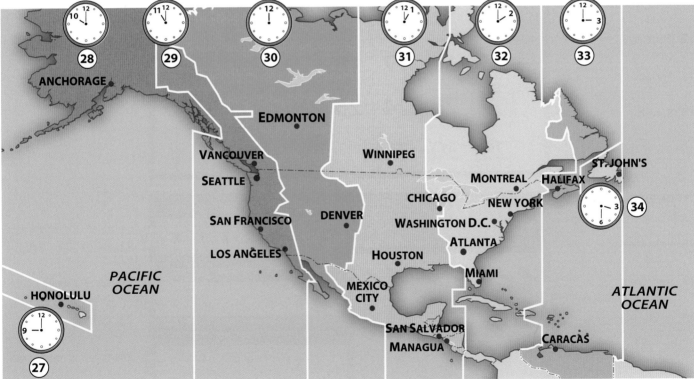

27. Hawaii-Aleutian time
توقيت هاواي - ألوشيان

28. Alaska time
توقيت ألاسكا

29. Pacific time
توقيت المحيط الهادئ (الباسيفيكي)

30. Mountain time
التوقيت الجبلي

31. Central time
توقيت الولايات الوسطى

32. Eastern time
توقيت الولايات الشرقية

33. Atlantic time
التوقيت الأطلنطي

34. Newfoundland time
توقيت نيوفاوندلاند

Survey your class. Record the responses.
1. When do you watch television? study? relax?
2. Do you like to stay up after midnight?
Report: *Most of us... Some of us...*

Think about it. Discuss.
1. What is your favorite time of day? Why?
2. Do you think daylight saving time is a good idea?
3. What's good about staying up after midnight?

19

1. date
   تاريخ

2. day
   يوم

3. month
   شهر

4. year
   سنة

5. today
   اليوم

6. tomorrow
   الغد (غدا)

7. yesterday
   الأمس

Days of the Week
أيام الأسبوع

8. Sunday
   الأحد

9. Monday
   الاثنين

10. Tuesday
    الثلاثاء

11. Wednesday
    الأربعاء

12. Thursday
    الخميس

13. Friday
    الجمعة

14. Saturday
    السبت

15. week
    أسبوع

16. weekdays
    أيام الأسبوع

17. weekend
    نهاية الأسبوع (عطلة نهاية الأسبوع)

MAY

⑧ SUN	⑨ MON	⑩ TUE	⑪ WED	⑫ THU	⑬ FRI	⑭ SAT
1	2	3	4	5	6	7
8	9	10	11	12	13	14
15	16	17	18	19	20	21
22	23	24	25	26	27	28
29	30	31				

Frequency
التردد

18. last week
    الأسبوع الماضي

19. this week
    الأسبوع الحالي

20. next week
    الأسبوع القادم

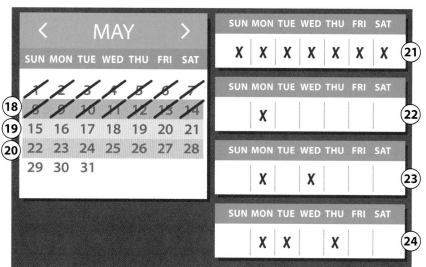

21. every day / daily
    كل يوم / يوميا

22. once a week
    مرة في الأسبوع

23. twice a week
    مرتان في الأسبوع

24. three times a week
    ثلاث مرات في الأسبوع

Ways to say the date

Today is <u>May 10th</u>. It's the <u>tenth</u>.
Yesterday was <u>May 9th</u>.
The party is on <u>May 21st</u>.

Pair practice. Make new conversations.

A: *The <u>test</u> is on <u>Friday</u>, <u>June 14th</u>.*
B: *Did you say <u>Friday</u>, the <u>fourteenth</u>?*
A: *Yes, the <u>fourteenth</u>.*

Months of the Year
شهور السنة

25. January
يناير / كانون الثاني

26. February
فبراير / شباط

27. March
مارس / آذار

28. April
إبريل / نيسان

29. May
مايو / أيار

30. June
يونيو / حزيران

31. July
يوليو / تموز

32. August
أغسطس / آب

33. September
سبتمبر / أيلول

34. October
أكتوبر / تشرين الأول

35. November
نوفمبر / تشرين الثاني

36. December
ديسمبر / كانون الأول

Seasons
فصول السنة

37. spring
الربيع

38. summer
الصيف

39. fall / autumn
الخريف

40. winter
الشتاء

Dictate to your partner. Take turns.

A: *Write Monday.*
B: *Is it spelled M-o-n-d-a-y?*
A: *Yes, that's right.*

Survey your class. Record the responses.

1. What is the busiest day of your week?
2. What is your favorite day?
Report: *Ten of us said Monday is our busiest day.*

21

1. birthday
عيد ميلاد

2. wedding
فرح / عرس

3. anniversary
عيد سنوي

4. appointment
موعد

5. parent-teacher conference
اجتماع آباء-معلمين

6. vacation
عطلة / أجازة

7. religious holiday
عيد ديني

8. legal holiday
عيد رسمي

Legal Holidays الأعياد الرسمية

Happy New Year!
JAN 1

I have a dream.
JAN

FEB

MAY

JUL 4

SEP
PROUD TO WORK

OCT

DEC 25

NOV

NOV

9. New Year's Day
عيد رأس السنة

10. Martin Luther King Jr. Day
عيد مارتن لوثر كنغ جونيور

11. Presidents' Day
عيد الرؤساء

12. Memorial Day
عيد الذكرى

**13. Fourth of July /
Independence Day**
عيد الرابع من يوليو / عيد الاستقلال

14. Labor Day
عيد العمال

15. Columbus Day
عيد كولومبس

16. Veterans Day
عيد المحاربين القدامى

17. Thanksgiving
عيد الشكر

18. Christmas
أعياد الميلاد (الكريسماس)

Pair practice. Make new conversations.

A: *When is your <u>birthday</u>?*
B: *It's on <u>January 31st</u>. How about yours?*
A: *It's on <u>December 22nd</u>.*

Internet Research: independence day

Type "independence day, world" in the search bar.
Report: <u>Peru</u> celebrates its independence on <u>7/28</u>.

1. **little** hand
يد صغيرة

2. **big** hand
يد كبيرة

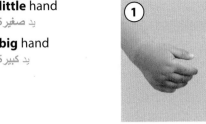
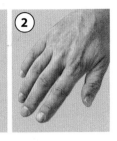

13. **heavy** box
صندوق ثقيل

14. **light** box
صندوق خفيف

3. **fast** speed
سرعة سريعة

4. **slow** speed
سرعة بطيئة

15. **same** color
نفس اللون (ألوان مشابهة)

16. **different** colors
ألوان مختلفة

5. **hard** chair
مقعد جامد (قاسي)

6. **soft** chair
مقعد طري (مريح)

17. **bad** news
أنباء سيئة

18. **good** news
أنباء سارة

There was an earthquake.

Everyone is OK!

7. **thick** book
كتاب سميك (غليظ)

8. **thin** book
كتاب رقيق (رفيع)

19. **expensive** ring
خاتم غالي

20. **cheap** ring
خاتم رخيص

9. **full** glass
كأس ممتلئ

10. **empty** glass
كأس فارغ

21. **beautiful** view
منظر بديع

22. **ugly** view
منظر قبيح

11. **noisy** children /
loud children
أطفال مزعجون

12. **quiet** children
أطفال هادئون

23. **easy** problem
مسألة سهلة

1+1=2

$$x^2 - 22\frac{1}{2}x =$$
$$-8\frac{1}{3}x^2 - 11\frac{2}{3}$$

24. **difficult** problem /
hard problem
مسألة صعبة

Survey your class. Record the responses.

1. Are you a slow walker or a fast walker?
2. Do you prefer loud parties or quiet parties?
Report: _Five of us prefer quiet parties._

Use the new words.

Look at pages 154–155. Describe the things you see.

A: _The subway is full._
B: _The motorcycle is noisy._

Basic Colors الألوان الأساسية

1. red
أحمر

2. yellow
أصفر

3. blue
أزرق

4. orange
برتقالي

5. green
أخضر

6. purple
أرجواني

7. pink
وردي

8. violet
بنفسجي

9. turquoise
فيروزي / تركواز

10. dark blue
أزرق غامق

11. light blue
أزرق فاتح

12. bright blue
أزرق لامع

Neutral Colors الألوان المحايدة

13. black
أسود

14. white
أبيض

15. gray
رمادي

16. cream / ivory
أصفر باهت / عاجي

17. brown
بني

18. beige / tan
بيج / أسمر مائل إلى الصفرة

Survey your class. Record the responses.

1. What colors are you wearing today?
2. What colors do you like? What colors do you dislike?
Report: *Most of us… Some of us…*

Use the new words. Look at pages 86–87.
Take turns naming the colors you see.

A: *His shirt is <u>blue</u>.*
B: *Her shoes are <u>white</u>.*

1. The yellow sweaters are **on the left**.
البلوفرات (الكنزات) الصفراء **على الجهة اليسرى**.

2. The purple sweaters are **in the middle**.
البلوفرات (الكنزات) الأرجوانية **في الجهة الوسطى**.

3. The brown sweaters are **on the right**.
البلوفرات (الكنزات) البنية **على الجهة اليمنى**.

4. The red sweaters are **above** the blue sweaters.
البلوفرات (الكنزات) الحمراء **فوق** البلوفرات (الكنزات) الزرقاء.

5. The blue sweaters are **below** the red sweaters.
البلوفرات (الكنزات) الزرقاء **تحت / أسفل** البلوفرات (الكنزات) الحمراء.

6. The turquoise sweater is **in** the box.
البلوفر (الكنزة) الفيروزي **في / داخل** الصندوق.

7. The white sweater is **in front of** the black sweater.
البلوفر (الكنزة) الأبيض **أمام** البلوفر (الكنزة) الأسود.

8. The black sweater is **behind** the white sweater.
البلوفر (الكنزة) الأسود **خلف** البلوفر (الكنزة) الأبيض.

9. The violet sweater is **next to** the gray sweater.
البلوفر (الكنزة) البنفسجي **بجانب** البلوفر (الكنزة) الرمادي.

10. The gray sweater is **under** the orange sweater.
البلوفر (الكنزة) الرمادي **تحت** البلوفر (الكنزة) البرتقالي.

11. The orange sweater is **on** the gray sweater.
البلوفر (الكنزة) البرتقالي **فوق / على** البلوفر (الكنزة) الرمادي.

12. The green sweater is **between** the pink sweaters.
البلوفر (الكنزة) الأخضر **بين** البلوفرات (الكنزات) الوردية.

More vocabulary

near: in the same area
far from: not near

Role play. Make new conversations.

A: *Excuse me. Where are the* <u>red</u> *sweaters?*
B: *They're* <u>on the left</u>, <u>above</u> *the* <u>blue</u> *sweaters.*
A: *Thanks very much.*

25

Coins العملة

1. $.01 = 1¢
   a penny / 1 cent
   بني / سنت واحد

2. $.05 = 5¢
   a nickel / 5 cents
   نيكل / ٥ سنتات

3. $.10 = 10¢
   a dime / 10 cents
   دَيْم / ١٠ سنتات

4. $.25 = 25¢
   a quarter / 25 cents
   كوارتر (ربع دولار) / ٢٥ سنتا

5. $.50 = 50¢
   a half dollar
   نصف دولار

6. $1.00
   a dollar coin
   عملة دولار فضي

Bills الورقات

7. $1.00
   a dollar
   دولار

8. $5.00
   five dollars
   خمسة دولارات

9. $10.00
   ten dollars
   عشرة دولارات

10. $20.00
    twenty dollars
    عشرون دولارا

11. $50.00
    fifty dollars
    خمسون دولارا

12. $100.00
    one hundred dollars
    مائة دولار

Do you have change for a dollar?

Yes, I do.

A

Can I borrow a dollar?

Sure. Here you go.

B   C

Thanks.

D

A. **Get** change.
احصل على فكّة.

B. **Borrow** money.
اقترض / استلف نقودا.

C. **Lend** money.
اقرض / سلّف نقودا.

D. **Pay back** the money.
سدّد النقود.

Pair practice. Make new conversations.

A: *Do you have change for a dollar?*
B: *Sure. How about two quarters and five dimes?*
A: *Perfect!*

Identify Mark's problem. Brainstorm solutions.

Mark doesn't like to lend money. His boss, Lia, asks, "Can I borrow $20.00?" What can Mark say? What will Lia say?

Ways to Pay طرق الدفع

A. pay cash
يدفع تقدا

B. use a credit card
يستخدم بطاقة انتمان

C. use a debit card
يستخدم بطاقة خصم من الحساب

D. write a (personal) check
يحرر شيكا (شخصيا)

E. use a gift card
يستخدم بطاقة إهداء

F. cash a traveler's check
يصرف شيكا سياحيا

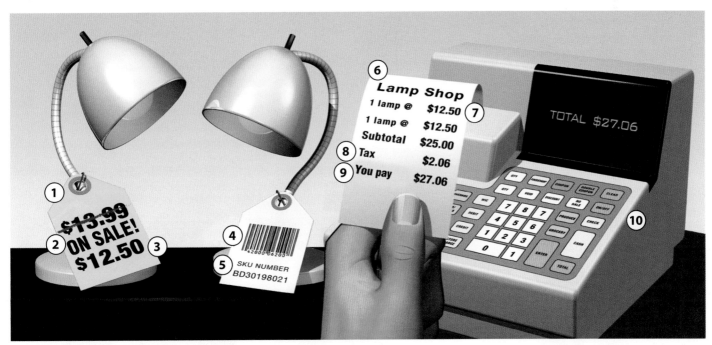

1. price tag
بطاقة السعر

3. sale price
سعر التنزيلات (المخفض)

5. SKU number
رقم تعريف السلعة (SKU)

7. price / cost
السعر / التكلفة

9. total
المجموع / الإجمالي

2. regular price
السعر العادي

4. bar code
شفرة القضبان

6. receipt
الإيصال / الوصل

8. sales tax
ضريبة مبيعات

10. cash register
آلة تسجيل النقود

G. buy / pay for
تشتري / تدفع حساب

H. return
ترجّع / ترد

I. exchange
يستبدل

1. twins
   توأمان

2. sweater
   بلوفر (كنزة)

3. matching
   مطابقان

4. disappointed
   الشعور بخيبة أمل

5. navy blue
   أزرق كحلي

6. happy
   سعيدتان

A. **shop**
   تَتَسوَّق

B. **keep**
   تحتفظ لنفسها

What do you see in the pictures?

1. Who is the woman shopping for?
2. Does she buy matching sweaters or different sweaters?
3. How does Anya feel about her green sweater? What does she do?
4. What does Manda do with her sweater?

Read the story.

Same and Different

Mrs. Kumar likes to <u>shop</u> for her <u>twins</u>. Today she's looking at <u>sweaters</u>. There are many different colors on sale. Mrs. Kumar chooses two <u>matching</u> green sweaters.

The next day, Manda and Anya open their gifts. Manda likes the green sweater, but Anya is <u>disappointed</u>. Mrs. Kumar understands the problem. Anya wants to be different.

Manda <u>keeps</u> her sweater, but Anya goes to the store. She exchanges her green sweater for a <u>navy blue</u> sweater. It's an easy answer to Anya's problem. Now the twins can be warm, <u>happy</u>, and different.

Reread the story.

1. Underline the last sentence in each paragraph. Why are these sentences important?
2. Retell the story in your own words.

What do you think?

3. Imagine you are Anya. Would you keep the sweater or exchange it? Why?

1. man
   رجل
2. woman
   امرأة
3. women
   نساء
4. men
   رجال
5. senior citizen
   مُسنَّة / عجوز

Listen and point. Take turns.

A: Point to _a woman_.

B: Point to _a senior citizen_.

A: Point to _an infant_.

Dictate to your partner. Take turns.

A: Write _woman_.

B: Is that spelled _w-o-m-a-n_?

A: Yes, that's right, _woman_.

6. infant
رضيع

7. baby
طفل

8. toddler
طفل في أول مراحل المشي

9. 6-year-old boy
ولد عمره ٦ سنوات

10. 10-year-old girl
بنت عمرها ١٠ سنوات

11. teenager / teen
مراهق / من ذوي السنوات
بين ١٣ و ١٩ من العمر

Ways to talk about age

1 month–3 months old = **infant**	13–19 years old = **teenager**
18 months–3 years old = **toddler**	18+ years old = **adult**
3 years old–12 years old = **child**	62+ years old = **senior citizen**

Pair practice. Make new conversations.

A: *How old is Sandra?*
B: *She's 13 years old.*
A: *Wow, she's a teenager now!*

31

Age السن

1. young
صغير(ة)

2. middle-aged
متوسط(ة)

3. elderly
عجوز / مسنّ(ة)

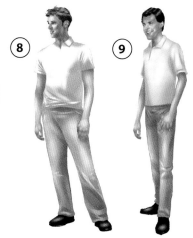

Height الطول

4. tall
طويل(ة)

5. average height
متوسط(ة) الطول

6. short
قصير(ة)

Weight الوزن

7. heavy / fat
بدين(ة)

8. average weight
متوسط(ة) الوزن

9. thin / slender
نحيف(ة)

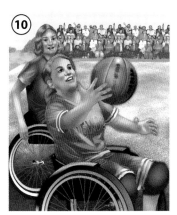

Prepositions of Motion

Disabilities حالات العجز

10. physically challenged
عاجز(ة)

11. sight impaired / blind
ضرير(ة)

12. hearing impaired / deaf
أصمّ / صمّاء

Appearance المظهر

13. attractive
وسيم(ة)

14. cute
جميل(ة)

15. pregnant
حامل

16. mole
شامة / خال

17. pierced ear
أذن مثقوبة

18. tattoo
وشم

Ways to describe people	**Use the new words.**
He's a <u>heavy</u>, <u>young</u> man.	Look at pages 44-45. Describe the people you see. Take turns.
She's a <u>pregnant</u> woman with <u>a mole</u>.	**A:** *This <u>elderly</u> woman is <u>short</u> and a little <u>heavy</u>.*
He's <u>sight impaired</u>.	**B:** *This <u>young</u> man is <u>physically challenged</u>.*

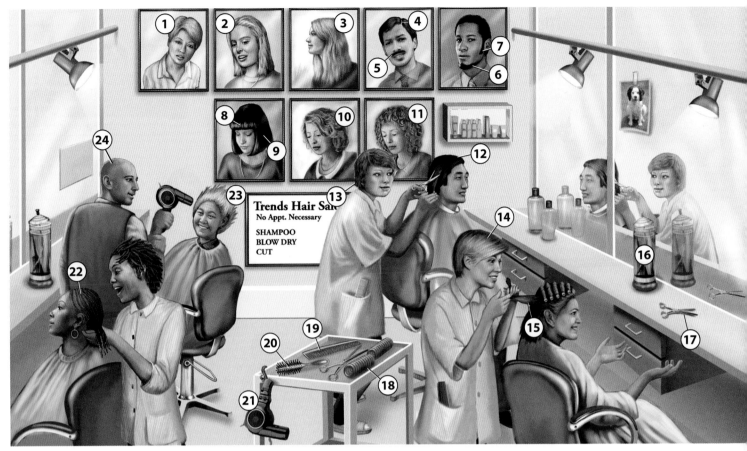

1. short hair شعر قصير	6. beard لحية	11. curly hair شعر مجعد	16. sanitizing jar برطمان تعقيم
2. shoulder-length hair شعر واصل للكتف	7. sideburns السبلة الخدية (سوالف)	12. black hair شعر أسود	17. shears مقص / مجز
3. long hair شعر طويل	8. bangs خصلة	13. red hair شعر أحمر	18. rollers بكرات شعر
4. part فرق الشعر	9. straight hair شعر ناعم	14. blond hair شعر أشقر	19. comb مشط
5. mustache شارب / شنب	10. wavy hair شعر مموج	15. brown hair شعر بني	20. brush فرشاة

21. blow dryer
مجفف شعر بالهواء الساخن (سيشوار)

22. cornrows
تضفير الشعر على فروة الرأس

23. gray hair
شعر شائب (أبيض)

24. bald
أصلع

Style Hair تصفيف الشعر

A. **cut** hair
يقص الشعر

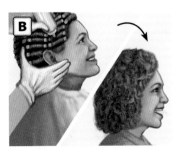

B. **perm** hair
يموّج الشعر

C. **add** highlights
أضف لونا للشعر

D. **color** hair / **dye** hair
يلوّن (يصبغ) الشعر

Ways to talk about hair

Describe hair in this order: length, style, and then color.
She has <u>long</u>, <u>straight</u>, <u>brown</u> hair.

Role play. Talk to a stylist.

A: *I need a new hairstyle.*
B: *How about <u>short</u> and <u>straight</u>?*
A: *Great. Do you think I should <u>dye</u> it?*

Families العائلات

1. grandmother
جدة

2. grandfather
جد

3. mother
أم

4. father
أب

5. sister
أخت

6. brother
أخ

7. aunt
عمة / خالة

8. uncle
عم / خال

9. cousin
بنت / ابن عم(ة) / خال(ة)

Tim Lee's Family

GRANDPARENTS — Min (1), Lu (2)
Immediate Family

PARENTS — Rose (3), Ken (4), Lynn (7), Dan (8)

CHILDREN — Tim, Lily (5), Alex (6), Emily (9)

10. mother-in-law
حماة

11. father-in-law
حمو

12. wife
زوجة

13. husband
زوج

14. daughter
ابنة

15. son
ابن

16. sister-in-law
سلفة (أخت الزوج أو الزوجة / زوجة الأخ)

17. brother-in-law
سلف (أخو الزوج أو الزوجة / زوج الأخت)

18. niece
ابنة الأخ أو الأخت

19. nephew
ابن الأخ أو الأخت

Ana Garcia's Family

Eva (10), Sam (11) — Extended Family
Ana (12), Tito (13), Marta (16), Carlos (17)
Sara (14), Felix (15), Alice (18), Eddie (19)

More vocabulary

Tim is Min and Lu's **grandson**.
Lily and Emily are Min and Lu's **granddaughters**.
Alex is Min's youngest **grandchild**.

Ana is Eva and Sam's **daughter-in-law**.
Carlos is Eva and Sam's **son-in-law**.
Note: Ana's married. = Ana **is** married.
Ana's **husband** = the man married to Ana

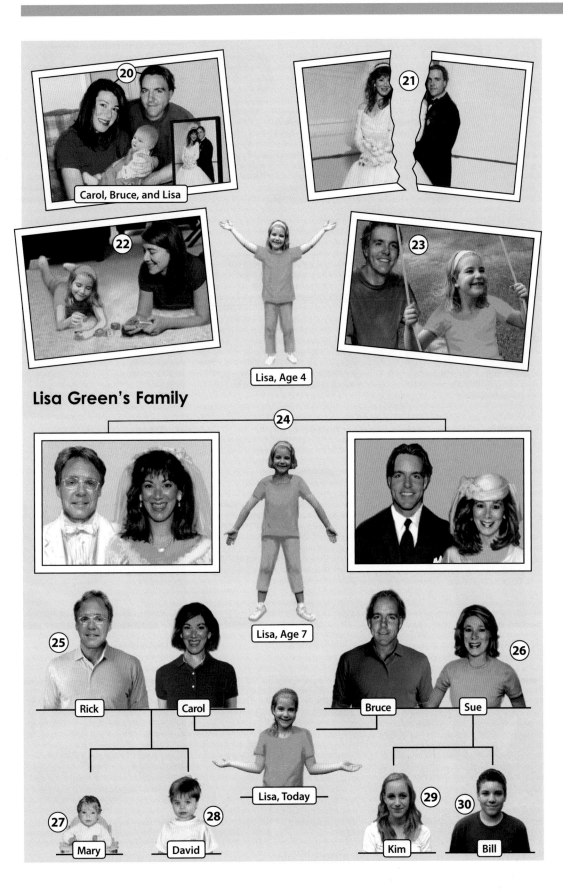

Carol, Bruce, and Lisa

Lisa, Age 4

Lisa Green's Family

Lisa, Age 7

Rick   Carol   Bruce   Sue

Lisa, Today

Mary   David   Kim   Bill

20. married couple
شخصان متزوجان

21. divorced couple
شخصان مطلقان

22. single mother
أم عزباء

23. single father
أب أعزب

24. remarried
متزوج للمرة الثانية

25. stepfather
زوج الأم

26. stepmother
زوجة الأب

27. half sister
أخت غير شقيقة

28. half brother
أخ غير شقيق

29. stepsister
أخت من زوجة الأب أو زوج الأم

30. stepbrother
أخ من زوجة الأب أو زوج الأم

More vocabulary

Bruce is Carol's **former husband** or **ex-husband**.
Carol is Bruce's **former wife** or **ex-wife**.
Lisa is the **stepdaughter** of both Rick and Sue.

Use the new words.

Ask and answer questions about Lisa's family.

A: *Who is Lisa's half sister?*
B: *Mary is. Who is Lisa's stepsister?*

35

A. hold
يحمل الطفل

B. nurse
ترضِع

C. feed
يطعم

D. rock
تهزّ

E. undress
تخلع ملابسه

F. bathe
تحمّي

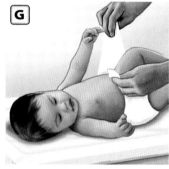

G. change a diaper
تغيّر الحفاض

H. dress
تلبّس

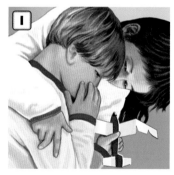

I. comfort
ترِّح / تهدّئ

Good job!

J. praise
تمدح

No!

K. discipline
تؤدّب

L. buckle up
يحزِم / يربط حزام الأمان

M. play with
تلعب معه

N. read to
يقرأ له

O. sing a lullaby
تغنّي له ترنيمة لتنويمه

P. kiss goodnight
يقبّله متمنيا له نوما مريحا

Look at the pictures.
Describe what is happening.

A: She's <u>changing her baby's diaper</u>.
B: He's <u>kissing his son goodnight</u>.

Talk about your experience.

I am great at <u>play**ing**</u> with toddlers.
I have a lot of experience <u>chang**ing** diapers</u>.
I know how to <u>hold an infant</u>.

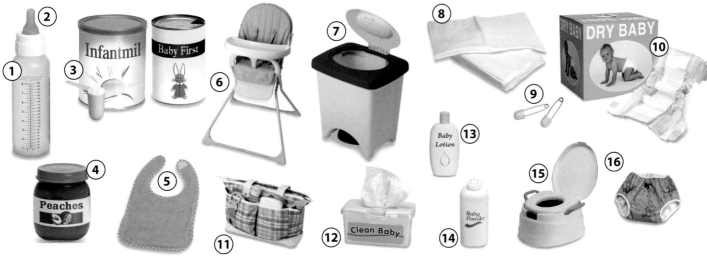

1. bottle
   زجاجة رضاعة

2. nipple
   حلمة زجاجة الرضاعة

3. formula
   بديل لبن الأم (حليب مستحضر)

4. baby food
   غذاء الأطفال

5. bib
   فوطة صدرية

6. high chair
   كرسي مرتفع

7. diaper pail
   دلو الحفاضات

8. cloth diaper
   حفاضات من القماش

9. safety pins
   دبابيس أمان

10. disposable diaper
    حفاض يلقى بعد الاستعمال

11. diaper bag
    حقيبة / كيس الحفاضات

12. wipes
    مناديل للتنظيف

13. baby lotion
    غسول أطفال

14. baby powder
    بودرة أطفال

15. potty seat
    نونية للأطفال

16. training pants
    بنطلون أطفال سهل الخلع

17. baby carrier
    حمالة أطفال

18. stroller
    متنزهة للأطفال

19. carriage
    عربة أطفال

20. car safety seat
    كرسي أمان لسلامة الأطفال بالسيارة

21. booster car seat
    كرسي أمان معزز لسلامة الأطفال بالسيارة

22. rocking chair
    كرسي هزاز

23. nursery rhymes
    أغاني تقليدية للأطفال

24. teddy bear
    دبة محشوة

25. pacifier
    عضاضة

26. teething ring
    حلقة تسنين

27. rattle
    خشخيشة

28. night light
    ضوء ليلي (نور سهّاري)

Dictate to your partner. Take turns.

A: *Write pacifier.*

B: *Was that pacifier, p-a-c-i-f-i-e-r?*

A: *Yes, that's right.*

Think about it. Discuss.

1. How can parents discipline toddlers? teens?

2. What are some things you can say to praise a child?

3. Why are nursery rhymes important for young children?

A. wake up
يستيقظ

B. get up
تقوم من السرير

C. take a shower
تستحمّ

D. get dressed
يلبس ثيابه

E. eat breakfast
يتناولون الإفطار

F. make lunch
تحضّر وجبة الغداء

G. take the children to school /
drop off the kids
يوصّل (يأخذ) الأطفال إلى المدرسة /
ينزل الأطفال عند باب المدرسة

H. take the bus to school
تأخذ (تركب) الأوتوبيس إلى المدرسة

I. drive to work / **go** to work
يقود السيارة إلى مكان العمل / يذهب إلى العمل

J. be in class
التواجد داخل الفصل

K. work
يعمل

L. go to the grocery store
تذهب إلى محل البقالة

M. pick up the kids
تُحضر الأطفال من المدرسة

N. leave work
يغادر العمل

Grammar Point: third-person singular

For *he* and *she*, add **-s** or **-es** to the verb:
He eat**s** breakfast.   He watch**es** TV.
She make**s** lunch.   She go**es** to the store.

For two-part verbs, put the **-s** on the first part: wake**s** up,
drop**s** off.
Be and *have* are different (irregular).
He **is** in bed at 5 a.m. He **has** breakfast at 7 a.m.

38

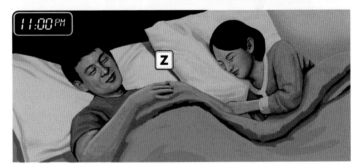

O. clean the house
ينظّفون المنزل

P. exercise
يمارس رياضة

Q. cook dinner / **make** dinner
تطبخ العشاء / **تحضّر** العشاء

R. come home / **get** home
يرجع / **يصل** إلى المنزل

S. have dinner / **eat** dinner
يتناولون العشاء

T. do homework
يعمل الواجب المدرسي

U. relax
يسترخي

V. read the paper
تقرأ الصحيفة

W. check email
تطلع على البريد الإلكتروني

X. watch TV
يشاهد التلفزيون

Y. go to bed
يذهب / **تذهب** للفراش

Z. go to sleep
ينام / **تنام**

Pair practice. Make new conversations.

A: *When does he go to work?*
B: *He goes to work at 8:00 a.m. When does she make dinner?*
A: *She makes dinner at 6:00 p.m.*

Internet Research: housework

Type "time survey, chart, housework" in the search bar.
Report: *According to the survey, men prepare food 17 minutes a day.*

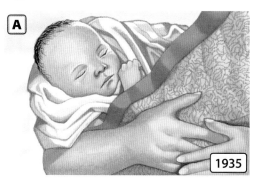

1935

A. be born
يولد

1940

B. start school
يدخل المدرسة

REGISTRO CIVIL
Acta de Nacimiento

MARTÍN PEREZ DE LÉON   B0983456
01-05-1935

Registro Civil
Acta de Nacimiento

1. birth certificate
شهادة ميلاد

DEPARTMENT OF IMMIGRATION

1950

C. immigrate
يهاجر / يهاجرون

1953

D. graduate
يتخرُّج

PERMANENT RESIDENT CARD
PEREZ, MARTIN   A043398414
01-05-1935

2. Resident Alien card / green card
بطاقة اقامة دائمة / البطاقة الخضراء

Los Angeles High School

Martin Perez

3. diploma
شهادة دبلوم

1953

E. learn to drive
يتعلَّم قيادة السيارة

1954

F. get a job
يحصل على وظيفة

CALIFORNIA
DRIVER LICENSE
M06188
MARTIN PEREZ

4. driver's license
رخصة قيادة سيارة

SOCIAL SECURITY
987-65-4321
MARTIN PEREZ

5. Social Security card
بطاقة ضمان اجتماعي

1954

G. become a citizen
يصبح مواطنا

1955

H. fall in love
يقع في غرام فتاة

THE UNITED STATES OF AMERICA
CERTIFICATE OF   NATURALIZATION

MARTIN PEREZ DE LEON

6. Certificate of Naturalization
شهادة جنسية

Grammar Point: past tense

start
learn   } + **ed**
travel

immigrate   retire
graduate   die   } + **d**

These verbs are different (irregular):

be – was	go – went	buy – bought
get – got	have – had	
become – became	fall – fell	

I. go to college
يلتحق بالجامعة

J. get engaged
يخطب حبيبته

7. college degree
شهادة جامعية

K. get married
يتزوَّج

L. have a baby
تنجب طفلا

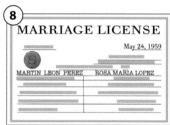

8. marriage license
عقد زواج

M. buy a home
يشتري منزلا

N. become a grandparent
يصير جدا

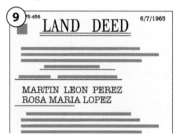

9. deed
صك ملكية

O. retire
يتقاعد

P. travel
يسافر

10. passport
جواز سفر

Q. volunteer
يتطوَّع

R. die
يتوفى / يموت

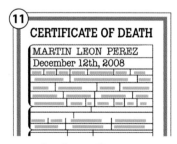

11. death certificate
شهادة وفاة

More vocabulary

When a husband dies, his wife becomes a **widow**.
When a wife dies, her husband becomes a **widower**.
Someone who is not living is **dead** or **deceased**.

Survey your class. Record the responses.

1. When did you start school? immigrate? learn to drive?
2. Do you want to become a citizen? travel? retire?
Report: *Most of us… Some of us…*

4

1. hot
   شاعر بالحَرّ / حرّان

2. thirsty
   ظامئ / عطشان

3. sleepy
   نعسان

4. cold
   شاعر بالبرد / بردان

5. hungry
   جائع / جوعان

6. full / satisfied
   ممتلئ / شبعان

7. disgusted
   مشمئزّ(ة)

8. calm
   هادئ(ة)

9. uncomfortable
   غير مرتاح

10. nervous
    متوتّر(ة)

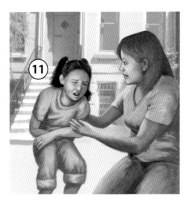

11. in pain
    متألّم(ة) / مصاب(ة) بألم

12. sick
    مريض(ة)

13. worried
    قلق(ة)

14. well
    معافى / معافية

15. relieved
    منفرج(ة)

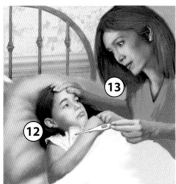

16. hurt
    مكسور الخاطر

17. lonely
    وحيد

18. in love
    محبّ / عاشق

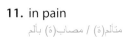

Pair practice. Make new conversations.

A: *How are you doing?*
B: *I'm hungry. How about you?*
A: *I'm hungry and thirsty, too!*

Use the new words.
Look at pages 40–41. Describe what each person is feeling.

A: *Martin is excited.*
B: *Martin's mother is proud.*

19. sad
حزين

20. homesick
مشتاق إلى الوطن / شاعر بالحنين للوطن

21. proud
فخورة)

22. excited
مثار

23. scared / afraid
خائف / متخوف

24. embarrassed
محرج

25. bored
مصاب بالملل / مسئوم

26. confused
محتار

27. frustrated
محبط

28. upset
متضايق / منزعج

29. angry
غضبان

30. surprised
مندهش

31. happy
سعيد / مسرور

32. tired
مرهق / تعبان

Identify Kenge's problem. Brainstorm solutions.

Kenge wants to learn English quickly, but it's difficult. He makes a lot of mistakes and gets frustrated. And he's homesick, too. What can he do?

More vocabulary

exhausted: very tired
furious: very angry
humiliated: very embarrassed

overjoyed: very happy
starving: very hungry
terrified: very scared

A Family Reunion اجتماع شمل الأسرة

LU FAMILY REUNION

1. banner
راية

2. baseball game
مباراة بيسبول

3. opinion
رأي

4. balloons
بالونات

5. glad
مسرور

6. relatives
أقارب / أقرباء

A. laugh
يضحك

B. misbehave
تسيء السلوك أو التصرف

I think large families are best.

What do you see in the picture?

1. How many relatives are there at this reunion?

2. How many children are there? Which children are misbehaving?

3. What are people doing at this reunion?

 Read the story.

A Family Reunion

Ben Lu has a lot of <u>relatives</u> and they're all at his house. Today is the Lu family reunion.

There is a lot of good food. There are also <u>balloons</u> and a <u>banner</u>. And this year there are four new babies!

People are having a good time at the reunion. Ben's grandfather and his aunt are talking about the <u>baseball game</u>. His cousins <u>are laughing</u>. His mother-in-law is giving her <u>opinion</u>. And many of the children <u>are misbehaving</u>.

Ben looks at his family and smiles. He loves his relatives, but he's <u>glad</u> the reunion is once a year.

Reread the story.

1. Find this sentence in the story: "He loves his relatives, but he's glad the reunion is once a year." Explain what this sentence means.

2. Retell the story in your own words.

What do you think?

3. You are at Ben's party. You see a child misbehave. No other guests see him. What do you do? What do you say?

The Home   المنزل

1. yard
فناء

2. roof
سقف

3. bedroom
غرفة نوم

4. door
باب

5. bathroom
حمّام

6. kitchen
مطبخ

7. floor
أرضية

8. dining area
غرفة الطعام

Listen and point. Take turns.

A: *Point to the kitchen.*
B: *Point to the living room.*
A: *Point to the basement.*

Dictate to your partner. Take turns.

A: *Write kitchen.*
B: *Was that k-i-t-c-h-e-n?*
A: *Yes, that's right, kitchen.*

9. attic
علّيّة

10. kids' bedroom
غرفة نوم الأطفال

11. baby's room /
nursery
غرفة الطفل الرضيع /
حجرة الأطفال

12. window
نافذة / شبّاك

13. living room
صالة الجلوس

14. basement
دور سفلي / تحتاني
(بدروم)

15. garage
جراج / كراج

Ways to give locations

*I'm **at** home.*

*I'm **in** the kitchen.*

*I'm **on** the roof.*

*It's **in** the laundry room.*

*It's **on** the floor.*

Pair practice. Ask and answer questions.

A: *Where's the <u>man</u>?*

B: *<u>He's</u> in the <u>attic</u>. Where's the <u>mother</u>?*

A: *<u>She's</u> in the <u>living room</u>.*

1. apartment search tool
أداة البحث عن الشقق

Oak Park News

Posen Street	$950
Apartment: 2BR 1 BA. 1st floor unit, central AC, laundry in unit	
$950/mo Call mgr eves **708-555-8941**	
Posted: **Today**	Category: **Rentals**

2. listing / classified ad
عرض المنزل للبيع على الإنترنت / إعلان مبوّب

Abbreviations

apt = apartment
bed, br = bedroom
ba, bath = bathroom
kit = kitchen
yd = yard
util = utilities
incl = included
mo = month
furn = furnished
unfurn = unfurnished
mgr = manager
eves = evenings
AC = air conditioning

3. furnished apartment
شقة مفروشة

4. unfurnished apartment
شقة غير مفروشة

GAS   WATER   ELECTRICITY   TRASH COLLECTION   CABLE   INTERNET ACCESS

5. utilities
مرافق

Renting an Apartment استئجار شقة

A. Call the manager.
تتصل بالمدير / المشرف.

Are utilities included?
No, they aren't.

B. Ask about the features.
تسأل عن المميزات.

Rental Application
Name: Maya Ramos
Telephone number: 818-555-2407

C. Submit an application.
تقدّم طلبا.

Rental Agreement
Maya Ramos

D. Sign the rental agreement.
توقّع عقد الإيجار.

E. Pay the first and last month's rent.
تدفع إيجار الشهرين الأول والأخير.

F. Move in.
تنتقل إلى الشقة.

More vocabulary

lease: a monthly or yearly rental agreement
redecorate: to change the paint and furniture in a home
move out: to pack and leave a home

Survey your class. Record the responses.

1. What features do you look for in a home?
2. How did you find your current home?
Report: *Most of us… Some of us…*

Buying a House شراء المنزل

G. Meet with a realtor.

يتقابل مع سمسار عقارات.

H. Look at houses.

يتفرّج على بيوت.

I. Make an offer.

يقدّم عرضا.

J. Get a loan.

يحصل على قرض.

K. Take ownership.

يتولى / يحصل على الملكية.

BEST BANK

Transfer Money & Make Payments

Send On	From Account
06/24/2018	CHECKING XXXXXX1785 (Avail. balance = $5,255.08)

SUBMIT

To Account

MORTGAGE XXX4219 (Amt. due on 07/01/2018 = $1,137.90)

L. Make a mortgage payment.

يسدد دفعة الرهن العقاري.

Moving In الانتقال إلى المنزل

M. Pack.

تقوم بتعبئة الصناديق.

N. Unpack.

تقوم بتفريغ الصناديق.

We have a new address.

O. Put the utilities in your name.

يطلب تسجيل المنافع العامة باسمه.

P. Paint.

يدهن / يطلي.

Q. Arrange the furniture.

يرتّب الأثاث.

Welcome!

R. Meet the neighbors.

يقابل / تقابل الجيران.

Ways to ask about a home's features

Are <u>utilities</u> included?
Is <u>the kitchen</u> large and sunny?
Are <u>the neighbors</u> quiet?

Role play. Talk to an apartment manager.

A: *Hi. I'm calling about <u>the apartment</u>.*
B: *OK. It's <u>unfurnished</u> and rent is $<u>800</u> a month.*
A: *Are utilities included?*

49

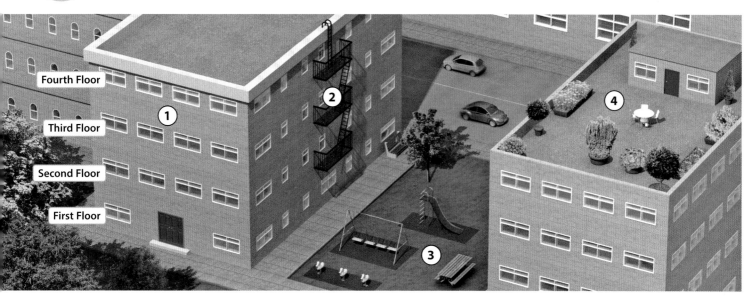

Fourth Floor

Third Floor

Second Floor

First Floor

1. **apartment building**
بناية شقق / عمارة سكنية

2. **fire escape**
سلّم النجاة من الحريق

3. **playground**
ملعب

4. **roof garden**
حديقة على السطح

Entrance المدخل

Apartment Available
2BR + 2BA
555-4263

5. **intercom / speaker**
نظام اتصال داخلي (إنتركوم)

6. **tenant**
مستأجر / ساكن

7. **vacancy sign**
لافتة شقة خالية

8. **manager / superintendent**
مدير / مشرف

Lobby البهو

9. **elevator**
مصعد

10. **stairs / stairway**
سلالم / دَرَج

11. **mailboxes**
صناديق للبريد

Basement الدور السفلي / التحتاني (البدروم)

LAUNDRY ROOM

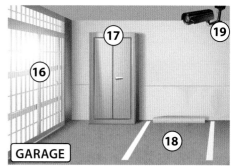

RECREATION ROOM

GARAGE

12. **washer**
غسالة

13. **dryer**
مجففة

14. **big-screen TV**
تلفيزيون بشاشة كبيرة

15. **pool table**
طاولة بلياردو

16. **security gate**
بوابة أمن

17. **storage locker**
مخزن

18. **parking space**
مكان لوقوف السيارة

19. **security camera**
كاميرا للأمن

Grammar Point: *Is there...? / Are there...?*

Is there a rec room?
Yes, there is.
No, there isn't.

Are there stairs?
Yes, there are.
No, there aren't.

Look at the pictures.
Describe the apartment building.

A: There's <u>a pool table</u> in <u>the recreation room</u>.
B: There **are** <u>parking spaces</u> in <u>the garage</u>.

APARTMENT COMPLEX

20. balcony
شرفة / بلكونة

21. courtyard
حوش / فناء / صحن الدار

22. swimming pool
مسبح / حمّام سباحة

23. trash bin
وعاء مهملات / صفيحة زبالة

24. alley
زقاق

Hallway الرواق

FIRE EXIT

25. emergency exit
مخرج للطوارئ

26. trash chute
فتحة أنبوب النفايات

Rental Office مكتب التأجير

Rental Agreement

27. landlord
صاحب الملك

28. lease / rental agreement
عقد الإيجار

29. prospective tenant
مستأجر / ساكن محتمل

An Apartment Entryway مدخل الشقة

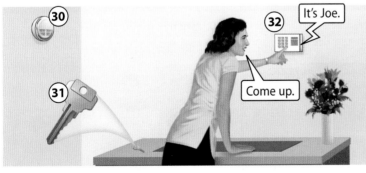

It's Joe.

Come up.

30. smoke detector
كاشف أدخنة

31. key
مفتاح

32. buzzer
رنّان

33. peephole
ثقب الباب / عين سحرية

34. door chain
سلسلة أمان للباب

35. deadbolt lock
قفل بمزلاج ثابت

More vocabulary

upstairs: the floor(s) above you
downstairs: the floor(s) below you
fire exit: another name for emergency exit

Role play. Talk to a landlord.

A: *Is there a swimming pool in this complex?*
B: *Yes, there is. It's near the courtyard.*
A: *Is there…?*

1. the city / an urban area
المدينة / منطقة حضرية

2. the suburbs
الضاحية (الضواحي)

3. a small town / a village
بلدة صغيرة / قرية

4. the country / a rural area
الريف / منطقة ريفية

5. condominium / condo
شقة تمليك

6. townhouse
بيت في مدينة

7. mobile home
بيت متنقل

8. college dormitory / dorm
مساكن الطلاب

9. farm
مزرعة

10. ranch
مزرعة كبيرة

11. senior housing
مساكن المسنين

12. nursing home
بيت للعجزة

13. shelter
ملجأ

More vocabulary

co-op: an apartment building owned by residents
duplex: a house divided into two homes
two-story house: a house with two floors

Think about it. Discuss.

1. Compare life in a city and a small town.
2. Compare life in a city and the country.

Front Yard and House الفناء الأمامي والمنزل

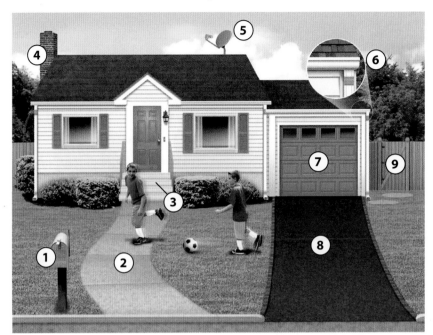

Front Porch الشرفة (الفراندة) الأمامية

1. mailbox صندوق للبريد	**4. chimney** مدخنة	**7. garage door** باب الجراج
2. front walk ممر المدخل الرئيسي	**5. satellite dish** صحن ساتليت	**8. driveway** ممر الجراج
3. steps سلالم / دَرَج	**6. gutter** مزراب	**9. gate** بوابة

10. storm door باب حاجز (مضاد للعواصف)	**13. porch light** مصباح الشرفة (الفراندة)
11. front door باب أمامي	**14. doorbell** جرس الباب
12. doorknob قبضة (أكرة) الباب	**15. screen door** باب منخلي (سلكي)

Backyard الفناء الخلفي

16. patio فناء مرصوف في الهواء الطلق	**19. patio furniture** أثاث للفناء المرصوف	**22. sprinkler** مِرَشّة	**25. compost pile** كومة سماد طبيعي	**A. take** a nap تأخذ قيلولة
17. grill شوّاية	**20. flower bed** حوض زهور	**23. hammock** أرجوحة شبكية للنوم	**26. lawn** مَخْضرة	**B. garden** يعمل في الحديقة
18. sliding glass door باب زجاجي منزلق	**21. hose** خرطوم	**24. garbage can** وعاء مهملات	**27. vegetable garden** بستان خضروات	

1. cabinet خزانة	**8. dishwasher** غسالة صحون	**15. toaster oven** فرن لتحميص الخبز	**22. counter** طاولة طويلة / منضدة
2. shelf رف	**9. refrigerator** ثلاجة	**16. pot** قدر طبخ	**23. drawer** دُرج / جارور
3. paper towels مناديل ورق	**10. freezer** حجرة التجميد في الثلاجة / فريزر	**17. teakettle** غلاية / برّاد شاي	**24. pan** طنجرة / مقلاة
4. sink حوض	**11. toaster** محمصة الخبز (توستر)	**18. stove** موقد	**25. electric mixer** خلاط كهربائي
5. dish rack رف أو صفاية صحون	**12. blender** خلاط	**19. burner** مضرم	**26. food processor** جهاز تحضير المأكولات
6. coffee maker صانع قهوة كهربائي	**13. microwave** فرن ميكروويف	**20. oven** فرن	**27. cutting board** لوحة تقطيع
7. garbage disposal وعاء لتصريف النفايات	**14. electric can opener** فتّاحة علب كهربائية	**21. broiler** مشواة	**28. mixing bowl** سلطانية للخلط

Ways to talk about location using *on* and *in*

Use **on** for the counter, shelf, burner, stove, and cutting board. *It's on the counter.* Use **in** for the dishwasher, oven, sink, and drawer. *Put it in the sink.*

Pair practice. Make new conversations.

A: *Please move the <u>blender</u>.*
B: *Sure. Do you want it <u>in the cabinet</u>?*
A: *No, put it <u>on the counter</u>.*

1

2

3

4

5

6

7

1. dish / plate
طبق / صحن

2. bowl
سلطانية

3. fork
شوكة

4. knife
سكين

5. spoon
ملعقة

6. teacup
فنجان للشاي

7. coffee mug
فنجان قهوة كبير

8. dining room chair
كرسي حجرة الطعام

9. dining room table
طاولة حجرة الطعام / سفرة

10. napkin
منديل مائدة

11. placemat
قطعة قماش مخرمة توضع تحت الطبق

12. tablecloth
مفرش الطاولة

13. salt and pepper shakers
مذرتا الملح والفلفل

14. sugar bowl
إناء للسكر

15. creamer
إناء للحليب

16. teapot
إبريق شاي

17. tray
صينية

18. light fixture
ضوء مثبت / تركيبة إنارة

19. fan
مروحة

20. platter
طبق كبير مسطح

21. serving bowl
سلطانية (طبق) تخديم

22. hutch
خزانة البوفيه العلوية

23. vase
زهرية

24. buffet
بوفيه / مقصف

Ways to make requests at the table

May I have <u>the sugar bowl</u>?
Would you pass <u>the creamer</u>, please?
Could I have <u>a coffee mug</u>?

Role play. Request items at the table.

A: *What do you need?*
B: *Could I have a <u>coffee mug</u>?*
A: *Certainly. And would you…?*

55

1. love seat أريكة / كنبة مزدوجة	**7. digital video recorder (DVR)** مسجل فيديو رقمي (دي في آر) DVR	**13. fireplace** مستوقد / مدفأة	**19. coffee table** طاولة قهوة
2. throw pillow وسادة كنبة للزينة	**8. stereo system** جهاز ستريو	**14. end table** طاولة طرفية أو جانبية	**20. candle** شمعة
3. basket سلة	**9. painting** لوحة فنية	**15. floor lamp** مصباح أرضي	**21. candle holder** قاعدة الشمعة
4. houseplant نبات منزلي	**10. wall** جدار / حائط	**16. drapes / curtains** ستائر / اسدال	**22. armchair / easy chair** كرسي ذو مسندين / فوتيه
5. entertainment center رف الأجهزة الصوتية والمرئية	**11. mantle** رف المستوقد (المدفأة)	**17. window** نافذة / شباك	**23. ottoman** مسند
6. TV (television) تلفزيون	**12. fire screen** حاجز منخلي للمستوقد (حاجب النار)	**18. sofa / couch** كنبة / أريكة	**24. carpet** سجادة

More vocabulary

light bulb: the light inside a lamp

magazine rack: a piece of furniture for magazines

sofa cushions: the pillows that are part of the sofa

Internet Research: furniture prices

Type any furniture item and the word "price" in the search bar.

Report: *I found a sofa for $300.00.*

1. hamper	**8. faucet**	**15. towel rack**	**22. medicine cabinet**
سلة الملابس (سبت للغسيل)	حنفية	حمالة فوط / مناشف	دولاب أدوية
2. bathtub	**9. hot water**	**16. bath towel**	**23. toothbrush**
حوض الاستحمام (بانيو)	ماء ساخن	منشفة للاستحمام	فرشاة أسنان
3. soap dish	**10. cold water**	**17. hand towel**	**24. toothbrush holder**
صحن صابون	ماء بارد	فوطة يد	إناء لفرشاة الأسنان
4. soap	**11. grab bar**	**18. mirror**	**25. sink**
صابون	قضيب للتمسك	مرآة	حوض
5. rubber mat	**12. tile**	**19. toilet paper**	**26. wastebasket**
بساطة أو حصيرة مطاطية	بلاط / قيشاني	ورق تواليت	سلة مهملات
6. washcloth	**13. showerhead**	**20. toilet brush**	**27. scale**
فوطة / منشفة صغيرة	رأس الدش	فرشاة التواليت	ميزان
7. drain	**14. shower curtain**	**21. toilet**	**28. bath mat**
مصرف المياه / بلاعة	ستار الدش	تواليت / مرحاض	حصيرة حمام

More vocabulary

stall shower: a shower without a bathtub
half bath: a bathroom with no shower or tub
linen closet: a closet for towels and sheets

Survey your class. Record the responses.

1. Is your toothbrush on the sink or in the medicine cabinet?
2. Do you have a bathtub or a shower?
Report: *Most of us… Some of us…*

1. dresser / bureau خزانة ملابس بمرآة وأدراج	**8. mini-blinds** ستائر معدنية أو خشبية صغيرة	**15. blanket** بطّانية	**22. rug** سجادة
2. drawer دُرج / جارور	**9. bed** سرير / فراش	**16. quilt** لحاف	**23. night table / nightstand** طاولة جانبية / كومودينو
3. photos صور فوتوغرافية	**10. headboard** رأس السرير	**17. dust ruffle** كشكشة مانعة للأتربة	**24. alarm clock** منبّه
4. picture frame اطار للصور / برواز	**11. pillow** وسادة / مخدة	**18. bed frame** قاعدة السرير	**25. lamp** مصباح (أباجورة)
5. closet دولاب / خزانة	**12. fitted sheet** ملاءة مفصلة	**19. box spring** صندوق زنبركي تحت السرير	**26. lampshade** قبعة أو شمسية المصباح
6. full-length mirror مراة كاملة الطول	**13. flat sheet** ملاءة	**20. mattress** مرتبة / فراش	**27. light switch** مفتاح الضوء
7. curtains ستائر	**14. pillowcase** كيس وسادة / مخدة	**21. wood floor** أرضية خشبية	**28. outlet** مأخذ التيار

Look at the pictures.
Describe the bedroom.

A: *There's a lamp on the nightstand.*
B: *There's a mirror in the closet.*

Survey your class. Record the responses.

1. Do you prefer a hard or a soft mattress?
2. How many pillows do you like on your bed?
Report: *All of us… A few of us…*

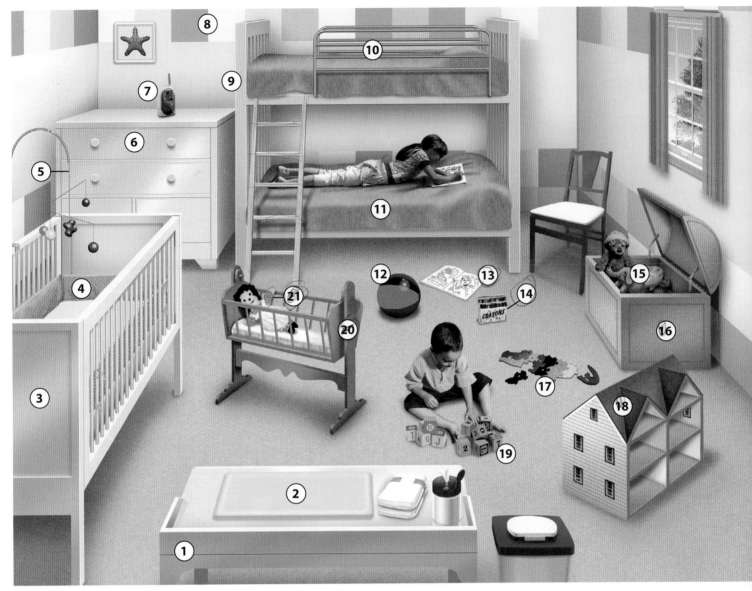

Furniture and Accessories أثاث وإكسسوارات

1. changing table
طاولة لتغيير ملابس الطفل

2. changing pad
لبادة لتغيير حفاض الطفل

3. crib
سرير طفل رضيع

4. bumper pad
لبادة وقائية للطفل

5. mobile
لعبة دوارة بزنبرك

6. chest of drawers
خزانة ذات أدراج

7. baby monitor
أداة مراقبة الطفل

8. wallpaper
ورق حائط

9. bunk beds
كناديس (سرير مزدوج)

10. safety rail
قضيب أمان

11. bedspread
مفرش سرير / شرشف

Toys and Games لعب وألعاب

12. ball
كرة

13. coloring book
كتاب تلوين

14. crayons
أقلام ألوان شمعية

15. stuffed animals
حيوانات محشوة

16. toy chest
صندوق اللعب

17. puzzle
لغز

18. dollhouse
بيت للدمى

19. blocks
مكعبات

20. cradle
مهد

21. doll
دمية

Pair practice. Make new conversations.

A: *Where's the changing pad?*

B: *It's on the changing table.*

Think about it. Discuss.

1. Which toys help children learn? How?
2. Which toys are good for older and younger children?
3. What safety features does this room need? Why?

A. **dust** the furniture
تمسح / تزيل التراب عن الأثاث

B. **recycle** the newspapers
يعد الصحف للاستعمال ثانية

C. **clean** the oven
تنظّف الفرن

D. **mop** the floor
يمسح الأرضية

E. **polish** the furniture
تلمّع الأثاث

F. **make** the bed
يرتّب (يسوّي) السرير

G. **put away** the toys
يضع اللعب في مكانها

H. **vacuum** the carpet
يكنس السجاد بالمكنسة الكهربائية

I. **wash** the windows
تغسل النوافذ

J. **sweep** the floor
يكنس الأرضية بالمقشة

K. **scrub** the sink
تنظّف الحوض بالفرشاة

L. **empty** the trash
يفرّغ سلة المهملات

M. **wash** the dishes
يغسل الأطباق أو الصحون

N. **dry** the dishes
تجفف / تنشف الأطباق

O. **wipe** the counter
تمسح المنضدة

P. **change** the sheets
تغيّر الملاءات

Q. **take out** the garbage
يلقي القمامة

Pair practice. Make new conversations.

A: *Let's clean this place. First, I'll <u>sweep the floor</u>.*
B: *I'll <u>mop the floor</u> when you finish.*
A: *OK. After that we can…*

Think about it. Discuss.

1. Rank housework tasks from difficult to easy.
2. Categorize housework tasks by age: children, teens, adults.

   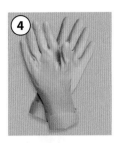 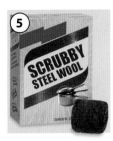 

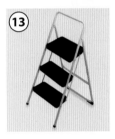     

1. feather duster
ريشة تنظيف

2. recycling bin
وعاء للمهملات المعاد تدويرها

3. oven cleaner
منظف الفرن

4. rubber gloves
قفازات مطاطية

5. steel-wool soap pads
قطع سلك للتنظيف

6. sponge mop
ممسحة إسفنجية

7. bucket / pail
دلو / جردل

8. furniture polish
ملمّع الأثاث

9. cleaning cloths
أقمشة للتنظيف

10. vacuum cleaner
مكنسة كهربائية

11. vacuum cleaner attachments
ملحقات المكنسة الكهربائية

12. vacuum cleaner bag
كيس المكنسة الكهربائية

13. stepladder
سلم درجي

14. glass cleaner
منظف زجاج

15. squeegee
مسّاحة مطاطية (سكويجي)

16. broom
مقشة / مكنسة

17. dustpan
جاروف / لقّاطة الكناسة

18. multipurpose cleaner
منظف متعدد الاستعمالات

19. sponge
إسفنجه

20. scrub brush
فرشاة مسح وحك

21. dishwashing liquid
سائل غسل الأطباق

22. dish towel
فوطة تجفيف الأطباق

23. disinfectant wipes
مناديل مطهّرة

24. trash bags
أكياس مهملات

Ways to ask for something

Please hand me <u>the squeegee</u>.
Can you get me <u>the broom</u>?
I need <u>the sponge mop</u>.

Pair practice. Make new conversations.

A: *Please hand me <u>the sponge mop</u>.*
B: *Here you go. Do you need <u>the bucket</u>?*
A: *Yes, please. Can you get me <u>the rubber gloves</u>, too?*

1. The water heater is **not working**.
سخان الماء **لا يعمل**.

2. The power is **out**.
التيار الكهربائي **مقطوع**.

3. The roof is **leaking**.
السقف **يسرب / يرشح**.

4. The tile is **cracked**.
البلاط **مشقوق**.

5. The window is **broken**.
النافذة **مكسورة**.

6. The lock is **broken**.
القفل مكسور.

7. The steps are **broken**.
الدرج **مكسور**.

8. roofer
أخصائي تصليح أسقف البيوت

9. electrician
كهربائي

10. repairperson
مُصلّح / عامل تصليح

11. locksmith
مُصلّح أقفال

12. carpenter
نجّار

13. fuse box
صندوق المصاهر الكهربائية (الفيوزات)

14. gas meter
عداد الغاز

More vocabulary

fix: to repair something that is broken
pests: termites, fleas, rats, etc.
exterminate: to kill household pests

Pair practice. Make new conversations.

A: The _faucet is leaking_.
B: I think I can fix it.
A: I think we should call _a plumber_.

15. The furnace is **broken**.

الفرن / التنور **متعطل**.

16. The pipes are **frozen**.

المواسير **مجمدة**.

17. The faucet is **dripping**.

الحنفية **تنقّط / تقطر**.

18. The sink is **overflowing**.

الحوض **طافح / مسدود**.

19. The toilet is **stopped up**.

المرحاض (التواليت) **مسدود**.

20. plumber

سبّاك / سمكري

21. exterminator

شخص متخصص في إبادة الحشرات

22. termites

نملة بيضاء (نمل أبيض)

23. ants

نملة (نمل)

24. bedbugs

بقة (بق)

25. fleas

برغوث (براغيث)

26. cockroaches / roaches

صرصور (صراصير)

27. rats

جرذ (جرذان)

28. mice*

فأر (فئران)

*Note: one mouse, two mice

Ways to ask about repairs

How much will it cost?

When can you begin?

How long will it take?

Role play. Talk to a repairperson.

A: *Can you <u>fix the roof</u>?*

B: *Yes, but it will take <u>two weeks</u>.*

A: *How much will it cost?*

1. roommates	3. music	5. noise	7. rules	9. invitation
رفقاء شقة	موسيقى	ضجيج	قواعد	دعوة / عزومة
2. party	4. DJ	6. irritated	8. mess	A. dance
حفلة	مشغّل الأسطوانات (دي جاي)	مهتاج / متهيج	لخبطة / خربطة	يرقصون

What do you see in the pictures?

1. What happened in apartment 2B? How many people were there?

2. How did the neighbor feel? Why?

3. What rules did they write at the tenant meeting?

4. What did the roommates do after the tenant meeting?

Read the story.

The Tenant Meeting

Sally Lopez and Tina Green are <u>roommates</u>. They live in apartment 2B. One night they had a big <u>party</u> with <u>music</u> and a <u>DJ</u>. There was a <u>mess</u> in the hallway. Their neighbors were very unhappy. Mr. Clark in 2A was very <u>irritated</u>. He hates <u>noise</u>!

The next day there was a tenant meeting. Everyone wanted <u>rules</u> about parties and loud music. The girls were very embarrassed.

After the meeting, the girls cleaned the mess in the hallway. Then they gave each neighbor an <u>invitation</u> to a new party. Everyone had a good time at the rec room party. Now the tenants have two new rules and a new place to <u>dance</u>.

Reread the story.

1. Find the word "irritated" in paragraph 1. What does it mean in this story?

2. Retell the story in your own words.

What do you think?

3. Imagine you are the neighbor in 2A. What do you say to Tina and Sally?

4. What are the most important rules in an apartment building? Why?

65

Back from the Market العودة من السوق

1. fish
   سمك

2. meat
   لحم

3. chicken
   دجاج

4. cheese
   جبن

5. milk
   حليب

6. butter
   زبد

7. eggs
   بيض

8. vegetables
   خضروات

Listen and point. Take turns.

A: *Point to the vegetables.*
B: *Point to the bread.*
A: *Point to the fruit.*

Dictate to your partner. Take turns.

A: *Write vegetables.*
B: *Please spell vegetables for me.*
A: *V-e-g-e-t-a-b-l-e-s.*

9. fruit
فاكهة

10. rice
أرز

11. bread
خبز / عيش

12. pasta
باستا (ضرب من المعكرونة)

13. grocery bag / shopping bag
كيس البقالة / كيس التسوق

14. shopping list
قائمة التسوق

15. coupons
كوبونات

Ways to talk about food.

Do we need <u>eggs</u>?

Do we have any <u>pasta</u>?

We have some <u>vegetables</u>, but we need <u>fruit</u>.

Role play. Talk about your shopping list.

A: *Do we need <u>eggs</u>?*

B: *No, we have some.*

A: *Do we have any...?*

67

1. apples	**9.** tangerines
تفاح	يوسفي
2. bananas	**10.** peaches
موز	خوخ
3. grapes	**11.** cherries
عنب	كرز
4. pears	**12.** apricots
كمثرى	مشمش
5. oranges	**13.** plums
برتقال	برقوق
6. grapefruit	**14.** strawberries
ليمون الجنة (كريب فروت)	فراولة / فريز
7. lemons	**15.** raspberries
ليمون (ليمون أصفر)	توت شوكي
8. limes	**16.** blueberries
ليم (ليمون أخضر أو حامض)	توت العنبية

17. blackberries	**25.** raisins
توت العليق	زبيب
18. watermelons	**26.** prunes
بطيخ	قراصيا (برقوق مجفف)
19. melons	**27.** figs
شمام	تين
20. papayas	**28.** dates
ببايا	تمر / بلح
21. mangoes	**29.** a bunch of bananas
مانجو	حزمة موز
22. kiwi	**30.** **ripe** banana
كيوي	موز **ناضج**
23. pineapples	**31.** **unripe** banana
أناناس	موز **غير ناضج (نيئ)**
24. coconuts	**32.** **rotten** banana
جوز الهند	موز **عفن**

Pair practice. Make new conversations.

A: *What's your favorite fruit?*
B: *I like apples. Do you?*
A: *I prefer bananas.*

Survey your class. Record the responses.

1. What kinds of fruit are common in your native country?
2. What kinds of fruit are uncommon?
Report: *According to Luis, papayas are common in Peru.*

1. lettuce
خس

2. cabbage
كرنب / ملفوف

3. carrots
جزر

4. radishes
فجل

5. beets
بنجر / شمندر

6. tomatoes
طماطم / قوطة / بندورة

7. bell peppers
فلفل رومي / فلفل حلو

8. string beans
فاصوليا

9. celery
كرفس

10. cucumbers
خيار

11. spinach
سبانخ

12. corn
ذُرة

13. broccoli
بروكلي (نوع من القرنبيط)

14. cauliflower
قرنبيط

15. bok choy
بوك تشوي

16. turnips
لفت

17. potatoes
بطاطا / بطاطس

18. sweet potatoes
بطاطا حلوة

19. onions
بصل

20. green onions / scallions
بصل أخضر / كرّاث أندلسي

21. peas
بسلة (بازلا)

22. artichokes
خرشوف

23. eggplants
باذنجان

24. squash
قرع

25. zucchini
كوسا

26. asparagus
هليون

27. mushrooms
فطر (عيش غراب)

28. parsley
بقدونس

29. chili peppers
فلفل حار

30. garlic
ثوم

31. a **bag of** lettuce
كيس خس

32. a **head of** lettuce
رأس خس

Pair practice. Make new conversations.

A: *Do you eat* <u>broccoli</u>?
B: *Yes. I like most vegetables, but not* <u>peppers</u>.
A: *Really? Well, I don't like* <u>cauliflower</u>.

Survey your class. Record the responses.

1. Which vegetables do you prefer to eat raw?
2. Which vegetables do you prefer to eat cooked?
Report: ____ *of us prefer* <u>raw carrots</u>. ____ *of us prefer* <u>cooked carrots</u>.

69

MEAT

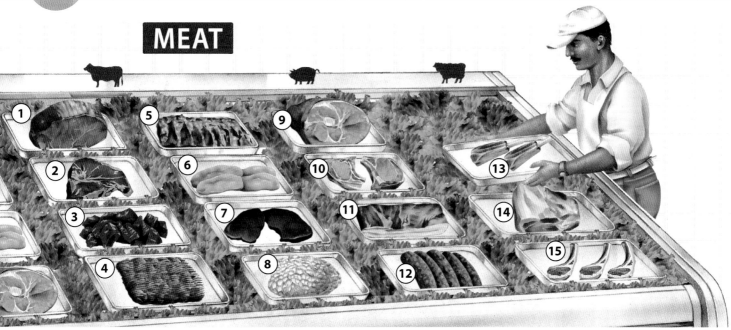

Beef لحم بقر

1. roast
   لحم معد للشواء (روستو)

2. steak
   شريحة لحم (بفتيك)

3. stewing beef
   لحم للسلق (لحم معدّ لليخنة)

4. ground beef
   لحم مفروم

5. beef ribs
   ريش (ضلوع) لحم بقري

6. veal cutlets
   شرائح لحم عجل (بتلو)

7. liver
   كبدة

8. tripe
   الكرش (كرشة)

Pork لحم الخنزير

9. ham
   لحم فخذ خنزير

10. pork chops
    شرائح لحم خنزير

11. bacon
    لحم خنزير مملح (بيكون)

12. sausage
    سجق / نقانق

Lamb لحم الحمل (الضأن)

13. lamb shanks
    ساق حمل

14. leg of lamb
    فخذة حمل

15. lamb chops
    شرائح لحم حمل

POULTRY

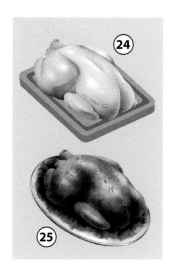

Poultry الدواجن

16. chicken	18. duck	20. wings	22. thighs	24. **raw** turkey
دجاج	بط	أجنحة	أفخاذ / أوراك	دجاج **نيئ**
17. turkey	19. breasts	21. legs	23. drumsticks	25. **cooked** turkey
ديك رومي	صدور	أرجل	دبابيس (وصلة الفخذ بالكاحل)	دجاجة **مطهوة**

More vocabulary

boneless: meat and poultry without bones
skinless: poultry without skin
vegetarian: a person who doesn't eat meat

Ways to ask about meat prices

*How much **is** that <u>roast</u>?*
*How much **are** those <u>cutlets</u>?*
*How much **is** the <u>ground beef</u>?*

SEAFOOD

Fish أسماك

1. trout
سمك التروتة المرقّط

2. catfish
سمك الصلور

3. whole salmon
سلمون كامل

4. salmon steak
شريحة (فيليه) سلمون

5. swordfish
سمك أبو سيف

6. halibut steak
شريحة (فيليه) هلبوت

7. tuna
التونة

8. cod
سمك القد (بكلاه)

Shellfish محار

9. crab
سرطان البحر (كابوريا)

10. lobster
جراد البحر (استاكوزة)

11. shrimp
جمبري / ربيان

12. scallops
أسقلوب

13. mussels
بلح البحر

14. oysters
محار رخوي

15. clams
صدف البطلنيوس

16. **fresh** fish
سمك **طازج**

17. **frozen** fish
سمك **مجمد**

DELI

18. white bread
خبز أبيض

19. wheat bread
خبز قمحي

20. rye bread
خبز جاوداري

21. roast beef
قطعة لحم بقري مشوي (روزبيف)

22. corned beef
لحم بقري مملح (بلوبيف)

23. pastrami
بسطرمة

24. salami
لانشون السلامي

25. smoked turkey
ديك رومي مدخّن

26. American cheese
جبن أمريكي

27. Swiss cheese
جبن سويسري

28. cheddar cheese
جبن شيدر

29. mozzarella cheese
جبن موتساريلا

Ways to order at the counter

I'd like some roast beef.
I'll have a halibut steak and some shrimp.
Could I get some Swiss cheese?

Pair practice. Make new conversations.

A: *What can I get for you?*
B: *I'd like some roast beef. How about a pound?*
A: *A pound of roast beef coming up!*

71

A Grocery Store محل البقالة

SEAFOOD

DAIRY

POULTRY

MEAT

FROZEN FOODS

2A | 2B

1. **customer**
زبون

2. **produce section**
قسم المنتجات الزراعية

3. **scale**
ميزان

4. **grocery clerk**
بائع في محل البقالة

5. **stocker**
عامل مخازن

6. **pet food**
طعام الحيوانات المنزلية

7. **aisle**
ممر

8. **manager**
مدير

Canned Foods
معلبات

17. **beans**
فول

18. **soup**
شوربة / حساء

19. **tuna**
علبة سمك التونة

Dairy
منتجات الألبان

20. **margarine**
مرجرين (سمن نباتي)

21. **sour cream**
قشدة (كريمة) حامضة

22. **yogurt**
زبادي / لبن

Grocery Products
منتجات بقالة

23. **aluminum foil**
ورق تغليف ألمونيوم

24. **plastic wrap**
ورق تغليف بلاستيكي

25. **plastic storage bags**
أكياس تخزين بلاستيكية

Frozen Foods
مأكولات مجمدة

26. **ice cream**
أيس كريم / بوظة / جيلاتي

27. **frozen vegetables**
خضروات مجمدة

28. **frozen dinner**
وجبة عشاء مجمدة

Ways to ask for information in a grocery store

Excuse me, where are <u>the carrots</u>?
Can you please tell me where to find <u>the dog food</u>?
Do you have any <u>lamb chops</u> today?

Pair practice. Make new conversations.

A: <u>*Can you please tell me where to find the dog food*</u>?
B: *Sure. It's in <u>aisle 1B</u>. Do you need anything else?*
A: *Yes, where are <u>the carrots</u>?*

9. shopping basket سلة التسوق	**11.** line صف / طابور	**13.** checkstand مركز الدفع	**15.** bagger مكيّس / معبّئ أكياس
10. self-checkout دفع الحساب ذاتيا	**12.** cart عربة تسوق	**14.** cashier / checker أمين صندوق / صراف	**16.** cash register آلة تسجيل النقود

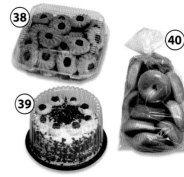

Baking Products منتجات للخبز	**Beverages** مشروبات	**Snack Foods** مأكولات خفيفة	**Baked Goods** أطعمة مخبوزة
29. flour دقيق	**32.** apple juice عصير تفاح	**35.** potato chips رقائق بطاطس مقلية (شيبس)	**38.** cookies بسكويت (كعك رقيق محلى)
30. sugar سكر	**33.** coffee قهوة	**36.** nuts مكسرات	**39.** cake كعكة
31. oil زيت	**34.** soda / pop مشروبات غازية / صودا	**37.** candy bar قطعة من الحلوى	**40.** bagels بيغل (أقراص من الخبز)

Survey your class. Record the responses.

1. What is your favorite grocery store?
2. Do you prefer to shop alone or with someone?
Report: *Most of us… Some of us…*

Think about it. Discuss.

1. Compare small grocery stores and large supermarkets.
2. Categorize the foods on this page as healthy or unhealthy. Explain your answers.

 **1. bottles**
زجاجة

 **2. jars**
برطمان / مرطبان

 **3. cans**
علبة (علب) معدنية

 **4. cartons**
علبة كرتون (كراتين)

 **5. containers**
حاوية / وعاء

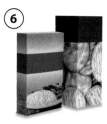 **6. boxes**
علبة / صندوق (صناديق)

 **7. bags**
كيس (أكياس)

 **8. packages**
رزمة (رزم)

 **9. six-packs**
علبة حاوية ست زجاجات أو علب

 **10. loaves**
رغيف (أرغفة)

 **11. rolls**
لفة (لفافات)

 **12. tubes**
أنبوب (أنابيب)

 **13.**

 **14.**

 15.

 **16.**

 **17.**

 **18.**

 19.

 **20.**

 **21.**

 **22.**

 **23.**

 **24.**

13. a bottle of water
زجاجة ماء

14. a jar of jam
برطمان مربى

15. a can of beans
علبة فول

16. a carton of eggs
كرتون(ة) بيض

17. a container of cottage cheese
وعاء / حاوية جبن حلوم

18. a box of cereal
علبة حبوب (سيريال)

19. a bag of flour
كيس دقيق

20. a package of cookies
رزمة بسكويت

21. a six-pack of soda (pop)
علبة حاوية ست زجاجات صودا

22. a loaf of bread
رغيف خبز

23. a roll of paper towels
لفة مناديل ورقية

24. a tube of toothpaste
أنبوب معجون أسنان

Grammar Point: count and noncount

Some foods can be counted: *an apple, two apples.*
Some foods can't be counted: *some rice, some water.*
For noncount foods, count containers: *two bags of rice.*

Pair practice. Make new conversations.

A: *How many boxes of cereal do we need?*
B: *We need two boxes.*

A. Measure the ingredients.
تعاير المقادير.

B. Weigh the food.
تزِن الطعام.

C. Convert the measurements.
تحوّل المكاييل.

1 cup = 237 milliliters

Liquid Measures مقادير السوائل

1 fl. oz.

1 c.

1 pt.

Milk 1 qt.

1 gal.

1. a fluid ounce of milk
أونصة سائلية من الحليب

2. a cup of oil
كوب زيت

3. a pint of frozen yogurt
باينت زبادي (لبن) مجمد

4. a quart of milk
كوارت حليب

5. a gallon of water
جالون ماء

Dry Measures مقادير المواد الجافة

 1 tsp.

1 TBS.

 1/4 c.

 1/2 c.

 1 c.

6. a teaspoon of salt
ملعقة شاي من الملح

7. a tablespoon of sugar
ملعقة طعام (سفرة) من السكر

8. a quarter cup of brown sugar
ربع كوب من السكر البني

9. a half cup of raisins
نصف كوب من الزبيب

10. a cup of flour
كوب من الدقيق

Weight الأوزان

11. an ounce of cheese
أونصة من الجبن

12. a pound of roast beef
باوند (رطل) من شرائح لحم البقر

Equivalencies	
3 tsp. = 1 TBS.	2 c. = 1 pt.
2 TBS. = 1 fl. oz.	2 pt. = 1 qt.
8 fl. oz. = 1 c.	4 qt. = 1 gal.

Volume
1 fl. oz. = 30 ml
1 c. = 237 ml
1 pt. = .47 L
1 qt. = .95 L
1 gal. = 3.79 L

Weight
1 oz. = 28.35 grams (g)
1 lb. = 453.6 g
2.205 lbs. = 1 kilogram (kg)
1 lb. = 16 oz.

Food Preparation and Safety تحضير الطعام وسلامته

Food Safety سلامة الطعام

A. **clean**
نظّف

B. **separate**
افصل

C. **cook**
اطبخ

D. **chill**
جمّد / برّد

Clean counters!
20 SECONDS
Wash your hands!

Use separate cutting boards for vegetables and meat!

Cook to the right temperature!

Refrigerate leftovers quickly!

Ways to Serve Meat and Poultry طرق لتحضير اللحوم والدواجن

1. fried chicken
دجاج مقلي

2. barbecued / grilled ribs
ريش (ضلوع) مشوية / مشوية على الفحم

3. broiled steak
شريحة لحم مشوي

4. roasted turkey
ديك رومي مطهو في الفرن

5. boiled ham
لحم فخذ خنزير مسلوق

6. stir-fried beef
لحم بقري مقلي بالتقليب

Ways to Serve Eggs طرق لتحضير البيض

7. scrambled eggs
بيض مفري

8. hard-boiled eggs
بيض مسلوق جيدا

9. poached eggs
بيض مسلوق مفقوصا في الماء الغالي

10. eggs sunny-side up
بيض مقلي على شكل عيون

11. eggs over easy
بيض مقلي خفيفا ومقلوب

12. omelet
بيض أومليت (عجة)

More vocabulary

bacteria: very small living things that often cause disease
surface: a counter, a table, or the outside part of something
disinfect: to remove bacteria from a surface

Pair practice. Make new conversations.

A: *How do you like your eggs?*
B: *I like them* <u>scrambled</u>. *And you?*
A: *I like them* <u>hard-boiled</u>.

Cheesy Tofu Vegetable Casserole كسرولة (طبق) خضار بالتوفو الجبني

A. Preheat the oven.
سخّن الفرن مسبقا.

B. Grease a baking pan.
شحّم طنجرة / طاسة خبز.

C. Slice the tofu.
قطع التوفو في شرائح.

D. Steam the broccoli.
اطهِ البروكولي على البخار.

E. Sauté the mushrooms.
اقلِ الفطر بسرعة وفي قليل من الدهن.

F. Spoon sauce on top.
ضع صلصة بالملعقة على السطح.

G. Grate the cheese.
ابشر الجبن.

H. Bake.
اخبز في الفرن.

Easy Chicken Soup شوربة دجاج سهلة

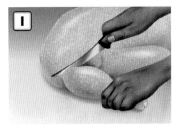

I. Cut up the chicken.
قطّع الدجاج إلى قطع صغيرة.

J. Dice the celery.
قطّع الكرفس إلى مكعبات.

K. Peel the carrots.
قشّر الجزر.

L. Chop the onions.
قطّع (قرّط) البصل.

M. Boil the chicken.
اسلق الدجاج.

N. Add the vegetables.
أضف الخضروات.

O. Stir.
قلّب.

P. Simmer.
اطهِ ببطء (على نار هادئة).

Quick and Easy Cake كعكة سريعة وسهلة

Q. Break 2 eggs into a microwave-safe bowl.
اكسر بيضتين في سلطانية آمنة الاستعمال في ميكروويف.

R. Mix the ingredients.
اخلط المكونات.

S. Beat the mixture.
اضرب الخليط.

T. Microwave for 5 minutes.
اطهِ في الميكروويف لمدة ٥ دقائق.

Kitchen Utensils   أدوات المطبخ

1. can opener
   فتّاحة علب

2. grater
   مبشرة

3. steamer
   وعاء الطهي بالبخار

4. storage container
   حاوية تخزين

5. frying pan
   طنجرة / مقلاة

6. pot
   إناء / قِدْرة

7. ladle
   مغرفة

8. double boiler
   إناء مزدوج للغلي (غلاية مزدوجة)

9. wooden spoon
   ملعقة خشبية

10. casserole dish
    طبق كبير / طبق كسرولة

11. garlic press
    معصرة ثوم

12. carving knife
    سكين لتقطيع اللحوم

13. roasting pan
    طنجرة / إناء للشوي

14. roasting rack
    شبكة للشوي

15. vegetable peeler
    قشّارة خضروات

16. paring knife
    سكين تقشير

17. colander
    مصفاة

18. kitchen timer
    ساعة توقيت للمطبخ

19. spatula
    ملعقة مبسطة

20. eggbeater
    مخففة (مضرب) بيض

21. whisk
    مخففة

22. strainer
    مصفاة (للسوائل)

23. tongs
    ملقطة

24. lid
    غطاء

25. saucepan
    قدر صغير

26. cake pan
    إناء الكعك

27. cookie sheet
    صينية لخبز الحلوى (البسكويت)

28. pie pan
    صينية فطائر

29. potholders
    ممسكات الآنية الساخنة

30. rolling pin
    مرقاق العجين / شوبك

31. mixing bowl
    سلطانية (وعاء) خلط

Pair practice. Make new conversations.

A: *Please hand me <u>the whisk</u>.*
B: *Here's <u>the whisk</u>. Do you need anything else?*
A: *Yes, pass me <u>the casserole dish</u>.*

Use the new words.

Look at page 77. Name the kitchen utensils you see.

A: *This is <u>a grater</u>.*
B: *This is <u>a mixing bowl</u>.*

1. hamburger	7. nachos	13. ice-cream cone	19. plastic utensils
سندوتش همبورجر (لحم البقر)	ناتشوز	آيس كريم في كوز من البسكويت	أدوات طعام بلاستيكية
2. French fries	8. taco	14. milkshake	20. sugar substitute
بطاطس مقلية	تاكو	لبن / حليب مخفوق	بديل السكر
3. cheeseburger	9. burrito	15. donut	21. ketchup
سندوتش همبورجر مع الجبن	بوريتو	كعكة الدونات	صلصة طماطم (كاتشب)
4. onion rings	10. pizza	16. muffin	22. mustard
حلقات بصل مقلي	بيتزا	فطيرة مدورة (موفينية)	صلصة خردل (موستردة)
5. chicken sandwich	11. soda	17. counterperson	23. mayonnaise
سندوتش دجاج	مشروب غازي / صودا	عامل المنضدة (الكاونتر)	مايونييز
6. hot dog	12. iced tea	18. straw	24. salad bar
سجق (هوت دوج)	شاي مثلج	شفاطة / ماصة	بوفيه / ركن السلاطات

Grammar Point: yes/no questions (do)

Do you like hamburgers? Yes, I do.
Do you like nachos? No, I don't.
Practice asking about the food on the page.

Think about it. Discuss.

1. Which fast foods are healthier than others? How do you know?
2. Compare the benefits of a fast food lunch and a lunch from home.

79

1. bacon
لحم خنزير مملح (بيكون)

2. sausage
سجق (نقانق)

3. hash browns
بطاطس مقلية ومفرومة

4. toast
خبز محمص (توست)

5. English muffin
موفينية إنجليزية

6. biscuits
فطيرة بسكويت

7. pancakes
فطيرة محلاة (بانكيك)

8. waffles
فطير الوافل

9. hot cereal
حبوب (سيريال) ساخنة

10. grilled cheese sandwich
سندوتش جبن مشوي

11. pickle
خيار مخلل

12. club sandwich
سندوتش النادي (كلوب سندوتش)

13. spinach salad
سلاطة سبانخ

14. chef's salad
سلاطة الشيف / سلاطة رئيس الطهاة

15. house salad / garden salad
سلاطة بيتي / سلاطة الحديقة

16. soup
شوربة / حساء

17. rolls
أقراص خبز

18. coleslaw
سلاطة كرنب (كولسلو)

19. potato salad
سلاطة بطاطس

20. pasta salad
سلاطة معكرونة (باستا)

21. fruit salad
سلاطة فواكه

Menu

Breakfast Special
Served 6 a.m. to 11 a.m.

Two egg omelet with one side

Lunch
Served 11 a.m. to 2 p.m • All sandwiches come with soup or salad.

Side salads

Dressings
Thousand Island · Ranch · Italian · Blue Cheese

Survey your class. Record the responses.
1. Do you prefer soup or salad?
2. Which do you prefer, tea or coffee?
Report: _Five_ of us prefer _tea_. _Most_ of us prefer _soup_.

Pair practice. Make new conversations.
A: What's your favorite _side salad_?
B: I like _coleslaw_. How about you?
A: I like _potato salad_.

Dinner

Desserts

Beverages

22. roast chicken
دجاج مطهو في الفرن

23. mashed potatoes
بطاطس مهروسة (بوريه)

24. steak
شريحة لحم بقري مشوي (ستيك)

25. baked potato
بطاطس مطهوة في الفرن

26. spaghetti
معكرونة رفيعة وطويلة (اسباجتي)

27. meatballs
كبب لحم (كبيبة)

28. garlic bread
خبز بالثوم

29. grilled fish
سمك مشوي على الفحم

30. rice
أرز

31. meatloaf
لحم مفروم مطبوخ في قالب

32. steamed vegetables
خضروات مطبوخة على البخار

33. layer cake
كعكة من طبقات

34. cheesecake
كعكة جبن

35. pie
فطيرة

36. mixed berries
توت مشكَّل

37. coffee
قهوة

38. decaf coffee
قهوة بدون كافيين

39. tea
شاي

40. herbal tea
شاي أعشاب

41. cream
قشدة / قشدة حليب

42. low-fat milk
حليب خفيض الدسم

Ways to order from a menu

I'd like _a grilled cheese sandwich_.
I'll have _a bowl of tomato soup_.
Could I get _the chef's salad_ with _ranch dressing_?

Role play. Order a dinner from the menu.

A: _Are you ready to order?_
B: _I think so. I'll have_ _the roast chicken_.
A: _Would you also like…?_

1. **dining room**
صالة الطعام

2. **hostess**
مضيفة

3. **high chair**
كرسي مرتفع

4. **booth**
مائدة بين مقعدين طويلين مرتفعي الظهر

5. **to-go box**
علبة لأخذ الطعام إلى المنزل

6. **patron / diner**
زبون / شخص يتناول الطعام

7. **menu**
قائمة الطعام

8. **server / waiter**
نادل / جرسون

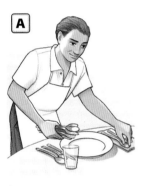

A. **set** the table
يحضّر الطاولة

B. **seat** the customer
تُجلس الزبون

C. **pour** the water
يسكب الماء

D. **order** from the menu
يطلب من قائمة الطعام

E. **take** the order
يسجّل الطلب

F. **serve** the meal
يقدّم الوجبة

G. **clear / bus** the dishes
يزيل الأطباق من على الطاولة / ينظف الطاولة

H. **carry** the tray
يحمل الصينية

I. **pay** the check
يدفع الفاتورة (الحساب)

J. **leave** a tip
يترك بقشيشا

More vocabulary

eat out: to go to a restaurant to eat
get takeout: to buy food at a restaurant and take it home to eat

Look at the pictures.
Describe what is happening.

A: She's _seating the customer_.
B: He's _taking the order_.

9. server / waitress
نادلة / جرسونة

10. dessert tray
صينية أطباق الحلو

11. breadbasket
سلة الخبز

12. busser
مساعد النادل (الجرسون)

13. dish room
غرفة الصحون

14. dishwasher
غسّال الصحون

15. kitchen
مطبخ

16. chef
رئيس الطهاة (شيف)

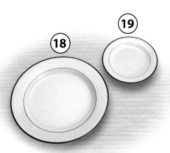

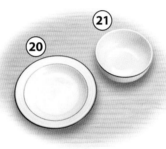

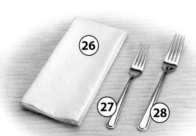

17. place setting
تجهيز سفرة الطعام

18. dinner plate
صحن طعام مفلطح

19. bread-and-butter plate
صحن الخبز والزبدة

20. salad plate
طبق السلاطة

21. soup bowl
سلطانية الشوربة

22. water glass
كأس للماء

23. wine glass
كأس للنبيذ

24. cup
فنجان

25. saucer
صحن للفنجان

26. napkin
منديل قماش للمائدة

27. salad fork
شوكة السلاطة

28. dinner fork
شوكة طعام

29. steak knife
سكين لقطع اللحم

30. knife
سكين

31. teaspoon
ملعقة شاي

32. soup spoon
ملعقة شوربة

Pair practice. Make new conversations.

A: *Excuse me, this <u>spoon</u> is dirty.*
B: *I'm so sorry. I'll get you a clean <u>spoon</u> right away.*
A: *Thanks.*

Role play. A new busser needs help.

A: *Do the <u>salad forks</u> go on <u>the left</u>?*
B: *Yes. They go <u>next to the dinner forks</u>.*
A: *What about the…?*

83

The Farmers' Market

GREEN FARMS

USDA ORGANIC

$1.00 each

1, 2, 3, 4...

4 for $3.00 USDA ORGANIC

Take One

BASIL

1. live music
موسيقى حية

2. organic
منتجات مزروعة بسماد طبيعي

3. lemonade
عصير ليمون (ليمونادة)

4. sour
مذاق حمضي / مُر

5. samples
عيّنات

6. avocados
أفوكاته / زبدية

7. vendors
بائعون

8. sweets
حلويات

9. herbs
أعشاب

A. count
تحصى / تعُدّ

84

What do you see in the picture?

1. How many vendors are at the market today?

2. Which vegetables are organic?

3. What are the children eating?

4. What is the woman counting? Why?

 Read the story.

The Farmers' Market

On Saturdays, the Novaks go to the farmers' market. They like to visit the <u>vendors</u>. Alex Novak always goes to the hot food stand for lunch. His children love to eat the fruit <u>samples</u>. Alex's father usually buys some <u>sweets</u> and <u>lemonade</u>. The lemonade is very <u>sour</u>.

Nina Novak likes to buy <u>organic</u> <u>herbs</u> and vegetables. Today, she is buying <u>avocados</u>. The market worker <u>counts</u> eight avocados. She gives Nina one more for free.

There are other things to do at the market. The Novaks like to listen to the <u>live music</u>. Sometimes they meet friends there. The farmers' market is a great place for families on a Saturday afternoon.

Reread the story.

1. Read the first sentence of the story. How often do the Novaks go to the farmers' market? How do you know?

2. The story says, "The farmers' market is a great place for families." Find examples in the story that support this statement.

What do you think?

3. What's good, bad, or interesting about shopping at a farmers' market?

4. Imagine you are at the farmers' market. What will you buy?

Everyday Clothes
الملابس اليومية

1. shirt
قميص

2. jeans
بنطلون جينز

3. dress
فستان

4. T-shirt
قميص تي شيرت

5. baseball cap
برنيطة (قبعة) بيسبول

6. socks
جوارب قصيرة

7. sneakers
أحذية رياضة / أحذية كاوتش

A. tie
تربط رباط الحذاء

Listen and point. Take turns.

A: *Point to the dress.*
B: *Point to the T-shirt.*
A: *Point to the baseball cap.*

Dictate to your partner. Take turns.

A: *Write dress.*
B: *Is that spelled d-r-e-s-s?*
A: *Yes, that's right.*

ONE NIGHT ONLY

DOORS OPEN AT 8:00

8. blouse
بلوزة

9. handbag
حقيبة / شنطة يد

10. skirt
تنورة (جونلا)

11. suit
بدلة

12. slacks / pants
بنطلون / سروال

13. shoes
أحذية

14. sweater
بلوفر (كنزة)

B. **put on**
ترتدي البلوفر

Ways to compliment clothes

That's a pretty <u>dress</u>!

Those are great <u>shoes</u>!

I really like your <u>baseball cap</u>!

Role play. Compliment a friend.

A: <u>*That's a pretty dress!*</u> <u>*Green*</u> *is a great color on you.*

B: *Thanks! I really like your…*

Casual Clothes الملابس غير الرسمية

1. cap
   قلنسوة / برنيطة

2. cardigan sweater
   بلوفر (كنزة) من صوف محبوك

3. pullover sweater
   بلوفر (كنزة) صوفي يلبس من طريق الرأس

4. sport shirt
   سترة رياضية

5. maternity dress
   فستان للحوامل

6. overalls
   الوزرة (أوفرول)

7. knit top
   سترة صوفية تريكو

8. capris
   بنطلون كابري (بنطلون ضيق مطاط)

9. sandals
   صندل

Work Clothes ملابس العمل

10. uniform
    زي مُوحّد

11. business suit
    بدلة أعمال

12. tie
    رابطة عنق (كرافتة)

13. briefcase
    حقيبة أوراق

More vocabulary

in fashion / in style: clothes that are popular now
outfit: clothes that look nice together
three-piece suit: matching jacket, vest, and slacks

Describe the people. Take turns.

A: *She's wearing a maternity dress.*
B: *He's wearing a uniform.*

Casual, Work, and Formal Clothes

Formal Clothes الملابس الرسمية

14. sport jacket / sport coat
جاكتة سبور / معطف سبور

15. vest
صدرة

16. bow tie
وردة عنق / بمباغ / بابيون

17. tuxedo
بدلة سهرة رسمية للرجال

18. evening gown
فستان سهرة

19. clutch bag
حقيبة أصابع / شنطة سهرة

20. cocktail dress
فستان شبه رسمي

21. high heels
أحذية ذات كعب عالٍ

Exercise Wear ملابس التمرينات الرياضية

22. sweatshirt / hoodie
كنزة فضفاضة / سترة رياضية بغطاء للرأس

23. sweatpants
سروال فضفاض / بنطلون رياضة

24. tank top
قميص قصير بدون أكمام وبفتحات كبيرة
للذراعين (قميص داخلي)

25. shorts
بنطلون قصير (شورت)

Survey your class. Record the responses.

1. Do you prefer to wear formal or casual clothes?

2. Do you prefer to exercise in shorts or sweatpants?

Report: _25% of the class prefers to…_

Think about it. Discuss.

1. Look at pages 170–173. Which jobs require uniforms?

2. What's good and what's bad about wearing a uniform?

3. Describe a popular style. Do you like it? Why or why not?

1. hat
قبعة

2. (over)coat
معطف (خارجي) / بلطو (خارجي)

3. headband
شريط للرأس

4. leather jacket
جاكتة (سترة) جلدية

5. winter scarf
وشاح شتوي

6. gloves
قفازات

7. headwrap
ملفوف حول الرأس

8. jacket
جاكتة

9. parka
بَرْكة (سترة فرائية مقلنسة)

10. mittens
قفازات صوفية بلا أصابع

11. ski hat
قبعة التزحلق على الجليد

12. leggings
الطَّماق / كساء للساق

13. earmuffs
وقاء للأذن من البرد

14. down vest
صدرة من زغب أو وبر

15. ski mask
قناع التزحلق على الجليد

16. down jacket
جاكتة طويلة من زغب أو وبر

17. umbrella
شمسية

18. raincoat
معطف (بلطو) مطر

19. poncho
البُنْش (معطف شبه عباءة)

20. rain boots
حذاء عالي الساق (جزمة) للمطر

21. trench coat
المُمطر (معطف واقٍ من المطر)

22. swimming trunks
شورت للسباحة للرجال (مايوه)

23. straw hat
قبعة من القش

24. windbreaker
سترة قصيرة واقية من الرياح

25. cover-up
غطاء خارجي

26. swimsuit / bathing suit
بدلة سباحة / بدلة استحمام للنساء (مايوه)

27. sunglasses
نظارة شمس (واقية من الشمس)

Grammar Point: should

*It's raining. You **should** take an umbrella.*
*It's snowing. You **should** put on a scarf.*
*It's sunny. You **should** wear a straw hat.*

Pair practice. Make new conversations.

A: *It's <u>snowing</u>. You should put on <u>a scarf</u>.*
B: *Don't worry. I'm wearing my <u>parka</u>.*
A: *Good, and don't forget your <u>mittens</u>!*

Unisex Underwear
ملابس داخلية لكلا الجنسين

1. undershirt
   قميص داخلي (فانيلا)
2. thermal undershirt
   قميص داخلي حراري
3. long underwear
   ملابس داخلية طويلة

Men's Underwear
ملابس داخلية للرجال

4. boxer shorts
   شورت داخلي (شورت ملاكمين)
5. briefs
   سروال تحتاني قصير
6. athletic supporter / jockstrap
   رباط رياضي للجوارب / سروال رياضي

Unisex Socks
جوارب قصيرة لكلا الجنسين

7. ankle socks
   جوارب كاحلية
8. crew socks
   جوارب رياضية
9. dress socks
   جوارب رسمية

Women's Socks
جوارب للنساء

10. low-cut socks
    جوارب قصيرة الارتفاع
11. anklets
    جوارب بارتفاع الكاحل
12. knee highs
    جوارب بارتفاع الركبتين

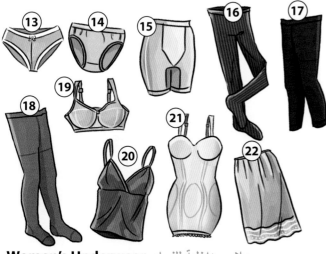

Women's Underwear ملابس داخلية للنساء

13. (bikini) panties
    قميصول (سترة نسائية قصيرة)
14. briefs / underpants
    سروال تحتي قصير رجالي / سروال تحتي
15. body shaper / girdle
    مِشَدّ

16. tights
    بنطلون ضيق جدا
17. footless tights
    رداء ضيق جدا بدون أقدام
18. pantyhose
    جورب سروالي نسائي
19. bra
    صديرية للثدين (سوتيان)

20. camisole
    قميصول (سترة نسائية قصيرة)
21. shapewear slip / slimming slip
    سترة داخلية للتنحيف / سترة داخلية لشد الخصر
22. half slip
    سترة داخلية بنصف طول

Sleepwear ملابس النوم

23. pajamas
    بيجاما
24. nightgown
    قميص نوم للنساء
25. slippers
    شبشب / خف

26. blanket sleeper
    مريلة نوم للأطفال / بيجاما ذات قدمين
27. nightshirt
    قميص طويل للنوم
28. robe
    ثوب حمام / برنس

More vocabulary

lingerie: underwear or sleepwear for women
loungewear: very casual clothing for relaxing around the home

Survey your class. Record the responses.

1. What color socks do you prefer?
2. What type of socks do you prefer?
Report: _Joe prefers white crew socks._

Construction Worker

Road Worker

Automotive Painter

Food Processor

1. hard hat
قبعة صلبة

2. work shirt
قميص عمل / قميص شغل

3. tool belt
حزام أدوات

4. high visibility safety vest
صديرية أمان يمكن رؤيتها عن بعد

5. work pants
بنطلون عمل (شغل)

6. steel toe boots
جزمة عالية الساق ذات مقدّم من الفولاذ

7. ventilation mask
قناع تهوية وتنفس

8. coveralls
منزر(ثوب عمل ذو كمين)

9. bump cap
برنيطة مضادة للصدمة

10. safety glasses
نظارات أمان

11. apron
مريلة

Manager   **Salesperson**

Farmworker

Ranch Hand

12. blazer
جاكتة خفيفة (بليزر)

13. tie
رابطة عنق (كرافتة)

14. polo shirt
فانلا قطن او تريكو

15. name tag
بطاقة عليها الاسم

16. bandana
منديل رأس مزدان بالرسوم

17. work gloves
قفازات عمل

18. cowboy hat
قبعة راعي البقر

19. jeans
بنطلون جينز

Use the new words.
Look at pages 170–173. Name the workplace clothing you see.

A: *Look at #37. She's wearing* a hard hat.
B: *Look at #47. He's wearing* a lab coat.

Pair practice. Make sentences.
Dictate them to your classmates.

A. *Farmworkers* wear *jeans* to work.
B. *A manager* often wears *a tie* to work.

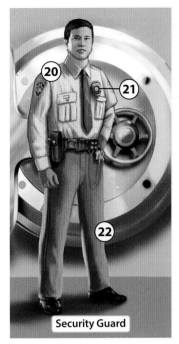

Security Guard

Emergency Worker

Counterperson

Chef

Line Cook

20. security shirt
قميص خاص لموظف الأمن

21. badge
شارة

22. security pants
بنطلون خاص لموظف الأمن

23. helmet
خوذة

24. jumpsuit
جوبية (سترة يرتديها العمال)

25. hairnet
شبكة للشعر

26. smock
سَمَق

27. disposable gloves
قفازات تلقى بعد الاستعمال

28. chef's hat
قبعة رئيس الطهاة (الشيف)

29. chef's jacket
جاكتة رئيس الطهاة (الشيف)

30. waist apron
مريلة خصرية

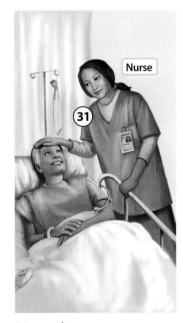

Nurse

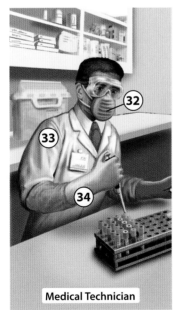

Medical Technician

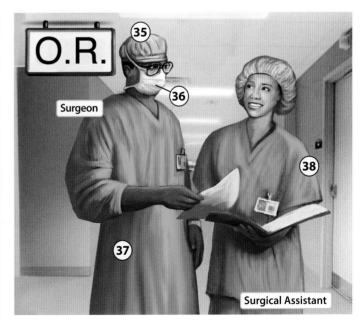

O.R.

Surgeon

Surgical Assistant

31. scrubs
ثياب الجراحين والممرضات

32. face mask
قناع الوجه

33. lab coat
سترة المختبر

34. medical gloves
قفازات طبية

35. surgical scrub cap
قبعة الجراح

36. surgical mask
قناع الجراح

37. surgical gown
رداء الجراح

38. surgical scrubs
ثياب غرفة العمليات

Identify Anya's problem. Brainstorm solutions.

Anya works at a sandwich counter. Her bus ride to work is an hour. She has to wear a hairnet at work, but today she forgot it at home. What can she do?

Think about it. Discuss.

1. What other jobs require helmets? disposable gloves?
2. Is it better to have a uniform or wear your own clothes at work? Why?

93

A. purchase
تشتري

B. wait in line
ينتظر (يقف) في الطابور

1. suspenders
حمالة البنطلون

2. purses / handbags
حقائب يد / جزدانات

3. salesclerk
بائعة أو بائع

4. customer
زبون

5. display case
صندوق معروضات زجاجي

6. belts
أحزمة

13. wallet
محفظة

14. change purse / coin purse
جزدان / كيس نقود

15. cell phone case
حقيبة / غطاء هاتف محمول (جوال)

16. (wrist)watch
ساعة (يد)

17. shoulder bag
حقيبة كتف نسائية

18. backpack
حقيبة تحمل على الظهر

19. tote bag
حقيبة نقل

20. belt buckle
إبزيم (مشبك) الحزام

21. sole
نعل الحذاء

22. heel
كعب الحذاء

23. toe
مقدّم (اصبع قدم) الحذاء

24. shoelaces
رباط الحذاء

More vocabulary

athletic shoes: tennis shoes, running shoes, etc.

gift / present: something you give to or receive from friends or family for a special occasion

Grammar Point: object pronouns

*My **sister** loves jewelry. I'll buy **her** a necklace.*
*My **dad** likes belts. I'll buy **him** a belt buckle.*
*My **friends** love scarves. I'll buy **them** scarves.*

7. shoe department
قسم الأحذية

8. jewelry department
قسم المجوهرات

9. bracelets
أساور

10. necklaces
قلائد / عقود

11. hats
قبعات

12. scarves
أوشحة

C. try on shoes
يلبس الحذاء لقياسها

D. assist a customer
يساعد زبونا

25. high heels
حذاء ذو كعب عالٍ

26. pumps
حذاء نسائي

27. flats
أحذية نسائية بدون كعب

28. boots
جزمة (حذاء عالي الساق)

29. oxfords
حذاء أكسفورد

30. loafers
حذاء شبيه بالموكاسان

31. hiking boots
جزمة (حذاء عالي الساق) للتسلق

32. tennis shoes
حذاء تنس (كرة المضرب)

33. chain
سلسلة

34. beads
خرز

35. locket
مُدَلاة

36. pierced earrings
حلق لأذن مثقوبة

37. clip-on earrings
حلق بمشبك

38. pin
دبوس

39. string of pearls
عقد لؤلؤ

40. ring
خاتم

Ways to talk about accessories

I need <u>a hat</u> to wear with <u>this scarf</u>.
I'd like a pair of <u>earrings</u> to match <u>this necklace</u>.
Do you have <u>a belt</u> that would go with my <u>shoes</u>?

Role play. Talk to a salesperson.

A: *Do you have <u>boots</u> that would go with <u>this skirt</u>?*
B: *Let me see. How about <u>these brown ones</u>?*
A: *Perfect. I also need…*

Describing Clothes وصف الملابس

Sizes مقاسات

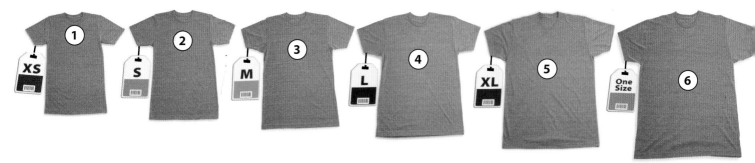

1. extra small	2. small	3. medium	4. large	5. extra large	6. one-size-fits-all
صغير جدا	صغير	متوسط	كبير	كبير جدا	مقاس واحد للجميع

Styles أزياء

7. crewneck sweater
بلوفر (كنزة) ذو رقبة عالية

8. V-neck sweater
بلوفر (كنزة) ذو رقبة على شكل حرف V

9. turtleneck sweater
بلوفر (كنزة) ذو رقبة عالية جدا

10. scoop neck sweater
بلوفر (كنزة) ذو رقبة مقوّرة

11. sleeveless shirt
قميص بدون أكمام

12. short-sleeved shirt
قميص ذو أكمام قصيرة (نصف كم)

13. 3/4-sleeved shirt
قميص ذو ٤ / ٣ (ثلاثة أرباع) كم

14. long-sleeved shirt
قميص ذو أكمام طويلة

15. miniskirt
تنورة قصيرة جدا (ميني)

16. short skirt
تنورة قصيرة

17. mid-length / calf-length skirt
تنورة متوسطة الطول / تنورة بطول بطن الساق

18. long skirt
تنورة طويلة

Patterns تصميمات مرسومة

19. solid	21. polka-dotted	23. print	25. floral
سادة / مصمت	منقّط	منقوش	مزهّر (ذو أشكال وردية)
20. striped	22. plaid	24. checked	26. paisley
مخطط / مقلم	مربعات ملوّنة	كاروهات	بيسلي (نسيج مزركش بالرسوم)

Survey your class. Record the responses.

1. What type of sweater do you prefer?
2. What patterns do you prefer?
Report: _Three_ out of _ten_ prefer ____.

Role play. Talk to a salesperson.

A: *Excuse me. I'm looking for this <u>V-neck sweater</u> in <u>large</u>.*
B: *Here's a <u>large</u>. It's on sale for $<u>19.99</u>.*
A: *Wonderful! I'll take it. I'm also looking for…*

Comparing Clothing مقارنة الملبوسات

27. **heavy** jacket
جاكتة ثقيلة

28. **light** jacket
جاكتة خفيفة

29. **tight** pants
بنطلون ضيق

30. **loose / baggy** pants
بنطلون واسع / فضفاض

31. **low** heels
كعب واطئ

32. **high** heels
كعب عالٍ

33. **plain** blouse
بلوزة سادة (بسيطة)

34. **fancy** blouse
بلوزة مُزيَّنة (مزركشة)

35. **narrow** tie
رابطة عنق (كرافتة) رفيعة

36. **wide** tie
رابطة عنق (كرافتة) عريضة

Clothing Problems مشاكل خاصة بالملبوسات

37. It's **too small**.
إنه أصغر من اللازم.

38. It's **too big**.
إنه أكبر من اللازم.

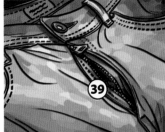

39. The zipper is **broken**.
الزمام المنزلق (السوستة) مكسور.

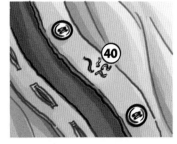

40. A button is **missing**.
هناك زر مفقود.

41. It's **ripped / torn**.
إنه ممزق / مقطوع.

42. It's **stained**.
إنه مبقّع.

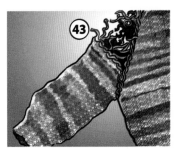

43. It's **unraveling**.
إنه يتمزق / تنحلّ خيوطه.

44. It's **too expensive**.
إنه أغلى من اللازم.

More vocabulary

complaint: a statement that something is not right
customer service: the place customers go with their complaints
refund: money you get back when you return an item to the store

Role play. Return an item to a salesperson.

A: *Welcome to Shopmart. How may I help you?*
B: *This sweater is new, but it's unraveling.*
A: *I'm sorry. Would you like a refund?*

Types of Material أنواع الخامات

1. cotton
قطن

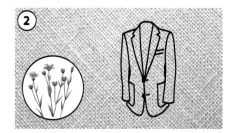

2. linen
كتّان

3. wool
صوف

4. cashmere
كشمير

5. silk
حرير

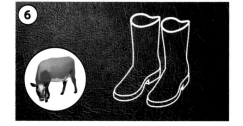

6. leather
جلد

A Garment Factory مصنع ملابس

Parts of a Sewing Machine
أجزاء ماكينة الخياطة

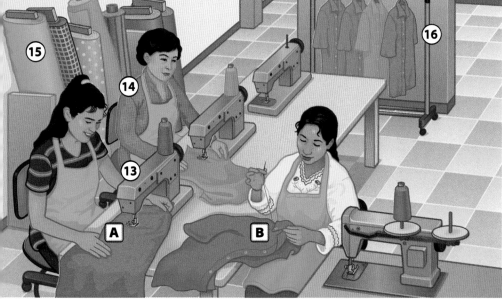

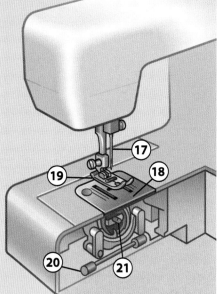

A. sew by machine تخيّط بماكينة الخياطة	**14.** sewing machine operator عامل(ة) ماكينة الخياطة	**17.** needle إبرة	**20.** feed dog / feed bar كلب إمداد / قضيب إمداد
B. sew by hand تخيّط باليد	**15.** bolt of fabric ثوب قماش	**18.** needle plate صفيحة معدنية للإبرة	**21.** bobbin مكوك / بكرة
13. sewing machine ماكينة خياطة	**16.** rack حامل / رف لتعليق الملابس	**19.** presser foot قدم ضاغط	

More vocabulary

fashion designer: a person who draws original clothes
natural materials: cloth made from things that grow in nature
synthetic materials: cloth made by people, such as nylon

Use the new words.

Look at pages 86–87. Name the materials you see.

A: Look at _her pants_. They're _denim_.
B: Look at _his shoes_. They're _leather_.

Types of Material أنواع الخامات

7. denim
الدنيم (قماش قطني متين)

8. suede
السويد (جلد أو قماش مزأبر)

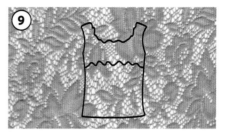

9. lace
دنتلة

10. velvet
قطيفة

11. corduroy
قطيفة مضلّعة

12. nylon
نايلون

A Fabric Store محل أقمشة

Closures أدوات للغلق

Trim التزيين

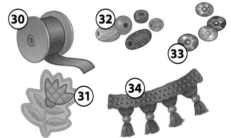

22. pattern
نموذج للتفصيل (باترون)

23. thread
خيط

24. button
زر

25. zipper
زمام منزلق (سوستة)

26. snap
كبسول أو طبّاقة

27. hook and eye
عقيفة وعروة (مشبك وفتحة)

28. buckle
إبزيم (مشبك)

29. hook and loop fastener
رابط بعقيفة وحلقة

30. ribbon
شريط

31. appliqué
تطريز أبليكيه

32. beads
خرز

33. sequins
ترتر

34. fringe
مزيّن بهداب (شراشيب)

Survey your class. Record the responses.

1. Can you sew?
2. What's your favorite type of material to wear?
Report: *Five* of us can't sew. *Most* of us like to wear *denim*.

Think about it. Discuss.

1. Which jobs require sewing skills?
2. You're going to make a shirt. What do you do first?
3. Which is better, hand sewn or machine sewn? Why?

Making Alterations   تعديل الثياب

An Alterations Shop   محل تعديل الثياب

1. dressmaker
خيّاطة

2. dressmaker's dummy
تمثال (مانيكان) الخيّاطة

3. tailor
خياط (ترزي)

4. collar
ياقة

5. waistband
حزام أو نطاق تنورة أو بنطلون

6. sleeve
كُم

7. pocket
جيب

8. hem
حاشية (هدب)

9. cuff
ثنية ساق البنطلون

Sewing Supplies   أدوات الخياطة

10. needle
إبرة

11. thread
خيط

12. (straight) pin
دبوس مستقيم

13. pincushion
مخدة دبابيس / مدبسة

14. safety pin
دبوس بمشبك

15. thimble
كستبان

16. pair of scissors
مقص

17. tape measure
شريط قياس (مازورة)

18. seam ripper
ممزّق الدروز (أداة فك الخياطة)

Alterations   تعديل الثياب

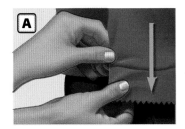

A. Lengthen the pants.
يطوّل البنطلون.

B. Shorten the pants.
يقصّر البنطلون.

C. Let out the pants.
يوسّع البنطلون.

D. Take in the pants.
يضيّق البنطلون.

Pair practice. Make new conversations.

A: *Would you hand me* <u>*the thread*</u>?
B: *OK. What are you going to do?*
A: *I'm going to* <u>*take in*</u> <u>*these pants*</u>.

Survey your class. Record the responses.

1. How many pockets do you have?
2. How many pairs of scissors do you have at home?
Report: <u>*Most*</u> *of us have* <u>*two*</u> ____.

100

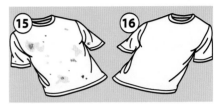

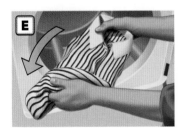
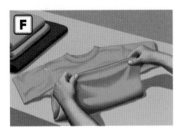
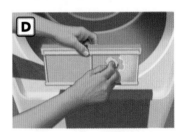
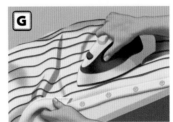

1. laundry
ملابس للغسل

2. laundry basket
سلة ملابس

3. washer
غسالة ملابس

4. dryer
نشافة ملابس

5. dryer sheets
أوراق نشافة

6. fabric softener
مطرّي للنسيج

7. bleach
مسحوق الغسيل

8. laundry detergent
مبيّض

9. clothesline
منشر الغسيل

10. clothespin
مشبك الملابس

11. hanger
حمالة الثياب

12. spray starch
رشاش النشا

13. iron
مكواة

14. ironing board
طاولة الكي

15. dirty T-shirt
تي شيرت **متسخ**

16. clean T-shirt
تي شيرت **نظيف**

17. wet shirt
تي شيرت **مبتلّ**

18. dry shirt
تي شيرت **جاف**

19. wrinkled shirt
قميص **متجعد (متكرمش)**

20. ironed shirt
قميص **مكوي**

A. Sort the laundry.
تفرز الغسيل.

B. Add the detergent.
تضيف مسحوق الغسيل.

C. Load the washer.
تضع الغسيل في الغسالة.

D. Clean the lint trap.
تنظّف مكان تجمع النسالة.

E. Unload the dryer.
تفرّغ مجفف الملابس.

F. Fold the laundry.
تطوي الملابس.

G. Iron the clothes.
تكوي الملابس.

H. Hang up the clothes.
تعلّق الملابس.

wash in cold water

no bleach

line dry

dry clean only, do not wash

Pair practice. Make new conversations.

A: *I have to <u>sort the laundry</u>. Can you help?*
B: *Sure. Here's <u>the laundry basket</u>.*
A: *Thanks a lot!*

101

1. flyer
نشرة إعلانية

2. used clothing
ملابس مستعملة

3. sticker
لاصق

4. folding card table
طاولة قابلة للطي لألعاب الورق أو الشدة

5. folding chair
كرسي قابل للطي

6. clock radio
راديو بساعة

7. VCR
جهاز فيديو+و

8. CD / cassette player
جهاز تشغيل أقراص مدمجة (سي دي) CD / شرائط كاسيت

A. **bargain**
تقاول على السعر

B. **browse**
يستعرض السلع المعروضة للبيع

What do you see in the pictures?

1. What kinds of used clothing do you see?
2. What information is on the flyer?
3. Why are the stickers different colors?
4. How much is the clock radio? the VCR?

Read the story.

A Garage Sale

Last Sunday, I had a garage sale. At 5:00 a.m., I put up <u>flyers</u> in my neighborhood. Next, I put price <u>stickers</u> on my <u>used clothing</u>, my <u>VCR</u>, my <u>CD / cassette player</u>, and some other old things. At 7:00 a.m., I opened my <u>folding card table</u> and <u>folding chair</u>. Then I waited.

At 7:05 a.m., my first customer arrived. She asked, "How much is the sweatshirt?"

"Two dollars," I said.

She said, "It's stained. I can give you seventy-five cents." We <u>bargained</u> for a minute and she paid $1.00.

All day people came to <u>browse</u>, bargain, and buy. At 7:00 p.m., I had $85.00.

Now I know two things: garage sales are hard work, and nobody wants to buy an old <u>clock radio</u>!

Reread the story.

1. Look at the conversation. Circle the punctuation you see. What do you notice?

What do you think?

2. Do you like to buy things at garage sales? Why or why not?
3. Imagine you want the VCR. How will you bargain for it?

1. **head**
   رأس

2. **hair**
   شَعر

3. **neck**
   رقبة

4. **chest**
   صدر

5. **back**
   ظهر

6. **nose**
   أنف

7. **mouth**
   فم

8. **foot**
   قدم

Listen and point. Take turns.

A: *Point to the chest.*
B: *Point to the neck.*
A: *Point to the mouth.*

Dictate to your partner. Take turns.

A: *Write hair.*
B: *Did you say hair?*
A: *That's right, h-a-i-r.*

9. leg
رجل

10. toe
إصبع قدم

11. eye
عين

12. ear
أذن

13. shoulder
كتف

14. arm
ذراع

15. hand
يد

16. finger
إصبع يد

Grammar Point: imperatives

*Please **touch** your right foot.*
***Put** your hands on your knees.*
***Don't put** your hands on your shoulders.*

Pair practice. Take turns giving commands.

A: <u>Raise</u> your <u>arms</u>.
B: <u>Touch</u> your <u>feet</u>.
A: <u>Put</u> your <u>hand</u> on your <u>shoulder</u>.

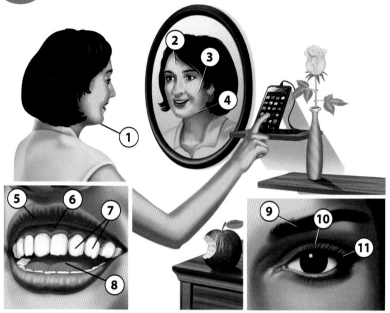

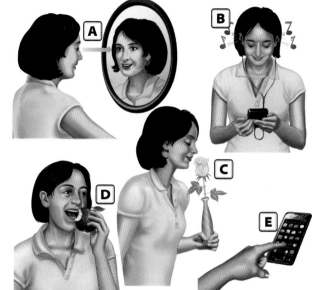

The Face
الوجه

1. chin
ذَقَن

2. forehead
جبهة

3. cheek
خذ

4. jaw
فك

The Mouth
الفم

5. lip
شفة

6. gums
لثة

7. teeth
أسنان

8. tongue
لسان

The Eye
العين

9. eyebrow
حاجب

10. eyelid
جفن

11. eyelashes
رموش

The Senses
الحواس

A. see
يرى

B. hear
يسمع

C. smell
يشم

D. taste
يتذوق

E. touch
يلمس (يحس باللمس)

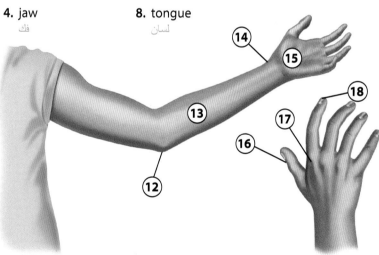

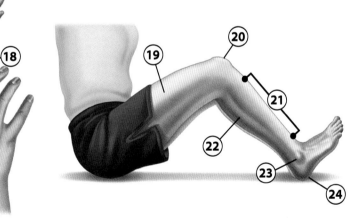

The Arm, Hand, and Fingers الذراع واليد وأصابع اليد

12. elbow
كوع

13. forearm
ساعد

14. wrist
رسغ

15. palm
كف

16. thumb
إبهام

17. knuckle
برجمة

18. fingernail
ظفر

The Leg and Foot الرجل والقدم

19. thigh
فخذ

20. knee
ركبة

21. shin
حرف الظنبوب

22. calf
ربلة أو بطة الساق

23. ankle
كاحل

24. heel
كعب

More vocabulary

torso: the part of the body from the shoulders to the pelvis
limbs: arms and legs
toenail: the nail on your toe

Pair practice. Make new conversations.

A: *Is your wrist OK?*
B: *Yes, but now my elbow hurts.*
A: *I'm sorry to hear that.*

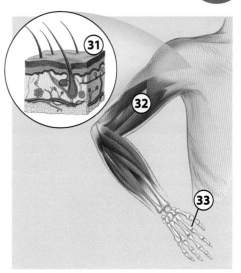

25. breast
ثدي

26. abdomen
بطن

27. hip
ورك

28. shoulder blade
لوح الكتف

29. lower back
الجزء السفلي من الظهر

30. buttocks
مقعدة / أرداف

31. skin
جلد

32. muscle
عضلة

33. bone
عظم

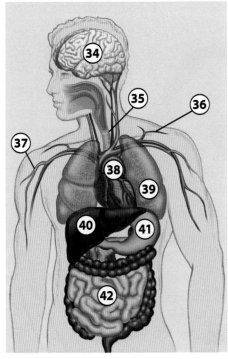

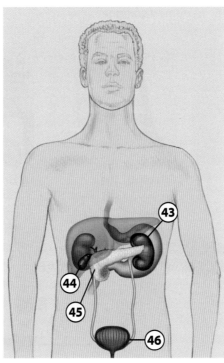

THE SKELETON

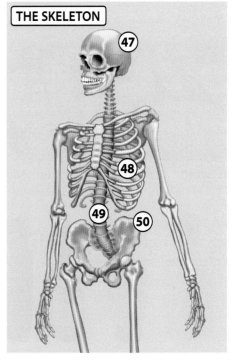

34. brain
مخ

35. throat
حنجرة

36. artery
شريان

37. vein
وريد

38. heart
قلب

39. lung
رئة

40. liver
كبد

41. stomach
معدة

42. intestines
أمعاء

43. kidney
كلية

44. gallbladder
مرارة

45. pancreas
بنكرياس

46. bladder
مثانة

47. skull
جمجمة

48. rib cage
قفص صدري

49. spinal column
عمود فقري

50. pelvis
حوض

A. take a shower / **shower**
يأخذ دشا / يغتسل

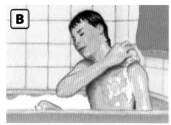
B. take a bath / **bathe**
يأخذ حماما / يستحمّ

C. use deodorant
يستعمل مزيل رائحة العرق

D. put on sunscreen
تضع واقيا من أشعة الشمس

1. shower cap
غطاء شعر للحمام

2. shower gel
جيل للدش

3. soap
صابون

4. bath powder
بودرة استحمام

5. deodorant / antiperspirant
مزيل رائحة العرق

6. perfume / cologne
كولونيا / عطر

7. sunscreen
واقٍ من أشعة الشمس

8. sunblock
مانع لأشعة الشمس

9. body lotion / moisturizer
كريم للجسم / مرطب للجلد

 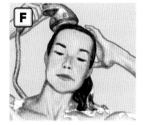  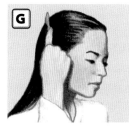 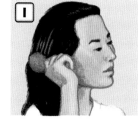

E. wash…hair
تغسل الشعر

F. rinse…hair
تشطف الشعر

G. comb…hair
تمشط (تسرّح) الشعر

H. dry…hair
تجفف الشعر

I. brush…hair
تصفف الشعر بالفرشاة

  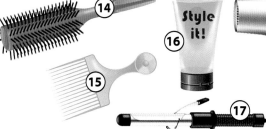 

10. shampoo
شامبو

11. conditioner
منعّم الشعر

12. hairspray
مثبّت الشعر

13. comb
مشط

14. brush
فرشاة

15. pick
مشط مدبب الأسنان

16. hair gel
جيل للشعر

17. curling iron
مكواة شعر

18. blow dryer
مجفف شعر بالهواء الساخن (سيشوار)

19. hair clip
دبوس شعر

20. barrette
مشبك شعر

21. bobby pins
دبابيس شعر محكمة

More vocabulary

hypoallergenic: a product that is better for people with allergies

unscented: a product without perfume or scent

Think about it. Discuss.

1. Which personal hygiene products are most important to use before a job interview? Why?

2. What is the right age to start wearing makeup? Why?

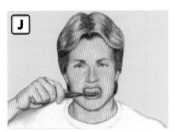

J. brush…teeth
يُنظّف الأسنان بالفرشاة

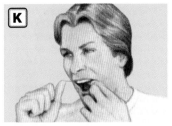

K. floss…teeth
يُنظّف الأسنان بالخيط

L. gargle
يتغرغر

M. shave
يحلق

 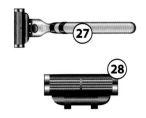 

22. toothbrush
فرشاة أسنان

23. toothpaste
معجون أسنان

24. dental floss
خيط لتنظيف الأسنان

25. mouthwash
مستحضر لغسل الفم

26. electric shaver
ماكينة حلاقة كهربائية

27. razor
ماكينة حلاقة

28. razor blade
موس حلاقة

29. shaving cream
معجون حلاقة

30. aftershave
كولونيا بعد الحلاقة

N. cut…nails
تقلّم الأظافر

O. polish…nails
تطلي الأظافر

P. put on / apply
تضع

Q. take off / remove
تزيل

Makeup مكياج

31. nail clippers
مقلمة أظافر

32. emery board
مبرد أظافر

33. nail polish
طلاء الأظافر

34. eyebrow pencil
قلم حواجب

35. eye shadow
قلم كحل

36. eyeliner
قلم تخطيط العين

37. blush
أحمر خدود

38. lipstick
أحمر الشفاء

39. mascara
مَسكرة (مستحضر تجميلي)

40. foundation
كريم أساس

41. face powder
بودرة للوجه

42. makeup remover
مزيل المكياج

 ①  ②  ③  **A**

 ④ 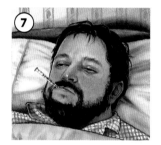 ⑤  ⑥  **B**

 ⑦  ⑧  ⑨  **C**

1. **headache**
صداع

2. **toothache**
وجع أسنان

3. **earache**
ألم في الأذن

4. **stomachache**
ألم في المعدة

5. **backache**
ألم في الظهر

6. **sore throat**
التهاب الحنجرة

7. **fever / temperature**
حمى / حرارة

8. **chills**
رعشة

9. **cough**
سعال

A. **feel** dizzy
يشعر / تشعر بالدوار (دوخة)

B. **feel** nauseous
تشعر بالغثيان

C. **throw up / vomit**
تتقيأ / يستفرغ ـ تستفرغ

 ⑩  ⑪  ⑫  ⑬

10. **insect bite**
لسعة حشرة

11. **bruise**
كدمة

12. **cut**
جرح

13. **sunburn**
سفعة (ضربة) شمس

 ⑭  ⑮ 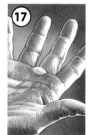 ⑯ 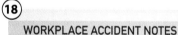 ⑰

14. **sprained ankle**
التواء الكاحل

15. **bloody nose**
نزيف في الأنف

16. **swollen finger**
ورم في الإصبع

17. **blister**
قرحة (كلّو)

⑱

WORKPLACE ACCIDENT NOTES

Name: Thiu An

Job Title: Packer

Date of accident: Monday, 9/18/17

Location of accident:
warehouse, aisle 3

Description of accident:
3 boxes fell on me

Was safety equipment used?
☑ yes   ☐ no

Were you injured? yes, sprained wrist
and some bruises

PLEASE FILL OUT A COMPLETE ACCIDENT
FORM AS SOON AS POSSIBLE.

18. **accident report**
تقرير عن حادث

Look at the pictures.
Describe the symptoms and injuries.

A: He has <u>a backache</u>.

B: She has <u>a toothache</u>.

Think about it. Discuss.

1. What do you recommend for a stomachache?
2. What is the best way to stop a bloody nose?
3. Who should stay home from work with a cold? Why?

In the Waiting Room في غرفة الانتظار

HEALTH FIRST
Name: Andre Zolmar
Group Number: 98765
Membership Number: 60756789

Health Form
Name: *Andre Zolmar*
Date of birth: *July 8, 1983*
Current symptoms: *stomachache*

Health History:

Childhood Diseases:
☑chicken pox
☑diphtheria
☑rubella
☑measles
☐mumps
☐other

Description of symptoms:
_____

1. appointment
موعد

2. receptionist
موظف استقبال

3. health insurance card
بطاقة تأمين صحي

4. health history form
استمارة التاريخ الصحي

In the Examining Room في غرفة الكشف

5. doctor
طبيب

6. patient
مريض

7. examination table
طاولة الكشف

8. nurse
ممرضة

9. blood pressure gauge
جهاز لقياس ضغط الدم

10. stethoscope
سماعة طبية

11. thermometer
مقياس حرارة (ترمومتر)

12. syringe
إبرة / سرنجة

Medical Procedures إجراءات طبية

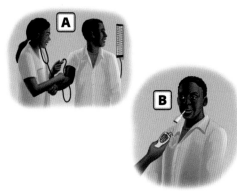

A. **check**...blood pressure
تفحص ضغط الدم

B. **take**...temperature
تفحص / تأخذ درجة الحرارة

C. **listen** to...heart
تستمع إلى نبض القلب

D. **examine**...eyes
تفحص العينين

E. **examine**...throat
تفحص الحنجرة

F. **draw**...blood
تسحب دما

Grammar Point: future tense with *will* + verb

To describe a future action, use *will* + verb.
The contraction of *will* is *-'ll*.
She will draw your blood. = She'll draw your blood.

Role play. Talk to a medical receptionist.

A: *Will the nurse <u>examine my eyes</u>?*
B: *No, but she'll <u>draw your blood</u>.*
A: *What will the doctor do?*

Patient

First name	Last name	Reason for visit
_____	_____	_____

Common Illnesses العلل الشائعة

  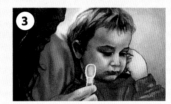 

1. cold
   برد

2. flu
   أنفلونزا

3. ear infection
   التهاب في الأذن

4. strep throat
   التهاب في الحنجرة

Medical History

Childhood and Infectious Diseases أمراض الطفولة والأمراض المعدية

Vaccination date
تاريخ التطعيم

5. measles   _____
   حصبة

6. chicken pox   _____
   جدري الماء (جديري)

7. mumps   _____
   نكاف / أبو كعب

8. shingles   _____
   الهربس النطاقي

9. hepatitis   _____
   التهاب الكبد

10. pneumonia   _____
    التهاب رئوي

11. allergies
    حساسية

 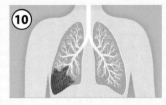

I am allergic to:

_____

_____

animals	shellfish	peanuts	drugs
حيوانات	محار	فول سوداني	عقاقير

_____

Survey your class. Record the responses.

1. Are you allergic to cats?
2. Are you allergic to shellfish?

Report: *Five of us are allergic to ____.*

Identify Omar's problem. Brainstorm solutions.

Omar filled out only half of the medical history form at the clinic. Many words on the form were new to him, and two questions were very personal. The nurse was upset.

Allergic Reactions تفاعلات نتيجة حساسية

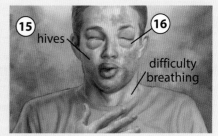

hives

difficulty breathing

12. sneezing
عطس

13. nasal congestion
احتقان في الأنف

14. rash
طفح جلدي

15. anaphylaxis
تأق

16. swelling
تورم

Medical Conditions حالات طبية

	Patient Yes	No	Family History			Patient Yes	No	Family History
17. cancer سرطان	☐	☐	_____	**23. TB / tuberculosis** سل		☐	☐	_____
18. asthma ربو	☐	☐	_____	**24. high blood pressure / hypertension** ضغط دم عالٍ / ارتفاع ضغط الدم		☐	☐	_____
19. dementia فقدان القوى العقلية (خبل)	☐	☐	_____	**25. intestinal parasites** دود معوي		☐	☐	_____
20. arthritis التهاب مفاصل	☐	☐	_____	**26. diabetes** مرض السكري		☐	☐	_____
21. HIV / AIDS فيروس نقص المناعة البشرية / الإيدز	☐	☐	_____	**27. kidney disease** مرض كلوي		☐	☐	_____
22. malaria ملاريا	☐	☐	_____	**28. heart disease** مرض القلب		☐	☐	_____

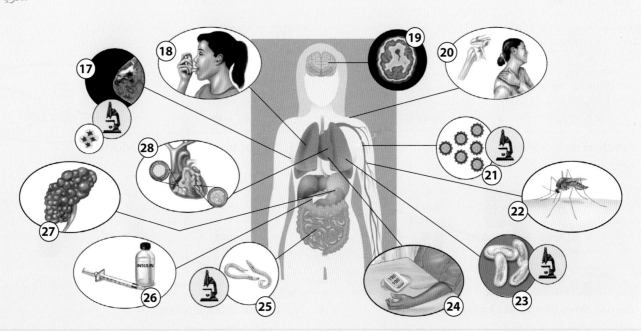

More vocabulary

AIDS (acquired immune deficiency syndrome): a medical condition that results from contracting the HIV virus
Alzheimer's disease: a disease that causes dementia

coronary disease: heart disease
infectious disease: a disease that is spread through air or water
influenza: flu

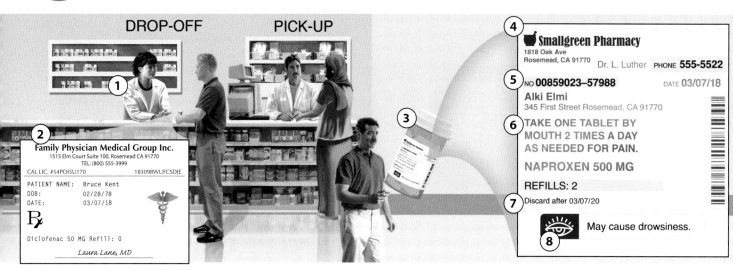

DROP-OFF   PICK-UP

Smallgreen Pharmacy
1818 Oak Ave
Rosemead, CA 91770
Dr. L. Luther   PHONE **555-5522**

NO **00859023–57988**   DATE **03/07/18**

Alki Elmi
345 First Street Rosemead, CA 91770

TAKE ONE TABLET BY
MOUTH 2 TIMES A DAY
AS NEEDED FOR PAIN.

NAPROXEN 500 MG

REFILLS: 2

Discard after 03/07/20

May cause drowsiness.

Family Physician Medical Group Inc.
1515 Elm Court Suite 100, Rosemead CA 91770
TEL: (800) 555-3999
CAL LIC. #54POI5U170   183098WUFCSDJE

PATIENT NAME: Bruce Kent
DOB: 02/28/78
DATE: 03/07/18

℞

Diclofenac 50 MG Refill: 0

Laura Lane, MD

1. pharmacist
   صيدلي
2. prescription
   وصفة طبية (روشتة)
3. prescription medication
   دواء موصوف طبيا
4. prescription label
   بطاقة الوصفة الطبية
5. prescription number
   رقم الوصفة الطبية
6. dosage
   جرعة
7. expiration date
   تاريخ انتهاء الصلاحية
8. warning label
   بطاقة تحذير

Medical Warnings تحذيرات طبية

A. **Take** with food or milk.
تناول مع أكل أو حليب.

B. **Take** one hour before eating.
تناول قبل ساعة من الأكل.

C. **Finish** all medication.
تناول كل الدواء حتى ينتهي.

D. **Do not take** with dairy products.
لا تتناوله مع منتجات ألبان.

E. **Do not drive or operate** heavy machinery.
لا تقود سيارة أو تشغل آلات ثقيلة.

F. **Do not drink** alcohol.
لا تشرب مشروبات كحولية.

More vocabulary

prescribe medication: to write a prescription
fill prescriptions: to prepare medications for patients
pick up a prescription: to get prescription medication

Role play. Talk to the pharmacist.

A: *Hi. I need to pick up a prescription for <u>Jones</u>.*
B: *Here's your medication, <u>Mr. Jones</u>. Take these <u>once a day with milk or food</u>.*

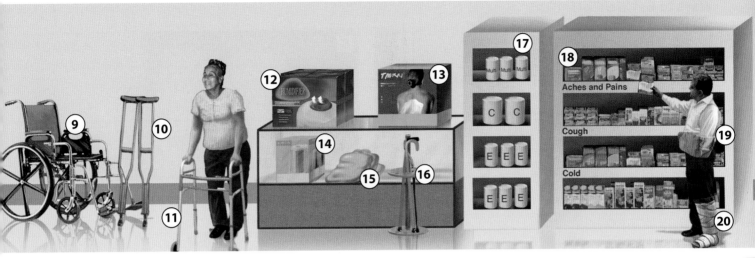

9. wheelchair كرسي بعجلات	13. heating pad لبادة تدفئة	17. vitamins فيتامينات
10. crutches عكاز	14. air purifier منقٍّ للهواء	18. over-the-counter medication أدوية مباعة بدون وصفة طبية
11. walker ممشاة (مشّاية)	15. hot water bottle كيس الماء الساخن	19. sling معلاق
12. humidifier مرطب للهواء	16. cane عصا	20. cast جبيرة / جبص

Types of Medication أنواع الأدوية

21. pill حبة	22. tablet قرص	23. capsule كبسولة	24. ointment مرهم	25. cream كريم / معجون

Over-the-Counter Medication الأدوية المباعة بدون وصفة طبية

26. pain reliever مسكن للآلام	28. antacid مضاد للحموضة	30. throat lozenges أقراص للمص ملطفة للحنجرة	32. nasal spray رشاش للأنف
27. cold tablets أقراص للبرد أو الزكام	29. cough syrup شراب للسعال	31. eye drops قطرة للعين	33. inhaler منشقة

Ways to talk about medication

Use **take** for pills, tablets, capsules, and cough syrup.
Use **apply** for ointments and creams.
Use **use** for drops, nasal sprays, and inhalers.

Identify Dara's problem. Brainstorm solutions.

Dara's father is 85 and lives alone. She lives nearby. Her dad has many prescriptions. He often forgets to take his medication or takes the wrong pills.

115

Ways to Get Well طرق الشفاء

A. Seek medical attention.
اطلب العناية الطبية.

B. Get bed rest.
ألزم الفراش.

C. Drink fluids.
اشرب سوائل.

D. Take medicine.
تعاطَ دواء.

Ways to Stay Well طرق المحافظة على صحتك

E. Stay fit.
حافظ على لياقتك البدنية.

F. Eat a healthy diet.
كلْ أطعمة صحية.

G. Don't smoke.
لا تدخَن.

Ms. Jones, you must stop smoking!

H. Have regular checkups.
اطلب إجراء كشوف طبية منتظمة.

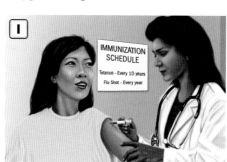

IMMUNIZATION SCHEDULE
Tetanus - Every 10 years
Flu Shot - Every year

I. Get immunized.
اطلب تحصينك بلقاحات ضد الأمراض.

J. Follow medical advice.
اتبع النصيحة الطبية.

More vocabulary

injection: medicine in a syringe that is put into the body
immunization / vaccination: an injection that stops
serious diseases

Survey your class. Record the responses.

1. How do you stay fit?
2. Which two foods are a part of your healthy diet?
Report: *I surveyed <u>ten</u> people who said they ____.*

Types of Health Problems أنواع المشاكل الصحية

1. vision problems
مشاكل في النظر

2. hearing loss
فقدان السمع

3. pain
ألم

4. stress
توتر / إجهاد

5. depression
اكتئاب

Help with Health Problems العون في المشاكل الصحية

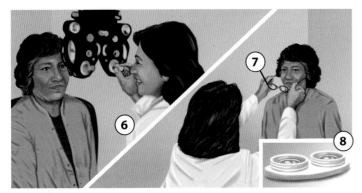

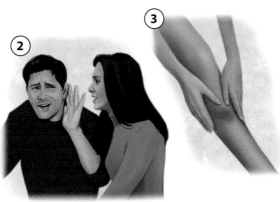

6. optometrist
مصحّح البصر

7. glasses
نظارات

8. contact lenses
عدسات لاصقة

9. audiologist
أخصائي سمع

10. hearing aid
سماعة أذن

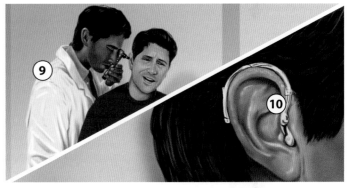

11. physical therapy
علاج طبيعي

12. physical therapist
أخصائي علاج طبيعي

13. talk therapy
علاج بالتكلم

14. therapist
معالج

15. support group
مجموعة دعم

Ways to ask about health problems

Are you in pain?
Are you having vision problems?
Are you experiencing depression?

Pair practice. Make new conversations.

A: *Do you know a good optometrist?*
B: *Why? Are you having vision problems?*
A: *Yes, I might need glasses.*

117

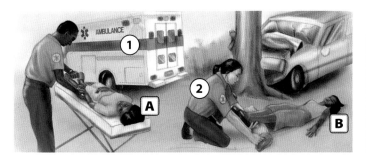

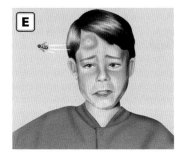

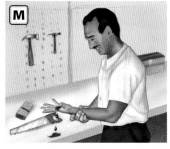

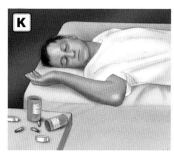
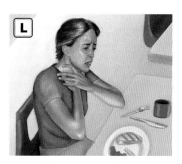

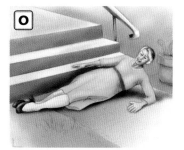
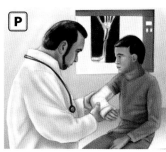

1. ambulance
سيارة إسعاف

2. paramedic
طاقم الإسعاف

A. **be** unconscious
يفقد الوعي

B. **be** in shock
يصاب بصدمة

C. **be** injured / **be** hurt
يصاب بإصابة / يصاب بأذى

D. **have** a heart attack
يصاب بنوبة قلبية

E. **have** an allergic reaction
يعاني من حساسية

F. **get** an electric shock
يصاب بصدمة كهربائية

G. **get** frostbite
يقرسها الصقيع

H. **burn** (your)self
يحرق نفسه

I. **drown**
يغرق

J. **swallow** poison
تبلع مادة سامة

K. **overdose** on drugs
يتناول كمية مفرطة من الدواء

L. **choke**
تختنق

M. **bleed**
ينزف

N. **can't breathe**
لا يستطيع التنفس

O. **fall**
تقع

P. **break** a bone
يكسر عظمة من عظامه

Grammar Point: past tense

For past tense, add *-d* or *-ed*.
burn**ed**, drown**ed**, swallow**ed**,
overdos**ed**, chok**ed**

These verbs are different (irregular):

be – was, were	bleed – bled	break – broke
have – had	can't – couldn't	
get – got	fall – fell	

First Aid إسعافات أولية

1. first aid kit
علبة إسعافات أولية

2. first aid manual
كتيب إسعافات أولية

3. medical emergency bracelet
أسورة طوارئ طبية

4. AED / automated external defibrillator
إيه إي دي (AED) / مزيل الرجفان الخارجي الآلي

Inside the Kit داخل العلبة

5. tweezers
ملقاط

6. adhesive bandage
ضمادة لاصقة

7. sterile pad
لبادة معقمة

8. sterile tape
شريط معقم

9. gauze
شاش

10. hydrogen peroxide
بيروكسيد الهيدروجين

11. antihistamine cream
كريم مضاد للهيستامين

12. antibacterial ointment
مرهم مضاد للجراثيم

13. elastic bandage
ضمادة مطاطية

14. ice pack
حزمة ثلج

15. splint
جبيرة لليد

First Aid Procedures إجراءات الإسعافات الأولية

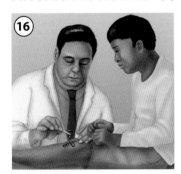
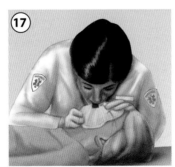
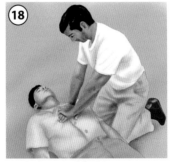
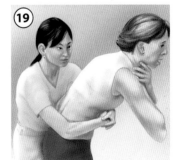

16. stitches
غرز / دروز

17. rescue breathing
تنفس إنقاذي

18. CPR (cardiopulmonary resuscitation)
إنعاش القلب والرئتين

19. Heimlich maneuver
طريقة هيمليك لمعالجة الاختناق

Pair practice. Make new conversations.

A: *What do we need in the first aid kit?*
B: *We need <u>tweezers</u> and <u>gauze</u>.*
A: *I think we need <u>sterile tape</u>, too.*

Internet Research: first aid class

Type "first aid," "class," and your ZIP code in the search bar. Look for a class near you.
Report: *I found a first aid class at ____.*

Dentistry الأسنان

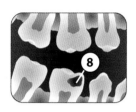
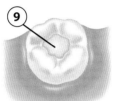

Orthodontics تقويم الأسنان

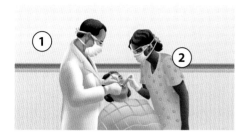

1. dentist
   طبيب / طبيبة أسنان

2. dental assistant
   مساعد طبيب أسنان

3. dental hygienist
   أخصائي صحة أسنان

4. dental instruments
   أدوات معالجة الأسنان

5. orthodontist
   طبيب تقويم الأسنان

6. braces
   طوق لتقويم الأسنان

7. clear aligner
   تركيبة شفافة لضبط استقامة الأسنان

Dental Problems مشاكل الأسنان

8. cavity / decay
   نخر / بلى

9. filling
   حشو

10. crown
    تاج

11. dentures
    طاقم أسنان اصطناعية

12. gum disease
    مرض اللثة

13. plaque
    لويحات البلاك

An Office Visit زيارة لعيادة أسنان

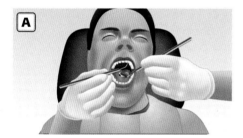

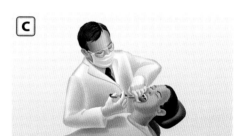

A. **clean** the teeth
   يُنظّف الأسنان

B. **take** X-rays
   يأخذ أشعة سينية

C. **numb** the mouth
   يخدّر الفم

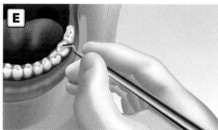
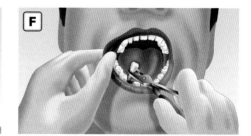

D. **drill** a tooth
   يحفر السن

E. **fill** a cavity
   يملأ النخر

F. **pull** a tooth
   يقتلع (يخلع) السن

Role play. Talk to a dentist.

A: *I think I have a cavity.*
B: *Let me see. Yes. I will need to drill that tooth.*
A: *Oh! How much will that cost?*

Identify Leo's problem. Brainstorm solutions.

Leo has a bad toothache. His wife says, "Call the dentist."
Leo doesn't want to call. He takes pain medication.
The toothache doesn't stop.

Insurance plans table:

	BRONZE	SILVER	GOLD
Monthly Premium	$	$$	$$$
Deductible	$5,000	$3,000	$1,500
Co-pay	$35	$30	none
Out-of-pocket Maximum	$10,000	$6,000	$3,000

Welcome to BEWELL — Summary of your BRONZE PLAN

BEWELL ONLINE PAYMENTS
JUNE 2018 PAID
JULY 2018 PAID
AUGUST 2018 DUE
BRONZE PLAN PREMIUM: $834.00
PAY NOW

That's $35. We'll bill your insurance for the other $115.

ABC RADIOLOGY

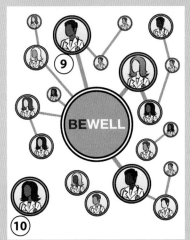

BEWELL

BEWELL HEALTH EXPLANATION OF BENEFITS

Claim submitted: 5/9/18   Provider: **ABC Radiology**

Claim processed: 6/1/18   Patient #5792321

Service Date	Type of Service	Total Billed	Allowable Amount	Co-pay	Amount Paid
5/9/18	X-ray	150.00	150.00	35.00	115.00

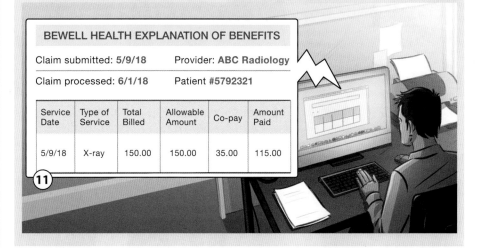

1. carrier
شركة التأمين

2. insurance plans
برامج التأمين

3. benefits
الاستحقاقات

4. insurance policy
بوليصة التأمين

5. insured / policyholder
المؤمّن عليه / صاحب البوليصة

6. dependents
المعالون

7. premium
القسط الشهري

8. co-pay
التغطية المشتركة الدفع

9. in-network doctor
طبيب داخل شبكة شركة التأمين

10. out-of-network doctor
طبيب خارج شبكة شركة التأمين

11. explanation of benefits / EOB
شرح الاستحقاقات / EOB (إي او بي)

A. **compare** plans
المقارنة بين البرامج المختلفة

B. **pay** a claim
دفع مطالبة بالتسديد

Medical Specialists أطباء أخصائيون

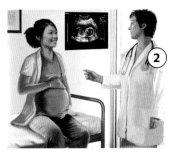

1. internist
طبيب باطني

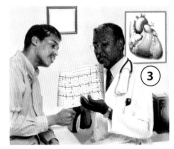

2. obstetrician
طبيب ولادة

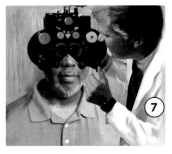

3. cardiologist
طبيب قلب

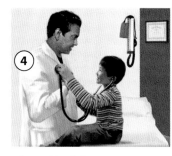

4. pediatrician
طبيب أطفال

5. oncologist
طبيب أورام

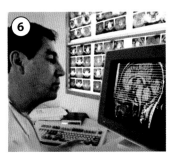

6. radiologist
طبيب أشعة

7. ophthalmologist
طبيب عيون

8. psychiatrist
طب أمراض نفسية

Nursing Staff هيئة التمريض

9. surgical nurse
ممرضة جراحة

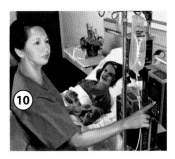

10. registered nurse (RN)
ممرضة مرخصة

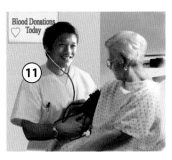

11. licensed practical nurse (LPN)
ممرضة ممارسة مرخصة

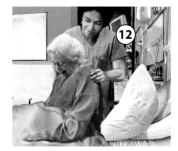

12. certified nursing assistant (CNA)
مساعد ممرضة معتمد

Hospital Staff العاملون بالمستشفى

13. administrator
إداري

14. admissions clerk
موظف الإدخال

15. dietician
أخصائي في شؤون التغذية

16. orderly
ممرض

More Vocabulary

Gynecologists examine and treat women.
Nurse practitioners can give medical exams.
Nurse midwives deliver babies.

Chiropractors move the spine to improve health.
Orthopedists treat bone and joint problems.
Dermatologists treat skin conditions.
Urologists treat bladder and kidney problems.

A Hospital Room غرفة بالمستشفى

Lab المختبر

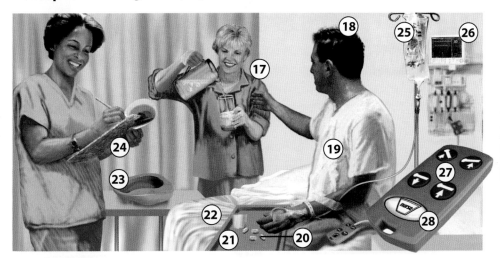

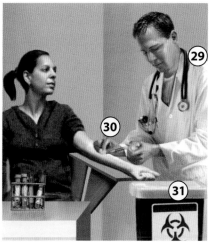

17. volunteer
متطوع

18. patient
مريض

19. hospital gown
رداء مستشفى

20. medication
دواء

21. bed table
طاولة سرير

22. hospital bed
سرير مستشفى

23. bedpan
وعاء للسرير / نونية

24. medical chart
ورقة بيانات طبية

25. IV (intravenous drip)
سائل تغذية يعطى في الوريد

26. vital signs monitor
مرقاب العلامات الحياتية

27. bed control
المتحكم في حركة السرير

28. call button
جرس الاستدعاء

29. phlebotomist
فصّاد

30. blood work / blood test
تحليل دم

31. medical waste disposal
سلة للمهملات الطبية

Emergency Room Entrance
مدخل غرفة الطوارئ

Operating Room غرفة العمليات

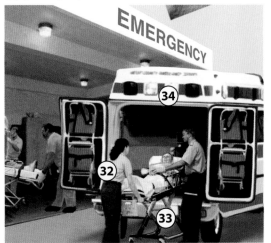

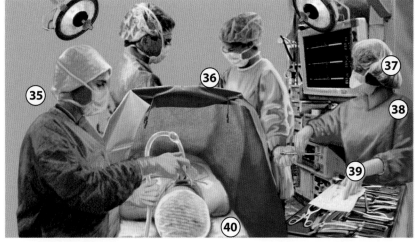

32. emergency medical technician (EMT)
أخصائي طبي لحالات الطوارئ

33. stretcher / gurney
نقالة مرضى

34. ambulance
سيارة إسعاف

35. anesthesiologist
طبيب تخدير

36. surgeon
جراح

37. surgical cap
قلنسوة غرفة العمليات

38. surgical gown
رداء غرفة العمليات

39. surgical gloves
قفازات غرفة العمليات

40. operating table
طاولة العملية الجراحية

Dictate to your partner. Take turns.

A: *Write this sentence: She's a volunteer.*
B: *She's a what?*
A: *Volunteer. That's v-o-l-u-n-t-e-e-r.*

Role play. Ask about a doctor.

A: *I need to find a good surgeon.*
B: *Dr. Jones is a great surgeon. You should call him.*
A: *I will! Please give me his number.*

123

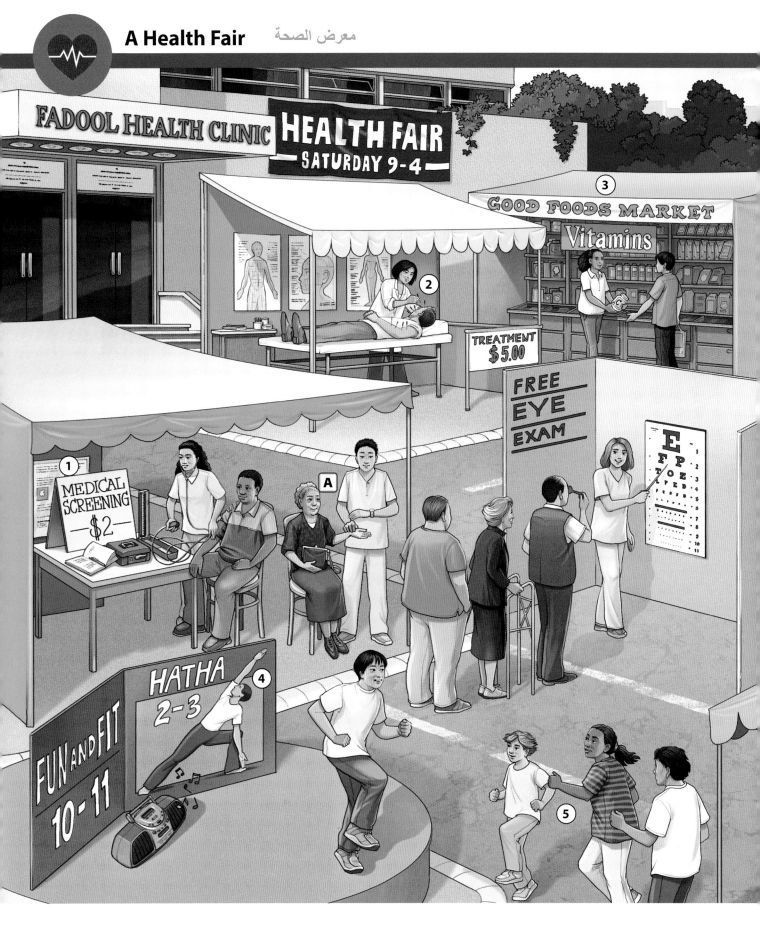

FADOOL HEALTH CLINIC

HEALTH FAIR
SATURDAY 9-4

GOOD FOODS MARKET

Vitamins

TREATMENT $5.00

FREE EYE EXAM

MEDICAL SCREENING —$2—

HATHA 2-3

FUN AND FIT 10-11

1. low-cost exam كشف قليل التكلفة	3. booth جناح	5. aerobic exercise تمرين حيهوائي	7. sugar-free خالٍ من السكر	A. **check**…pulse **يفحص** النبض
2. acupuncture علاج بالإبر الصينية	4. yoga اليوجا	6. demonstration عرض / تجربة حية	8. nutrition label بطاقة بيانات تغذوية	B. **give** a lecture **تلقي** محاضرة

124

What do you see in the picture?

1. Where is this health fair?

2. What kinds of exams and treatments can you get at this fair?

3. What kinds of lectures and demonstrations can you attend here?

4. How much money should you bring? Why?

Read the article.

A Health Fair

Once a month the Fadool Health Clinic has a health fair. You can get a low-cost medical exam at one booth. The nurses check your blood pressure and check your pulse. At another booth, you can get a free eye exam. And an acupuncture treatment is only $5.00.

You can learn a lot at the fair. This month a doctor is giving a lecture on nutrition labels. There is also a demonstration on sugar-free cooking. You can learn to do aerobic exercise and yoga, too.

Do you want to get healthy and stay healthy? Then come to the Fadool Health Clinic Fair! We want to see you there!

Reread the article.

1. Who wrote this article? How do you know?

2. What information in the picture is *not* in the article?

What do you think?

3. Which booths at this fair look interesting to you? Why?

4. Do you read nutrition labels? Why or why not?

Downtown وسط المدينة

1. parking garage
   جراج سيارات / موقف سيارات

2. office building
   مبنى خاص للمكاتب

3. hotel
   فندق

4. Department of
   Motor Vehicles
   دائرة تسجيل المركبات الآلية

5. bank
   بنك / مصرف

6. police station
   مخفر الشرطة

7. bus station
   محطة الأوتوبيس

8. city hall
   مبنى البلدية

THE SHELTON

DMV

DMV

RED LINE BUS CO.

Elm Street

FIRST U.S.

DOWNTOWN DIVISION

Grand Avenue

Listen and point. Take turns.

A: *Point to the bank*.

B: *Point to the hotel*.

A: *Point to the restaurant*.

Dictate to your partner. Take turns.

A: *Write bank*.

B: *Is that spelled b-a-n-k?*

A: *Yes, that's right.*

9. hospital
مستشفى

10. gas station
محطة بنزين

11. post office
مكتب بريد

12. fire station
إطفائية

13. courthouse
دار المحكمة

14. restaurant
مطعم

15. library
مكتبة

Grammar Point: *in* and *at* with locations

Use *in* when you are inside the building. *I am **in** (inside) the bank.* Use *at* to describe your general location. *I am **at** the bank.*

Pair practice. Make new conversations.

A: *I'm in the <u>bank</u>. Where are you?*
B: *I'm at the <u>bank</u>, too, but I'm outside.*
A: *OK. I'll meet you there.*

127

1. stadium
استاد

2. construction site
موقع إنشاءات

3. factory
مصنع

4. car dealership
معرض سيارات

5. mosque
مسجد

6. movie theater
دور عرض / سينما

7. shopping mall
مركز تسوق

8. furniture store
محل لبيع الأثاث

9. school
مدرسة

10. gym
جمنازيوم (قاعة الجمباز)

11. coffee shop
مقهى

12. motel
موتيل (فندق صغير)

Ways to state your destination using *to* and *to the*

Use ***to*** for schools, churches, and synagogues.
*I'm going **to** <u>school</u>.*
Use ***to the*** for all other locations. *I have to go **to the** <u>bakery</u>.*

Pair practice. Make new conversations.

A: *Where are you going today?*
B: *I'm going to <u>school</u>. How about you?*
A: *I have to go to the <u>bakery</u>.*

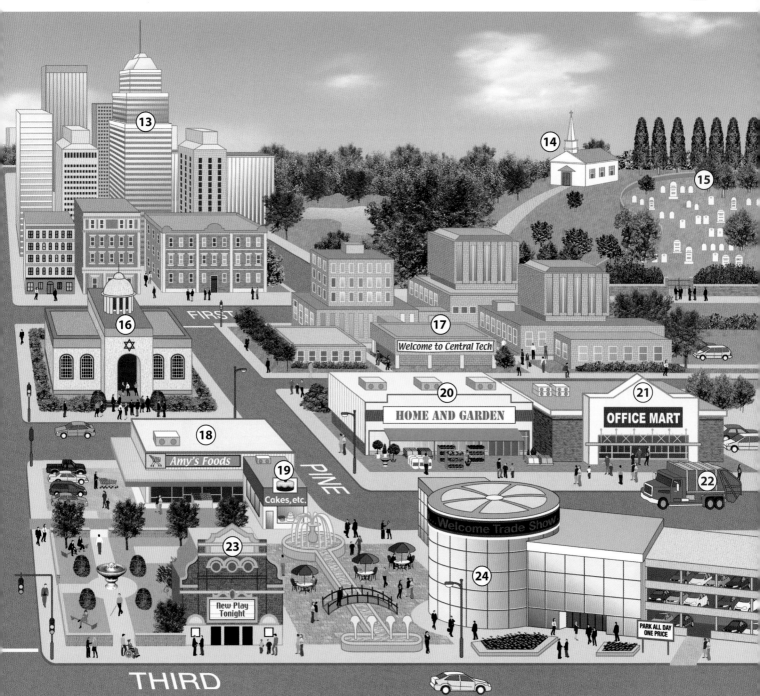

13. skyscraper / high-rise
ناطحة سحاب / بناية عالية الارتفاع

14. church
كنيسة

15. cemetery
مقبرة

16. synagogue
معبد يهودي

17. community college
كلية أهلية

18. supermarket
محل سوبرماركت

19. bakery
مخبز

20. home improvement store
محل أدوات لتحسين المنازل

21. office supply store
محل أدوات مكتبية

22. garbage truck
سيارة النفايات

23. theater
مسرح

24. convention center
مركز مؤتمرات

Ways to give locations

The mall is on Second Street.
The mall is on the corner of Second and Elm.
The mall is next to the movie theater.

Survey your class. Record the responses.

1. Do you have a favorite coffee shop? Which one?
2. Which supermarkets do you go to?
Report: *Nine* out of *ten* students go to ____.

129

1. laundromat مغسلة عامة	**7. corner** زاوية / ناصية	**13. mailbox** صندوق البريد
2. dry cleaners مصبغة / تنظيف جاف	**8. traffic light** إشارة مرور	**14. pedestrian** مشاة
3. convenience store بقالة صغيرة	**9. bus** أوتوبيس / حافلة	**15. crosswalk** ممر المشاة
4. pharmacy صيدلية	**10. fast food restaurant** مطعم وجبات سريعة	**A. cross** the street تعبر الشارع
5. parking space مكان لوقوف السيارة	**11. drive-thru window** نافذة تقديم الأطعمة للسيارات	**B. wait for** the light ينتظر الإشارة الضوئية
6. handicapped parking مكان مخصص للمعوقين لوقوف سياراتهم	**12. newsstand** كشك جرائد	**C. jaywalk** يعبر الطريق في غير المكان المخصص لذلك

More vocabulary

do errands: to make a short trip from your home to buy or pick up things

neighborhood: the area close to your home

Pair practice. Make new conversations.

A: *I have a lot of errands to do today.*

B: *Me too. First, I'm going to the* <u>laundromat</u>.

A: *I'll see you there after I stop at the* <u>copy center</u>.

130

16. bus stop	22. bike	28. cart
موقف أوتوبيس	دراجة	عربة يد
17. donut shop	23. pay phone	29. street vendor
محل لكعك الدونات	هاتف / تليفون بالأجرة (تليفون عمومي)	بائع متجول
18. copy center	24. sidewalk	30. childcare center
مطبعة / محل لتصوير مستندات	رصيف	مركز رعاية أطفال
19. barbershop	25. parking meter	D. **ride** a bike
حلاق	عداد موقف السيارة	تركب دراجة
20. used book store	26. street sign	E. **park** the car
محل لبيع الكتب المستعملة	لافتة شارع	يوقف سيارة
21. curb	27. fire hydrant	F. **walk** a dog
حافة رصيف	مطفئة حريق	يمشّي كلبا

Internet Research: finding business listings

Type "pharmacy" and your city in the search bar.
Count the pharmacy listings you see.
Report: *I found 25 pharmacies in Chicago.*

Think about it. Discuss.

1. How many different jobs are there at this intersection?
2. Which of these businesses would you like to own? Why?

1. music store محل موسيقى	5. toy store محل لعب	9. optician نظاراتي
2. jewelry store محل مجوهرات	6. pet store محل منتجات الحيوانات المنزلية	10. shoe store محل أحذية
3. nail salon صالون لتجميل الأظافر	7. card store محل بطاقات معايدة / محل كروت	11. play area منطقة للعب
4. bookstore محل بيع كتب	8. florist بائع زهور	12. guest services خدمات الضيوف

More vocabulary

beauty shop: hair salon

gift shop: a store that sells T-shirts, mugs, and other small gifts

men's store: men's clothing store

Pair practice. Make new conversations.

A: *Where is the florist?*

B: *It's on the first floor, next to the optician.*

13. department store	**17.** candy store	**21.** elevator
محل متعدد الأقسام	محل بيع الحلوى	مصعد
14. travel agency	**18.** hair salon	**22.** kiosk
مكتب سياحة / وكالة سفر	صالون حلاقة	كشك
15. food court	**19.** maternity store	**23.** escalator
ساحة الطعام	محل بيع ملابس الحوامل	سلم متحرك
16. ice cream shop	**20.** electronics store	**24.** directory
محل آيس كريم	محل أجهزة إلكترونية	الدليل

Ways to talk about plans

Let's go to the <u>card store</u>.
I have to go to the <u>card store</u>.
I want to go to the <u>card store</u>.

Role play. Talk to a friend at the mall.

A: *Let's go to the <u>card store</u>. I need to buy <u>a card</u> for Maggie's birthday.*
B: *OK, but can we go to the <u>shoe store</u> next?*

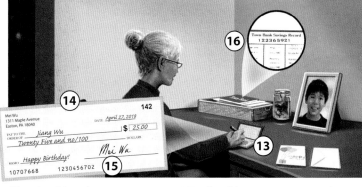

1. teller	3. deposit
أمينة الصندوق	إيداع
2. customer	4. deposit slip
زبون / عميل	بيان الإيداع

5. security guard	7. safety deposit box
حارس أمن	صندوق حفظ الودائع
6. vault	8. valuables
خزينة	نفائس / أشياء ثمينة

Bank Accounts الحسابات المصرفية

9. account manager	11. opening deposit
مدير حسابات	المبلغ المودع عند فتح الحساب
10. joint account	12. ATM card
حساب مشترك	بطاقة جهاز الصرف الآلي

13. checkbook	15. checking account number
دفتر شيكات	رقم الحساب الجاري
14. check	16. savings account number
شيك	رقم حساب التوفير

A. **Cash** a check.
يصرف شيكا.

B. **Make** a deposit.
يودع نقدا أو شيكا.

17. bank statement	18. balance
كشف الحساب البنكي	الرصيد

The ATM (Automated Teller Machine) جهاز الصرف الآلي

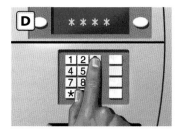

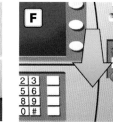

C. **Insert** your ATM card.
أدخل بطاقة إيه تي أم الخاصة بك.

D. **Enter** your PIN.*
أدخل رقمك السري.

E. **Withdraw** cash.
اسحب النقود.

F. **Remove** your card.
أخرج بطاقة إيه تي أم الخاصة بك.

*PIN = personal identification number

A. get a library card
يحصل على بطاقة مكتبة

B. look for a book
يبحث عن كتاب

C. check out a book
يستعير كتابا

D. return a book
يعيد كتابا

E. pay a late fine
يدفع غرامة تأخير

1. library clerk
كاتب / موظف مكتبة

2. circulation desk
مكتب تداول

3. library patron
مُرتاد مكتبة

4. periodicals
منشورات دورية

5. magazine
مجلة

6. newspaper
صحيفة

7. headline
عنوان رئيسي (مانشت)

8. atlas
أطلس

9. reference librarian
أمين مكتبة للمعلومات المرجعية

10. self-checkout
استعارة كتب ذاتيا

11. online catalog
كتالوج إلكتروني

12. picture book
كتاب مصور

13. biography
سيرة ذاتية

14. title
عنوان

15. author
مؤلف

16. novel
رواية

17. audiobook
كتاب صوتي

18. e-book
كتاب إلكتروني

19. DVD
قرص فيديو رقمي (دي في دي)

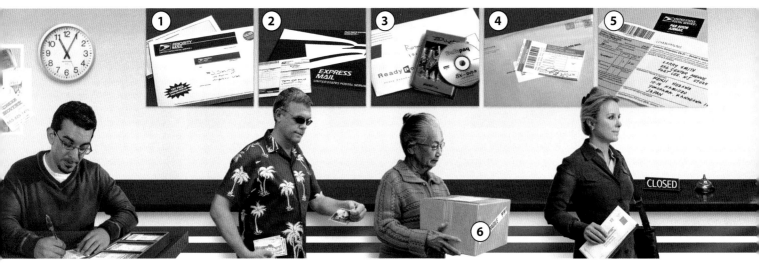

1. Priority Mail®
بريد مستعجل

2. Express Mail®
بريد سريع

3. Media Mail®
بريد الوسائط الإعلامية

4. Certified Mail™
بريد مسجل

5. airmail
بريد جوي

6. ground post / parcel post
بريد برّي

13. letter
خطاب / جواب

14. envelope
ظرف / مغلف

15. greeting card
بطاقة / كارت معايدة

16. postcard
بطاقة بريدية (كارت بوستال)

17. package
طرد

18. book of stamps
دفتر طوابع بريدية

19. postal forms
استمارات بريدية

20. letter carrier
ساعي البريد / حامل البريد

21. return address
عنوان المرسل

Sonya Enriquez
258 Quentin Avenue
Los Angeles, CA 90068-1416

23. stamp
طابع بريد

22. mailing address
عنوان المرسل إليه

Cindy Lin
807 Glenn Drive
Charlotte, NC 28201

24. postmark
ختم البريد

Ways to talk about sending mail

This letter has to <u>get there tomorrow</u>. (Express Mail®)
This letter has to <u>arrive in two days</u>. (Priority Mail®)
This letter can go in <u>regular mail</u>. (First Class)

Pair practice. Make new conversations.

A: *Hi. <u>This letter has to get there tomorrow</u>.*
B: *You can send it by <u>Express Mail</u>®.*
A: *OK. I need <u>a book of stamps</u>, too.*

7. postal clerk
موظف بريد

8. scale
ميزان

9. post office box (PO box)
صندوق بريد (ص. ب.)

10. automated postal center (APC)
مركز بريدي آلي

11. post office lobby drop
صندوق بريد موجود داخل مكتب البريد

12. mailbox
صندوق لإلقاء البريد

Sending a Card إرسال بطاقة / كارت

A. Write a note in a card.
تكتب رسالة في الكارت.

B. Address the envelope.
تكتب **العنوان** على الظرف.

C. Put on a stamp.
تضع طابع البريد.

D. Mail the card.
تلقي الكارت في صندوق البريد.

E. Deliver the card.
يوصّل البريد.

F. Receive the card.
تستلم الكارت.

G. Read the card.
تقرأ الكارت.

H. Write back.
تكتب إليها ردا على الكارت.

More vocabulary

junk mail: mail you don't want
overnight / next-day mail: Express Mail®
postage: the cost to send mail

Survey your class. Record the responses.

1. Do you send greeting cards by mail or online?
2. Do you pay bills by mail or online?
Report: _25%_ of us _send cards_ _by mail_.

137

Signs visible in image: No Talking • Quiet Please • BUCKLE UP IT'S THE LAW! • Forms • Handbooks • Information • CLOSED • Vehicle Registration → • 104 105 106 107 108 109 • California Driver Handbook

1. **DMV handbook**
كتيب دائرة تسجيل المركبات الآلية

2. **testing area**
منطقة الامتحان

3. **DMV clerk**
موظف دائرة تسجيل المركبات الآلية

4. **photo**
صورة فوتوغرافية

5. **fingerprint**
بصمة اصبع

6. **vision exam**
كشف نظر

7. **window**
نافذة / شبّاك

Pluto Auto Insurance — Proof of Insurance — Policyholder: Irene Pena — Policy No: 1119000555 — Make: Ford Taurus — Expiration Date: 9/25/21 — IMPORTANT: PLEASE PLACE IN DESIGNATED VEHICLE

CALIFORNIA DRIVER LICENSE — EXPIRES 07-29-25 — N57881049 — CLASS — Irene Pena 1313 Balboa Blvd, Van Nuys, CA 91064 — DONOR — DOB 7-29-70

AUG California 2021 — 30PD016

8. **proof of insurance**
إثبات التأمين

9. **driver's license**
رخصة قيادة سيارة

10. **expiration date**
تاريخ الانتهاء

11. **driver's license number**
رقم رخصة القيادة

12. **license plate**
لوحة الترخيص المعدنية

13. **registration sticker / tag**
لاصق / لصيقة التسجيل

More vocabulary

expire: A license is no good, or **expires**, after the expiration date.
renew a license: to apply to keep a license before it expires
vanity plate: a more expensive, personal license plate

Internet Research: DMV locations

Type "DMV" and your ZIP code in the search bar. How many DMVs are there?
Report: I found ____ DMV office(s) near me.

Getting Your First License الحصول على أول رخصة قيادة لك

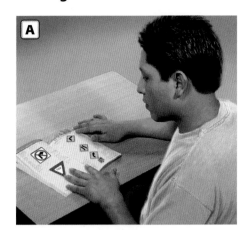

A. Study the handbook.
ذاكر الكتيب.

B. Take a driver education course.*
التحق بدورة لتعليم قيادة السيارات.

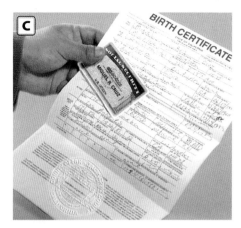

C. Show your identification.
أبرز بطاقة هويتك.

D. Pay the application fee.
ادفع رسم تقديم الطلب.

E. Take a written test.
تقدم للامتحان التحريري.

F. Get a learner's permit.
احصل على تصريح للمتعلم.

G. Take a driver's training course.*
التحق بدورة تدريب السائقين.

H. Pass a driving test.
انجح في امتحان قيادة السيارة.

I. Get your license.
تسلم رخصة القيادة الخاصة بك.

*Note: This is not required for drivers 18 and older.

Ways to request more information

What do I do next?
What's the next step?
Where do I go from here?

Role play. Talk to a DMV clerk.

A: *I want to apply for a driver's license.*
B: *Did you study the handbook?*
A: *Yes, I did. What do I do next?*

Federal Government (الحكومة الاتحادية (الفدرالية

Legislative Branch
السلطة التشريعية

1. U.S. Capitol
   الكابيتول (مقر الكونجرس الأمريكي في واشنطن)

2. Congress
   الكونجرس

3. House of Representatives
   مجلس النواب

4. congressperson
   عضو كونجرس

5. Senate
   مجلس الشيوخ

6. senator
   عضو مجلس شيوخ / سناتور

Executive Branch
السلطة التنفيذية

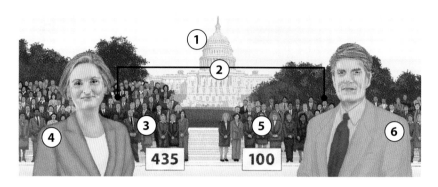

7. White House
   البيت الأبيض

8. president
   الرئيس

9. vice president
   نائب الرئيس

10. Cabinet
    الوزارة

Judicial Branch
السلطة القضائية

11. Supreme Court
    المحكمة العليا

12. justices
    قضاة

13. chief justice
    رئيس القضاة / رئيس المحكمة

State Government حكومة الولاية

14. governor
    الحاكم

15. lieutenant governor
    نائب الحاكم

16. state capital
    عاصمة الولاية

17. Legislature
    المجلس التشريعي للولاية

18. assemblyperson
    عضو المجلس التشريعي

19. state senator
    عضو مجلس شيوخ الولاية

City Government حكومة المدينة

20. mayor
    العمدة

21. city council
    مجلس المدينة / المجلس البلدي

22. councilperson
    عضو مجلس المدينة

The U.S. Military القوات المسلحة الأمريكية

23. **Pentagon**
وزارة الدفاع الأمريكية (البنتاغون)
24. **Secretary of Defense**
وزير الدفاع
25. **general**
جنرال / فريق أول
26. **admiral**
أميرال / قائد بحري
27. **officer**
ضابط

Military Service الخدمة العسكرية

A. **be** a recruit
أن تكون مجندا

B. **be** on active duty
أن تكون عاملا في الخدمة العسكرية

C. **be** on reserve
أن تكون في قوات الاحتياط

D. **be** a veteran
أن تكون من المحاربين القدامى

Branches of the Military فروع القوات المسلحة

28. **Army**
الجيش
29. **soldier**
جندي

30. **Navy**
البحرية
31. **seaman / sailor**
بحار / نوتي

32. **Air Force**
القوات الجوية
33. **airman**
طيار

34. **Marines**
سلاح مشاة البحرية (المارينز)
35. **marine**
جندي في مشاة البحرية

36. **Coast Guard**
خفر السواحل
37. **coast guardsman**
جندي في خفر السواحل

38. **National Guard***
الحرس الوطني
39. **national guardsman**
جندي في الحرس الوطني

*Each state has an Army National Guard. The national guardsmen are reservists.

Responsibilities الواجبات

A. vote
يصوت في الانتخابات

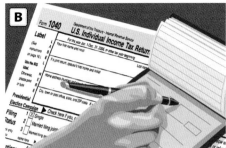

B. pay taxes
يدفع الضرائب

C. obey the law
يطيع القانون

D. register with Selective Service*
يسجل اسمه في الخدمة الانتقائية

E. serve on a jury
يؤدي الخدمة في هيئة محلفين

F. be informed
يبقى على اطلاع بما يجري

Citizenship Requirements متطلبات الحصول على الجنسية

G. be 18 or older
أن يكون عمره ١٨ سنة أو أكبر

H. live in the U.S. for five years
أن يكون مقيما في الولايات المتحدة لفترة ٥ سنوات

I. take a citizenship test
أن يتقدم لامتحان الجنسية

Rights الحقوق

1. peaceful assembly
التجمع السلمي

2. free speech
حرية الكلام

3. freedom of religion
حرية الدين أو العبادة

4. freedom of the press
حرية الصحافة

5. a fair trial
المحاكمة العادلة

*Note: All males 18 to 26 who live in the U.S. are required to register with Selective Service.

An Election انتخابات

J. run for office
يرشّح نفسه لمنصب عام

6. candidate
مرشح

K. campaign
يجري حملة انتخابية

7. rally
تجمع

L. debate
يدخل في مناظرة

8. opponent
المنافس / الخصم

9. ballot
ورقة اقتراع / ورقة تصويت

10. voting booth /
polling booth
كابينة تصويت / كابينة اقتراع

M. get elected
يفوز في الانتخابات

11. election results
نتائج الانتخابات

N. serve
يتولى منصبه

12. elected official
مسؤول منتخب

More vocabulary

political party: a group of people with the same
political goals

term: the period of time an elected official serves

Think about it. Discuss.

1. Should everyone have to vote? Why or why not?

2. Are candidate debates important? Why or why not?

3. Would you prefer to run for city council or mayor? Why?

A You have the right to remain silent…

A. arrest a suspect
يلقي القبض على شخص مشتبه فيه.

1. police officer
ضابط شرطة / شرطي

2. handcuffs
قيود / كلبشات

B

B. hire a lawyer / **hire** an attorney
يوكّل محاميا

3. guard
حارس

4. defense attorney
محامي دفاع

C Bail is set at $20,000.

C. appear in court
يمثل أمام القضاء

5. defendant
متهم / مدعى عليه

6. judge
قاضي

D

D. stand trial
يحاكم / يخضع للمحاكمة

7. courtroom
قاعة المحكمة

8. jury
هيئة محلفين

9. evidence
دليل / بينة

10. prosecuting attorney
المدعي العام / وكيل النيابة

11. witness
شاهد

12. court reporter
كاتب المحكمة

13. bailiff
حاجب المحكمة

E Guilty.

E. convict the defendant
يحكم بإدانة المتهم

14. verdict*
الحكم / القرار

F 7 years

F. sentence the defendant
يصدر الحكم بمعاقبة المتهم

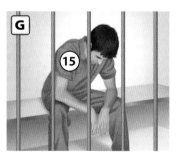

G

G. go to jail / **go** to prison
يسجن / يودع السجن

15. convict / prisoner
مدان (محكوم عليه) / سجين

H

H. be released
يفرج عنه / يطلق سراحه

*Note: There are two possible verdicts, "guilty" and "not guilty."

Look at the pictures.
Describe what happened.

A: The <u>police officer</u> <u>arrested a suspect</u>.
B: <u>He put handcuffs on him</u>.

Think about it. Discuss.

1. Would you want to serve on a jury? Why or why not?
2. Look at the crimes on page 145. What sentence would you give for each crime? Why?

1. vandalism
   تخريب متعمد
2. burglary
   سطو

3. assault
   اعتداء
4. gang violence
   عنف عصابات

5. drunk driving
   قيادة سيارة تحت تأثير الخمر
6. illegal drugs
   مخدرات ممنوعة

7. arson
   حرق متعمد
8. shoplifting
   سرقة معروضات المتجر

9. identity theft
   سرقة هويات الغير
10. victim
    ضحية / مجني عليه

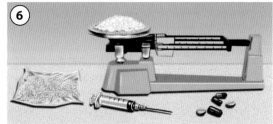

11. mugging
    اعتداء بهدف السلب
12. murder
    جريمة القتل
13. gun
    مسدس

More vocabulary

commit a crime: to do something illegal
criminal: someone who does something illegal
steal: to take money or things from someone illegally

Identify the tenants' problem. Brainstorm solutions.

The apartment tenants at 65 Elm Street are upset.
There were three burglaries on their block last month.
This month there were five burglaries and a mugging!

A. Walk with a friend.
امش مع صديق أو صديقة.

B. Stay on well-lit streets.
ابق في شوارع جيدة الإنارة.

C. Conceal your PIN number.
اخف رقمك السري الذي تستخدمه في جهاز الصرف الآلي.

D. Protect your purse or wallet.
حافظ على محفظتك أو حقيبة يدك.

E. Lock your doors.
اقفل أبوابك.

F. Don't **open** your door to strangers.
لا تفتح بابك للغرباء.

G. Don't **drink** and **drive**.
لا تشرب الخمر وتقود سيارة.

H. Shop on secure websites.
لا تتسوق إلا على مواقع إنترنت مؤمنة.

I. Be aware of your surroundings.
كن على دراية بالبيئة المحيطة بك.

J. Report suspicious packages.
بلّغ الشرطة عن أية علب أو طرود مشبوهة.

K. Report crimes to the police.
بلّغ الشرطة عن الجرائم.

L. Join a Neighborhood Watch.
انضم إلى هيئة أهل الحي لمراقبة الأعمال المشبوهة.

More vocabulary

sober: not drunk
designated drivers: sober drivers who drive drunk people home safely

Survey your class. Record the responses.

1. Do you always lock your doors?
2. Do you belong to a Neighborhood Watch?
Report: _75% of us always lock our doors._

Online Dangers for Children
الأخطار التي يواجهها الأطفال على الإنترنت

1. cyberbullying
البلطجة على الإنترنت

2. online predators
المفترسون على الإنترنت

3. inappropriate material
المواد غير اللائقة

Ways to Protect Children طرق حماية الأطفال

A. **Turn on** parental controls.
قم **بتشغيل** أدوات الرقابة الأبوية.

B. **Monitor** children's Internet use.
قم **بمراقبة** استعمال أطفالك للإنترنت.

C. **Block** inappropriate sites.
قم **بحجب أو إيقاف** المواقع الإلكترونية غير اللائقة.

Internet Crime جرائم الإنترنت

4. phishing
المخادعة الحاسوبية

5. hacking
القرصنة الحاسوبية

Safety Solutions حلول السلامة

D. **Create** secure passwords.
اخلق كلمات سر مؤمَّنة.

E. **Update** security software.
قم **بتحديث** البرمجيات الأمنية.

F. **Use** encrypted / secure sites.
استعمل مواقع إلكترونية مشفرة / مؤمَّنة.

G. **Delete** suspicious emails.
احذف رسائل البريد الإلكتروني المشبوهة.

1. lost child
   طفل ضائع

2. car accident
   حادث سيارة / حادث طريق

3. airplane crash
   تحطم طائرة

4. explosion
   انفجار

5. earthquake
   زلزال

6. mudslide
   انزلاق الطين

7. forest fire
   حريق غابات

8. fire
   حريق

9. firefighter
   إطفائي / رجل اطفاء

10. fire truck
    سيارة اطفاء

Ways to report an emergency

First, give your name. *My name is <u>Tim Johnson</u>.*
Then, state the emergency and give the address.
There was <u>a car accident</u> at <u>219 Elm Street</u>.

Role play. Call 911.

A: *911 emergency operator.*

B: *My name is <u>Lisa Diaz</u>. There is <u>a fire</u> at <u>323 Oak Street</u>.*
   Please hurry!

11. drought
جفاف / قحط

12. famine
مجاعة

13. blizzard
عاصفة ثلجية شديدة

14. hurricane
إعصار

15. tornado
زوبعة

16. volcanic eruption
انفجار بركاني

17. tidal wave / tsunami
موجة بحرية مدية / تسونامي

18. avalanche
تيهور / جرف ثلجي

19. flood
فيضان

20. search and rescue team
فريق البحث والإنقاذ

Survey your class. Record the responses.

1. Which natural disaster worries you the most?
2. Which natural disaster worries you the least?

Report: _Five_ of us are _most_ worried about _earthquakes_.

Think about it. Discuss.

1. What organizations can help you in an emergency?
2. What are some ways to prepare for natural disasters?
3. Where would you go in an emergency?

Before an Emergency قبل حدوث الحالة الطارئة

A. Plan for an emergency.
خطط للحالة الطارئة.

1. meeting place
مكان تجمع

2. out-of-state contact
معارف خارج الولاية

3. escape route
طريق للهرب / مهرب

4. gas shut-off valve
صمام غلق الغاز

5. evacuation route
طريق للإخلاء

B. Make a disaster kit.
اصنع / جهّز علبة بمستلزمات الكوارث.

6. warm clothes
ملابس ثقيلة للتدفئة

7. blankets
بطاطين

8. can opener
فتاحة علب

9. canned food
مأكولات معلبة

10. packaged food
أطعمة مغلفة

11. bottled water
زجاجات ماء

12. moist towelettes
فوط صغيرة رطبة

13. toilet paper
ورق تواليت

14. flashlight
مصباح بطارية

15. batteries
بطاريات

16. matches
كبريت

17. cash and coins
نقد وعملة

18. first aid kit
علبة إسعافات أولية

19. copies of ID and credit cards
نسخ مصورة من بطاقات الهوية وبطاقات الائتمان

20. copies of important papers
نسخ مصورة من الأوراق المهمة

Pair practice. Make new conversations.

A: *What do we need for our disaster kit?*
B: *We need blankets and matches.*
A: *I think we also need batteries.*

Survey your class. Record the responses.

1. Do you have a disaster kit?
2. Do you have an out-of-state contact?
Report: *Ten of us have a disaster kit.*

During an Emergency في أثناء الحالة الطارئة

C. **Watch** the weather.
راقب حالة الطقس.

hurricane watch

D. **Pay attention** to warnings.
انتبه للتحذيرات العامة.

hurricane watch

E. **Remain** calm.
ابقَ هادئًا.

Go to a shelter.

F. **Follow** directions.
اتبع الإرشادات.

Shelter

G. **Help** people with disabilities.
ساعد الناس المعوقين.

Shelter

H. **Seek** shelter.
ابحث عن مخبأ أو ملجأ.

I. **Stay away** from windows.
ابتعد عن النوافذ.

J. **Take** cover.
احتمِ.

K. **Evacuate** the area.
اخلِ المنطقة.

After an Emergency بعد حدوث الحالة الطارئة

We're OK.

Great.

L. **Call** out-of-state contacts.
اتصل بمعارفك خارج الولاية.

M. **Clean up** debris.
نظّف المكان من الأنقاض.

N. **Inspect** utilities.
فتّش على المرافق.

Ways to say you're OK	**Ways to say you need help**	**Role play. Prepare for an emergency.**
I'm fine.	*We need help.*	A: *They just issued a hurricane warning.*
We're OK here.	*Someone is hurt.*	B: *OK. We need to stay calm and follow directions.*
Everything's under control.	*I'm injured. Please get help.*	A: *What do we need to do first?*

1. graffiti

رسوم أو نقوش على الجدران

2. litter

مهملات ملقاة في الطرقات العامة

3. streetlight

عامود انارة الشارع

4. hardware store

محل الأدوات المعدنية /
محل أدوات الحدادة

5. petition

التماس / عريضة رسمية

A. **give** a speech

تلقي خطابا

B. **applaud**

تصفيق

C. **change**

تغيير

What do you see in the pictures?

1. What were the problems on Main Street?
2. What was the petition for?
3. Why did the city council applaud?
4. How did the volunteers change the street?

 Read the story.

Community Cleanup

Marta Lopez has a donut shop on Main Street. One day she looked at her street and was very upset. She saw graffiti on her donut shop and the other stores. Litter was everywhere. All the streetlights were broken. Marta wanted to fix the lights and clean up the street.

Marta started a petition about the streetlights. Five hundred people signed it. Then she gave a speech to the city council. The council members voted to repair the streetlights. Everyone applauded. Marta was happy, but her work wasn't finished.

Next, Marta asked for volunteers to clean up Main Street. The hardware store manager gave the volunteers free paint. Marta gave them free donuts and coffee. The volunteers painted and cleaned. They changed Main Street. Now Main Street is beautiful and Marta is proud.

Reread the story.

1. Find "repair" in paragraph 2. Find another word for "repair" in the story.

What do you think?

2. What are the benefits of being a volunteer?
3. What do you think Marta said in her speech? How do you know?

Basic Transportation

وسائل النقل الأساسية

1. car
   سيارة

2. passenger
   راكب

3. taxi
   سيارة أجرة / تاكسي

4. motorcycle
   دراجة بخارية / موتوسيكل

5. street
   شارع

6. truck
   شاحنة / لوري

7. train
   قطار

8. (air)plane
   طائرة

Listen and point. Take turns.

A: Point to <u>the motorcycle</u>.
B: Point to <u>the truck</u>.
A: Point to <u>the train</u>.

Dictate to your partner. Take turns.

A: Write <u>motorcycle</u>.
B: Could you repeat that for me?
A: I said <u>motorcycle</u>.

9. helicopter
طائرة عمودية / هليكوبتر

10. airport
مطار

11. subway station
محطة قطار نفقي /
محطة مترو أنفاق

12. subway
قطار نفقي / مترو أنفاق

13. bus stop
موقف أوتوبيس /
موقف حافلات

14. bus
أوتوبيس / حافلة

15. bicycle
دراجة / بسكيلته

SUBWAY

Mario's ITALIAN DELI

Ways to talk about using transportation

Use *take* for buses, trains, subways, taxis, planes, and helicopters. Use *drive* for cars and trucks. Use *ride* for bicycles and motorcycles.

Pair practice. Make new conversations.

A: *How do you get to school?*
B: *I take the bus. How about you?*
A: *I ride a bicycle to school.*

A Bus Stop   موقف أوتوبيس

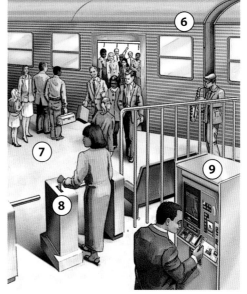

BUS 10 Northbound

Main	Elm	Oak
6:00	6:10	6:13
6:30	6:40	6:43
7:00	7:10	7:13
7:30	7:40	7:43

TRANSFER →
Valid for $2\frac{1}{2}$ hours

A Subway Station   محطة قطار نفقي

MetroCard

1. bus route
طريق سير الأوتوبيس

3. rider
راكب

5. transfer
تذكرة تحويل

2. fare
أجرة / تعريفة

4. schedule
جدول مواعيد

6. subway car
عربة قطار نفقي

7. platform
رصيف

8. turnstile
حاجز أفقي دوار

9. vending machine
آلة البيع

10. token
عملة رمزية

11. fare card
بطاقة الأجرة المدفوعة

A Train Station   محطة قطار

AMTRAK
LIZ   LK98S
KOENIG   3/12/2017
TRIP
CHICAGO, IL   5:15 PM
ST. LOUIS, MO   10:45 PM
RAIL FARE 70.00
PAYMENT STATUS PAID
RAIL PLANS G0517B
ISSUE CHICAGO UNION STATION
TICKET 1 OF 1

Fresno

Los Angeles

Fresno

Los Angeles

Airport Transportation   مواصلات إلى المطار

TAXIS

J&J Hotel

TAXI

1036081

12. ticket window
شباك تذاكر

13. conductor
قاطع التذاكر / كمسري

14. track
سكة

15. ticket
تذكرة

16. one-way trip
رحلة ذهاب فقط

17. round trip
ذهاب وعودة

18. taxi stand
موقف سيارات أجرة (تاكسي)

19. shuttle
وشيعة / مكوك

20. town car
سيارة صالون فاخرة / سيارة ليموزين

21. taxi driver
سائق سيارة أجرة / تاكسي

22. taxi license
رخصة تاكسي

23. meter
عدّاد

More vocabulary

hail a taxi: to raise your hand to get a taxi
miss the bus: to get to the bus stop after the bus leaves

Internet Research: taxi fares

Type "taxi fare finder" and your city in the search bar.
Enter a starting address and an ending address.
Report: *The fare from <u>my house</u> to <u>school</u> is <u>$10.00</u>.*

A. go under the bridge
تذهب (تسير) تحت الجسر

B. go over the bridge
يذهب (يسير) فوق الجسر

C. walk up the steps
تطلع / تصعد الدرجات مشيا على قدميها

D. walk down the steps
ينزل / يهبط الدرجات مشيا على قدميه

E. get into the taxi
تدخل إلى سيارة الأجرة (التاكسي)

F. get out of the taxi
يخرج من سيارة الأجرة (التاكسي)

G. run across the street
يركض عبر الشارع

H. run around the corner
تركض حول الزاوية

I. get on the highway
يدخل على الطريق السريع

J. get off the highway
يخرج من الطريق السريع

K. drive through the tunnel
يسوق عبر النفق

Grammar Point: *into, out of, on, off*

Use ***get into*** for taxis and cars.
Use ***get on*** for buses, trains, planes, and highways.

Use ***get out of*** for taxis and cars.
Use ***get off*** for buses, trains, planes, and highways.

1. stop
قِف

2. do not enter / wrong way
ممنوع الدخول / اتجاه خطأ

3. one way
اتجاه واحد

4. speed limit
السرعة القصوى

5. U-turn OK
مسموح الدوران

6. no outlet / dead end
بدون منفذ / طريق مسدود

7. right turn only
الانعطاف إلى اليمين فقط

8. no left turn
ممنوع الانعطاف إلى اليسار

9. yield
انتظر السيارات المارة

10. merge
اندماج

11. no parking
ممنوع الوقوف

12. handicapped parking
موقف للمعاقين

13. pedestrian crossing
عبور المشاة

15. school crossing
عبور مدرسة

17. U.S. route / highway marker
طريق بين ولايات / علامة طريق سريع

14. railroad crossing
عبور سكة حديد (مزلقان)

16. roadwork
منطقة عمل

18. hospital
مستشفى

Directions إرشادات

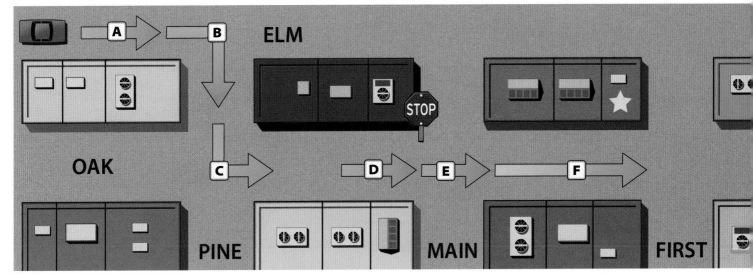

ELM

OAK

PINE

MAIN

FIRST

A. Go straight on Elm Street.
سر باتجاه **مستقيم** على شارع إلم.

B. Turn right on Pine Street.
انعطف يمينا على شارع باين.

C. Turn left on Oak Street.
انعطف يسارا على شارع أوك.

D. Stop at the corner.
قف عند الزاوية / الناصية.

E. Go past Main Street.
اعبر شارع مين.

F. Go one block to First Street.
سر مسافة ناصية إلى شارع فيرست.

Maps خرائط

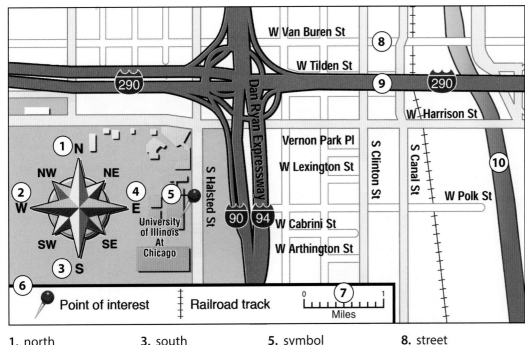

W Van Buren St

W Tilden St

Dan Ryan Expressway

290

290

W Harrison St

Vernon Park Pl

W Lexington St

S Halsted St

S Clinton St

S Canal St

W Polk St

90 94

W Cabrini St

W Arthington St

University of Illinois At Chicago

NW N NE
W E
SW S SE

Point of interest   Railroad track   0 ‖‖‖‖‖ 1 Miles

1. north
شمال

3. south
جنوب

5. symbol
رمز

8. street
شارع

11. GPS (global positioning system)
جي بي إس (نظام تحديد الموضع عالميا)

2. west
غرب

4. east
شرق

6. key
مفتاح

9. highway
طريق سريع

12. Internet map
خريطة إنترنت

7. scale
مقياس

10. river
نهر

Role play. Ask for directions.

A: *I'm lost. I need to get to Elm and Pine.*
B: *Go straight on Oak and make a right on Pine.*
A: *Thanks so much.*

Think about it. Discuss.

1. What are the pros and cons of using a GPS?
2. Which types of jobs require map-reading skills?

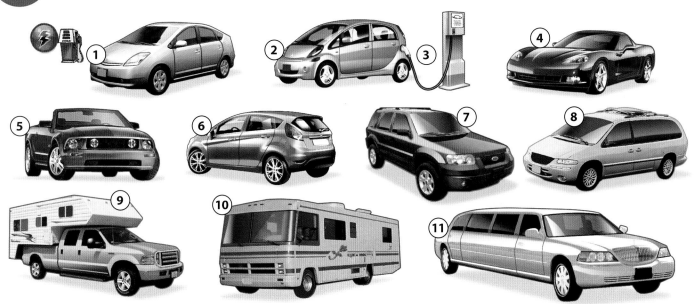

1. **hybrid**
   سيارة هييريد (تعمل بالبنزين والكهرباء)

2. **electric vehicle / EV**
   السيارة الكهربائية / EV (إي في)

3. **EV charging station**
   محطة شحن السيارة الكهربائية

4. **sports car**
   سيارة سبور (رياضية)

5. **convertible**
   سيارة مكشوفة (كابريوليه)

6. **hatchback**
   سيارة بباب خلفي

7. **SUV (sport utility vehicle)**
   سيارة رياضية متعددة الاستعمالات (إس يو في)

8. **minivan**
   سيارة فان صغيرة (ميني فان)

9. **camper**
   كارافان

10. **RV (recreational vehicle)**
    ار في (مركبة ترفيهية)

11. **limousine / limo**
    سيارة ليموزين

12. **pickup truck**
    شاحنة بيك اب

13. **cargo van**
    فان بضائع

14. **tow truck**
    سيارة قطر أو سحب

15. **tractor-trailer / semi**
    شاحنة مقطورة

16. **cab**
    كابينة الشاحنة

17. **trailer**
    عربة مقطورة

18. **moving van**
    سيارة فان للنقل

19. **dump truck**
    شاحنة نفايات

20. **tank truck**
    شاحنة صهريجية

21. **school bus**
    أوتوبيس مدرسة

More vocabulary

sedan: a 4-door car

coupe: a 2-door car

make and model: the car manufacturer and style: *Ford Fiesta*

Pair practice. Make new conversations.

A: *I have a new car!*

B: *Did you get <u>a hybrid</u>?*

A: *Yes, but I really wanted <u>a sports car</u>.*

Buying a Used Car شراء سيارة مستعملة

'09 compact. Only $8,500.

'13 sedan. Must sell. Great deal!

SEDAN. MUST SELL. GREAT DEAL!

A

A. **Look at** car ads.

انظر في إعلانات السيارات.

B How many miles does it have?

FOR SALE

B. **Ask** the seller about the car.

اسأل البائع عن السيارة.

It's in good condition.

C

C. **Take** the car to a mechanic.

خذ السيارة إلى ميكانيكي.

D It's $8,500.

I can give you $8,000.

D. **Negotiate** a price.

فاوض على سعر.

E

E. **Get** the title from the seller.

احصل على سند الملكية من البائع.

F

F. **Register** the car.

سجّل السيارة.

Taking Care of Your Car الاعتناء بسيارتك

G

G. **Fill** the tank with gas.

عبّئ خزان البنزين.

H

H. **Check** the oil.

افحص الزيت.

I

I. **Put in** coolant.

ضع سائل التبريد.

J 050·1HV

J. **Go** for a smog and safety check.*

اذهب لعمل فحص السلامة والغازات الملوثة.

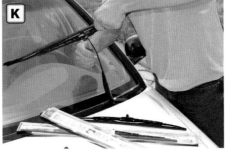

K

K. **Replace** the windshield wipers.

استبدل المسّاحات.

L

L. **Fill** the tires with air.

انفخ الإطارات بالهواء.

*smog check = emissions test

Ways to request service	Think about it. Discuss.
Please check the oil.	1. What's good and bad about a used car?
Could you fill the tank?	2. Do you like to negotiate car prices? Why or why not?
Put in coolant, please.	3. Do you know any good mechanics? Why are they good?

161

At the Dealer عند وكالة السيارات (معرض السيارات)

At the Mechanic عند الميكانيكي

1. windshield	5. tire
حاجب الريح الزجاجي	إطار / عجلة
2. windshield wipers	6. turn signal
المسّاحات	إشارة الانعطاف
3. side-view mirror	7. headlight
مرآة الرؤية الجانبية	مصباح أمامي
4. hood	8. bumper
غطاء محرك السيارة (كبّوت)	مخفف الصدمة

9. hubcap / wheel cover	13. taillight
غطاء محور العجلة	مصباح خلفي
10. gas tank	14. brake light
خزان البنزين	مصباح الفرملة
11. trunk	15. tailpipe
صندوق السيارة	ماسورة العادم
12. license plate	16. muffler
لوحة رقم السيارة	مخمّد الصوت (شكمان)

Under the Hood تحت غطاء المحرك (الكبّوت)

Inside the Trunk داخل صندوق السيارة

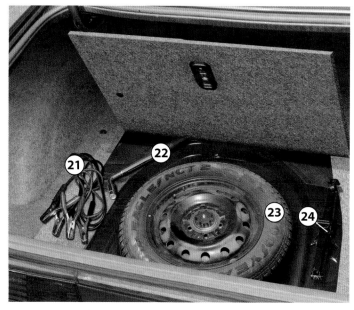

17. fuel injection system	19. radiator
نظام حقن الوقود	رادياتير (مشعاع)
18. engine	20. battery
محرك / موتور	بطارية

21. jumper cables	23. spare tire
كبل عبور الطاقة	إطار احتياطي (استبن)
22. lug wrench	24. jack
مفتاح ربط	مرفاع (كوريك)

The Dashboard and Instrument Panel تابلو السيارة ولوحة العدادات وأجهزة القياس

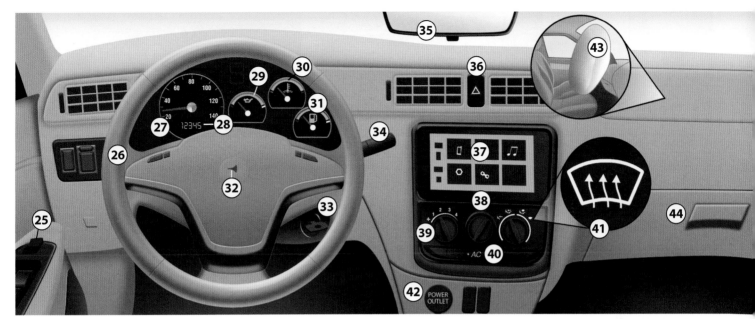

25. door lock
قفل الباب

26. steering wheel
عجلة القيادة

27. speedometer
عداد السرعة

28. odometer
أودومتر (عداد المسافة)

29. oil gauge
مقياس الزيت

30. temperature gauge
مقياس الحرارة

31. gas gauge
مقياس البنزين

32. horn
بوق (كلاكس)

33. ignition
إشعال

34. turn signal
إشارة الانعطاف

35. rearview mirror
مرآة للرؤية الخلفية

36. hazard lights
ضوء الوقوف للطوارئ

37. touch screen / audio display
شاشة تعمل باللمس / عرض النظام الصوتي

38. temperature control dial
مفتاح التحكم في درجة الحرارة

39. fan speed
سرعة المروحة

40. air conditioning / AC button
مكيّف الهواء / زر مكيّف الهواء

41. defroster
مزيل التجمد

42. power outlet
منفذ طاقة

43. airbag
كيس أمام هوائي

44. glove compartment
صندوق قفازات

An Automatic Transmission
ناقل حركة أوتوماتيكي

A Manual Transmission
ناقل حركة يدوي

Inside the Car
داخل السيارة

45. brake pedal
دواسة الفرملة

46. gas pedal / accelerator
دواسة البنزين

47. gearshift
ناقل التروس

48. handbrake
فرملة اليد

49. clutch
القابض (الدوبرياج)

50. stick shift
ذراع نقل السرعات (فتيس)

51. front seat
مقعد أمامي

52. seat belt
حزام أمان بالمقعد

53. child safety seat
مقعد أمان للطفل

54. back seat
مقعد خلفي

In the Airline Terminal في صالة المطار

At the Security Checkpoint
عند نقطة تفتيش الأمن

1. skycap
   حامل الحقائب

2. check-in kiosk
   كشك التسجيل

3. ticket agent
   وكيل تذاكر

4. screening area
   منطقة فرز وتفتيش

5. TSA* agent / security screener
   وكيل تي إس إيه / مفتش أمن

6. bin
   حاوية

Taking a Flight السفر في رحلة جوية

A. **Check in** electronically.
   قم بالتسجيل إلكترونيا.

B. **Check** your bags.
   سلّمي الحقائب.

C. **Show** your boarding pass and ID.
   أظهر بطاقة الصعود والهوية.

D. **Go through** security.
   مر عبر نقطة الأمن.

E. **Board** the plane.
   اصعد الطائرة.

F. **Find** your seat.
   أبحث عن مقعدك.

G. **Stow** your carry-on bag.
   خزّن حقيبة اليد الخاصة بك.

H. **Fasten** your seat belt.
   اربط حزام المقعد.

I. **Put** your cell phone in airplane mode.
   ضع هاتفك المحمول (الخلوي) في نمط الطيران.

J. **Take off**. / **Leave**.
   إقلاع / مغادرة.

K. **Land**. / **Arrive**.
   هبوط / وصول.

L. **Claim** your baggage.
   استردي أمتعتك.

* Transportation Security Administration

At the Gate عند البوابة

On the Airplane داخل الطائرة

At Customs عند الجمرك

7. arrival and departure monitors
شاشات الوصول والمغادرة

8. gate
بوابة

9. boarding area
منطقة الصعود إلى الطائرة

10. cockpit
كابينة الطيارين

11. pilot
طيار

12. flight attendant
مضيف / مضيفة طائرة

13. overhead compartment
حجرة حقائب علوية

14. emergency exit
باب خروج في حالات طوارئ

15. passenger
راكب

16. declaration form
استمارة إقرار جمركي

17. customs officer
موظف جمارك

18. luggage / bag
أمتعة / حقيبة

19. e-ticket
تذكرة إلكترونية

20. mobile boarding pass
بطاقة صعود إلكترونية على الهاتف المحمول (الخلوي)

21. tray table
صينية حاملة

22. turbulence
مطب هوائي / اضطراب جوي

23. baggage carousel
سير الأمتعة المتحرك

24. oxygen mask
قناع أكسيجين

25. life vest
صديرية النجاة

26. emergency card
بطاقة إرشادات للطوارى

27. reclined seat
مقعد مائل الظهر

28. upright seat
مقعد مستقيم الظهر

29. on time
في الموعد المحدد

30. delayed
متأخرة

More vocabulary

departure time: the time the plane takes off
arrival time: the time the plane lands
nonstop flight: a trip with no stops

Pair practice. Make new conversations.

A: *Excuse me. Where do I <u>check in</u>?*
B: *At the <u>check-in kiosk</u>.*
A: *Thanks.*

A Road Trip   رحلة على الطريق

★ Seattle, WA

YELLOWSTONE NATIONAL PARK

1. ranger
حارس الحديقة أو الغابة

2. wildlife
الأحياء البرية

3. stars
النجوم

4. scenery
المناظر الخلابة

5. automobile club card
بطاقة نادي السيارات

6. destination
جهة الوصول

A. **pack**
حضّر الحقيبة

B. **be** lost
أن تكون تائها

C. **have** a flat tire
يخلو إطار السيارة من الهواء / تنام العجلة

D. **get** a ticket
أن تحصل على مخالفة مرور

E. **run out** of gas
فرغ البنزين

F. **break down**
تتعطل السيارة

166

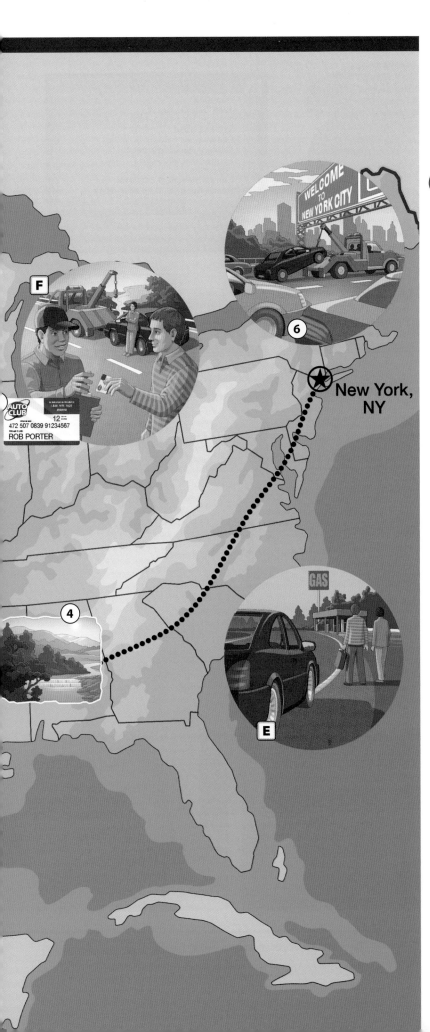

What do you see in the pictures?

1. Where are the young men from? What's their destination?

2. Do they have a good trip? How do you know?

 Read the story.

A Road Trip

On July 7, Joe and Rob <u>pack</u> their bags and start their road trip to New York City.

Their first stop is Yellowstone National Park. They listen to a <u>ranger</u> talk about the <u>wildlife</u> in the park. That night they go to bed under a sky full of <u>stars</u>, but Rob can't sleep. He's nervous about the wildlife.

The next day, their GPS breaks. "We're not going in the right direction!" Rob says. "<u>We're lost</u>!"

"No problem," says Joe. "We can take the southern route. We'll see some beautiful <u>scenery</u>."

But there are *a lot* of problems. They <u>have a flat tire</u> in west Texas and <u>get a</u> speeding <u>ticket</u> in east Texas. In South Carolina, they <u>run out of gas</u>. Then, five miles from New York City, their car <u>breaks down</u>. "Now, *this* is a problem," Joe says.

"No, it isn't," says Rob. He calls the number on his <u>automobile club card</u>. Help arrives in 20 minutes.

After 5,000 miles of problems, Joe and Rob finally reach their <u>destination</u>—by tow truck!

Reread the story.

1. Find the phrase "Help arrives." What does that phrase mean?

What do you think?

2. What is good, bad, or interesting about taking a road trip?

3. Imagine you are planning a road trip. Where will you go?

167

Job Search البحث عن وظيفة

A. **set** a goal
حدد هدفا

B. **write** a resume
اكتب خلاصة عن
مهاراتك وانجازاتك

C. **contact** references
اتصل بالمراجع

D. **research** local
companies
ابحث في الشركات المحلية

E. **talk** to friends /
network
تحدّث مع أصدقاء / كوّن
شبكة من الاتصالات

F. **go** to an employment
agency
اذهب إلى مكتب توظيف

G. **look** for help wanted
signs
ابحث عن لافتات الوظائف الشاغرة

H. **check** employment
websites
راجع المواقع الإلكترونية
الخاصة بإيجاد الوظائف

My Goals:
Now: Get a job in a market.
2 years: Manage a market.
5 years: Get a business degree.
10 years: Own a market.

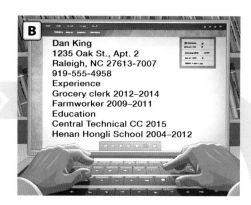

Dan King
1235 Oak St., Apt. 2
Raleigh, NC 27613-7007
919-555-4958
Experience
Grocery clerk 2012–2014
Farmworker 2009–2011
Education
Central Technical CC 2015
Henan Hongli School 2004–2012

#1 GROCERY COMPANY IN US

SUPERMARKETS!

May I put your number as a reference?

Of course.

I need a job.

I think S and K is hiring.

ABC Employment

We can get you a job!

HELP WANTED
INQUIRE WITHIN

WORKPOWER.COM
We help YOU get the job YOU want!
1,000 Matches for Grocery.

Listen and point. Take turns.

A: *Point to a resume.*
B: *Point to a help wanted sign.*
A: *Point to an application.*

Dictate to your partner. Take turns.

A: *Write contact.*
B: *Is it spelled c-o-n-t-a-c-t?*
A: *Yes, that's right, contact.*

I. **apply** for a job
التقدم بطلب لشغل وظيفة

J. **complete** an application
إكمال طلب الوظيفة

K. **write** a cover letter
اكتب خطابا تقديميا

L. **submit** an application
تقديم طلب

M. **set up** an interview
تحديد موعد لمقابلة شخصية

N. **go on** an interview
اذهب إلى المقابلة الشخصية

O. **get** a job /
be hired
الحصول على وظيفة /
يتم توظيفك

P. **start** a new job
البدء في وظيفة جديدة

Ways to talk about the job search

It's important to *set a goal*.
You have to *write a resume*.
It's a good idea to *network*.

Role play. Talk about a job search.

A: *I'm looking for a job. What should I do?*
B: *Well, it's important to set a goal.*
A: *Yes, and I have to write a resume.*

1. accountant
محاسبة

2. actor
ممثل

3. administrative assistant
مساعدة إدارية

4. appliance repairperson
أخصائي تصليح أدوات منزلية

5. architect
مهندسة معمارية

6. artist
فنّانة

7. assembler
أخصائي تجميع

8. auto mechanic
ميكانيكي سيارات

9. babysitter
حاضنة أطفال

10. baker
فرّانة / خبّازة

11. business owner
ربة أعمال / صاحبة أعمال

12. businessperson
رجل أعمال / سيدة أعمال

13. butcher
جزار / لحّام

14. carpenter
نجّار

15. cashier
صرّاف / أمين صندوق

16. childcare worker
أخصائية حضانة أطفال

Ways to ask about someone's job

What's <u>her</u> job?

What does <u>he</u> do?

What does <u>he</u> do for a living?

Pair practice. Make new conversations.

A: *What <u>does she</u> do for a living?*

B: *<u>She's an accountant</u>. What <u>do they</u> do?*

A: *<u>They're actors</u>.*

17. commercial fisher
صياد سمك تجاري

18. computer software engineer
مهندسة مبرمجات كمبيوتر (حاسوب)

19. computer technician
فني كمبيوترات (حواسيب)

We have that shirt in red.

20. customer service representative
مندوب خدمة عملاء

21. delivery person
عامل توصيل

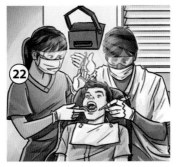

22. dental assistant
مساعدة طبيب أسنان

23. dock worker
عامل مراكب

24. electronics repairperson
أخصائي تصليح أجهزة إلكترونية

25. engineer
مهندس

26. firefighter
إطفائي

27. florist
بائعة زهور

28. gardener
بستاني / جنايني

29. garment worker
خياطة

30. graphic designer
مصمم فنون تخطيطية

31. hairdresser / hairstylist
مزينة شعر / مصففة شعر

32. home healthcare aide
مساعدة رعاية صحية منزلية

Ways to talk about jobs and occupations

Sue's <u>a garment worker</u>. She works **in** a factory.
Tom's <u>an engineer</u>. He works **for** a large company.
Luis is <u>a gardener</u>. He's self-employed.

Role play. Talk about a friend's new job.

A: Does your friend like <u>his</u> new job?
B: Yes, <u>he</u> does. <u>He's a graphic designer</u>.
A: Who does <u>he</u> work for?

171

33. homemaker
ربة منزل

34. housekeeper
مديرة منزل

你好

He says, "Hi."

35. interpreter / translator
مترجم شفهي / مترجم تحريري

36. lawyer
محامي

37. machine operator
عاملة ماكينات

38. manicurist
مزينة أظافر

39. medical records technician
فنية سجلات طبية

40. messenger / courier
مرسال / ساعي

41. model
عارضة أزياء

42. mover
عامل نقليات

43. musician
موسيقي

44. nurse
ممرضة

45. occupational therapist
أخصائية علاج مهني

46. (house) painter
دهّان (منازل)

47. physician assistant
مساعد طبيب

48. police officer
شرطية / ضابطة شرطة

Grammar Point: past tense of *be*

I **was** a machine operator for five years.
She **was** a model from 2010 to 2012.
Before they **were** movers, they **were** painters.

Pair practice. Make new conversations.

A: *What was your first job?*
B: *I was <u>a musician</u>. How about you?*
A: *I was <u>a messenger for a small company</u>.*

49. postal worker
موظف بريد

50. printer
عامل طباعة

51. receptionist
موظفة استقبال

52. reporter
مراسلة صحفية

53. retail clerk
موظف مبيعات

54. sanitation worker
عامل نظافة

55. security guard
حارسة أمن

56. server
نادلة

Here are some programs that will help you.

57. social worker
أخصائية اجتماعية

58. soldier
جندي

59. stock clerk
عامل جرد مخازن

Hello. I'm calling with a very special offer.

60. telemarketer
مسوّق بالهاتف / بالتليفون

61. truck driver
سائق شاحنة

62. veterinarian
طبيبة بيطرية

63. welder
لحام

64. writer / author
كاتبة / مؤلفة

Survey your class. Record the responses.

1. What is one job you don't want to have?
2. Which jobs do you want to have?
Report: _Tom wants to be a(n) ____, but not a(n) ____._

Think about it. Discuss.

Q: What kind of person makes a good <u>interpreter</u>? Why?
A: To be a(n) ____, you need to be able to ____ and have ____, because…

Planning and Goal Setting التخطيط وتحديد الأهداف

A. visit a career planning center
قم **بزيارة** مركز لتخطيط المسار الوظيفي

B. explore career options
استكشف الخيارات المتاحة لك للمسار الوظيفي

C. take an interest inventory
قم **بعمل** جرد لاهتماماتك

D. identify your technical skills
حدد مهاراتك التقنية

E. list your soft skills
أدرج مهاراتك الشخصية غير التقنية

F. consult with a career counselor
استشر أخصائيا في المسارات الوظيفية

G. set a long-term goal
حدد هدفا طويل المدى

H. set a short-term goal
حدد هدفا قصير المدى

I. attend a job fair
احضر معرضا لفرص العمل

J. speak with a recruiter
تحدّث مع اختصاصي توظيف

Career Path المسار الوظيفي

1. basic education
   التعليم الأساسي

2. entry-level job
   وظيفة لمبتدئ

3. training
   تدريب

4. new job
   وظيفة جديدة

5. college degree
   شهادة جامعية

6. career advancement
   التقدم في المسار الوظيفي

7. continuing education / professional development
   التعليم المستمر / التنمية المهنية

8. promotion
   ترقية

Types of Training أنواع التدريب

9. career and technical training / vocational training
   المسار الوظيفي والتدريب التقني / التدريب المهني

10. apprenticeship
    التلمذة أو التمرس بالمهنة

11. internship
    تدريب داخلي

12. on-the-job training
    تدريب أثناء أداء الوظيفة

13. online course
    دورة مقدمة على الإنترنت

14. workshop
    ورشة عمل

A. assemble components
يجمع / تجمع القطع

B. assist medical patients
يساعد المرضى

C. cook
يطبخ

D. do manual labor
يقوم بأعمال يدوية

E. drive a truck
يسوق شاحنة

F. fly a plane
يطير طائرة

G. make furniture
يصنع الأثاث

H. operate heavy machinery
يشغّل آلات ثقيلة

I. program computers
يبرمج كمبيوترات

J. repair appliances
يصلح أدوات منزلية

K. sell cars
يبيع سيارات

L. sew clothes
تخيّط ثيابا

M. solve math problems
تحلّ مسائل رياضيات

4% interest of 5K = x

N. speak another language
يتحدث لغة ثانية

ПРИВЕТ

O. supervise people
تشرف على موظفين

P. take care of children
تعتني بالأطفال

Q. teach
تعلّم / تدرّس

R. type
تطبع

S. use a cash register
تستخدم آلة تسجيل نقود

T. wait on customers
تقوم على خدمة الزبائن

Grammar Point: can, can't

I am a chef. I **can** cook.

I'm not a pilot. I **can't** fly a plane.

I **can't** speak French, but I **can** speak Spanish.

Role play. Talk to a job counselor.

A: Let's talk about your skills. Can you _type_?

B: _No, I can't, but_ I can _use a cash register_.

A: That's good. What else can you do?

Office Skills

مهارات للعمل في مكتب

Customers need better service…

A. **type** a letter
تطبع رسالة

B. **enter** data
يدخل بيانات

C. **transcribe** notes
يستنسخ ملاحظات

D. **make** copies
يصنع / يعمل نسخا

E. **collate** papers
يرتّب أوراقا

F. **staple**
يخرز / يدبّس

G. **fax** a document
يرسل وثيقة بالفاكس

H. **scan** a document
ينسخ وثيقة بماسحة

I. **print** a document
يطبع وثيقة على طابعة

Let's meet at 2:00.

Sure.

J. **schedule** a meeting
يحدد موعدا لاجتماع

K. **take** notes
يأخذ مذكرات بالإملاء

L. **organize** materials
تنظم المواد

Telephone Skills

مهارات هاتفية / تليفونية

Hello. ABC Company. How may I help you?

Please hold.

Mr. Perez, I'm transferring you.

M. **greet** the caller
تحيّي الطالب

N. **put** the caller on hold
تحوّل الطالب إلى الانتظار

O. **transfer** the call
تحوّل المكالمة

Hello. This is Sue Jones. Please call me.

Message Pad
Call From Ana Puerta
Tel: 555-1234
Message:
Please Call

This is Lee Tran. Please call me back.

P. **leave** a message
تترك رسالة

Q. **take** a message
تأخذ رسالة

R. **check** messages
تستمع إلى الرسائل

Leadership Skills · المهارات القيادية

A. solve problems
حل المشاكل

Which is better for us?

B. think critically
التفكير الناقد

Let's do this!

C. make decisions
صنع القرارات

Let's take five minutes to review our timeline.

D. manage time
إدارة الوقت

Interpersonal Skills · مهارات التعامل مع الآخرين

I have three suggestions.

E. communicate clearly
التواصل بوضوح

Let's start with line 15.

I'll get the data.

I can type.

F. cooperate with teammates
التعاون مع أعضاء فريقك

On line 15 or 50?

G. clarify instructions
توضيح التعليمات

Good, but fix page 5.

Thank you. I will.

H. respond well to feedback
التجاوب بشكل جيد مع آراء الغير

Personal Qualities · الصفات الشخصية

Your wait time is approximately ten minutes.

1. patient
الصبر

We can do this!

2. positive
الإيجابية

You need to sort by date.

Please show me how.

3. willing to learn
الاستعداد للتعلم

I think this is yours!

Thanks!

4. honest
الصدق والأمانة

Ways to talk about your skills
*I **can** solve problems. I communicate clearly.*
Ways to talk about your qualities
*I **am** patient and honest.*

Talk about your skills and abilities.
A: *Tell me about your leadership skills.*
B: *I can solve problems. How about you?*
A: *I can think critically.*

A. **Prepare** for the interview.
استعد للمقابلة.

B. **Dress** appropriately.
البس ملابس مناسبة.

C. **Be** neat.
كن مهندما.

D. **Bring** your resume and ID.
أحضر معك سيرتك الذاتية وهويتك.

E. **Don't be** late.
لا تتأخر عن الميعاد.

F. **Be** on time.
صِل في الموعد المحدد.

G. **Turn off** your cell phone.
أغلق هاتفك / تليفونك المحمول.

Hello, I'm Elias Ortiz.

Hello, Mr. Ortiz. I'm Mrs. Perez.

H. **Greet** the interviewer.
حيِّ الشخص القائم بالمقابلة.

I. **Shake** hands.
صافحها باليد.

Computer skills are important.

I have those skills.

I worked with computers on my last job.

J. **Make** eye contact.
انظر مباشرة في عينيها.

K. **Listen** carefully.
استمع إليها بعناية.

L. **Talk** about your experience.
تحدث عن خبرتك.

Do you offer training?

Thank you for your time.

Dear Mrs. Perez, Thank you for the opportunity to meet with you.

M. **Ask** questions.
اطرح أسئلة.

N. **Thank** the interviewer.
اشكر الشخص القائم بالمقابلة.

O. **Write** a thank-you note.
اكتب رسالة شكر.

More vocabulary

benefits: health insurance, vacation pay, or other things the employer can offer an employee

inquire about benefits: to ask about benefits

Identify Dan's problem. Brainstorm solutions.

Dan has an interview tomorrow. Making eye contact with strangers is hard for him. He doesn't like to ask questions. What can he do?

179

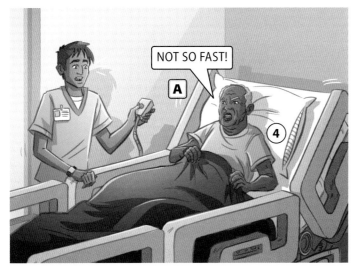

1. facility	**3.** team player	**5.** co-worker	**A. yell**	**C. direct**
المنشأة	لاعب ضمن الفريق	زميل / زميلة في العمل	يصيح / يصرخ	يوجه
2. staff	**4.** resident	**6.** shift	**B. complain**	**D. distribute**
الموظفون	نزيل	وردية	يشكو	يوزع

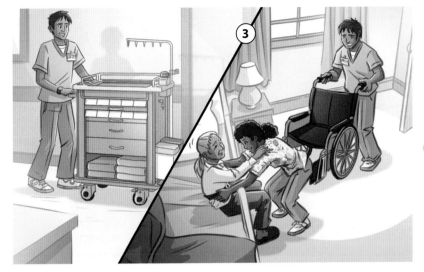

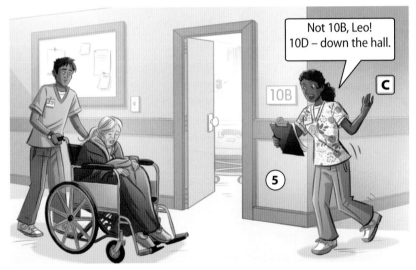

> Not 10B, Leo!
> 10D – down the hall.

> How did it go, Leo?

> I learned a lot!

FROM	TO	CNA STAFF
1st 7:00AM	3:30PM	MARY, LIZ, LEO
2nd 3:00PM	11:30PM	BEN, SARA, TOM
3rd 11:00PM	7:30AM	MEI, KARA, JOSH

What do you see in the pictures?

1. What time does Leo arrive at the nursing home?

2. What other types of workers are on the staff?

3. Is Leo a team player? How do you know?

4. How long was Leo's shift on his first day?

Read the story.

First Day on the Job

Leo Reyes arrives at the Lakeview nursing home <u>facility</u> at 7 a.m. It's his first day as a CNA. The nurse, Ms. Castro, introduces him to the <u>staff</u>. He meets Lakeview's receptionist, cook, social worker, physical therapists, and the other CNAs. Then it's time for work.

Leo has a positive attitude. He is a <u>team player</u>. He also makes mistakes.

One elderly <u>resident</u> <u>yells</u> at Leo. Another <u>complains</u> about him. Leo goes to the wrong room, but a <u>co-worker</u> <u>directs</u> him to the right one.

The afternoon is better. Leo listens to the residents talk about their careers. He drives the van to the mall. He helps another CNA <u>distribute</u> the afternoon snacks.

At the end of his <u>shift</u>, Ms. Castro asks Leo about his day. He tells her, "I worked hard, made mistakes, and learned a lot!" Ms. Castro smiles and says, "Sounds like a good first day!"

Reread the story.

1. Highlight the word "distribute" in paragraph 4. What other words can you use here?

2. Underline two examples of negative feedback in the story.

What do you think?

3. Should Leo respond to the residents' feedback? Why or why not?

1. entrance
   مدخل

2. customer
   زبون

3. office
   مكتب

4. employer / boss
   ربة العمل / رئيسة

5. receptionist
   موظفة استقبال

6. safety regulations
   لوائح السلامة

IRINA'S COMPUTER SERVICE

6 **OSHA**
HAZARDS
SPILLS
CALL 911
SAFETY FIRST

COMPUTER NEWS

Irina Sarkov Owner

Listen and point. Take turns.

A: *Point to the <u>front entrance</u>.*
B: *Point to the <u>receptionist</u>.*
A: *Point to the <u>time clock</u>.*

Dictate to your partner. Take turns.

A: *Can you spell <u>employer</u>?*
B: *I'm not sure. Is it <u>e-m-p-l-o-y-e-r</u>?*
A: *Yes, that's right.*

7. time clock
ساعة الدوام

8. supervisor
مشرف

9. employee
موظف

10. payroll clerk
موظفة جدول الرواتب

11. pay stub
كعب استلام راتب

12. wages
أجور

13. deductions
خصومات

14. paycheck
شيك الراتب

Ways to talk about wages

I **earn** $800 a week.
He **makes** $10 an hour.
I'm **paid** $2,000 a month.

Role play. Talk to an employer.

A: *Is everything correct on your paycheck?*
B: *No, it isn't. I make $619 a week, not $519.*
A: *Let's talk to the payroll clerk. Where is she?*

183

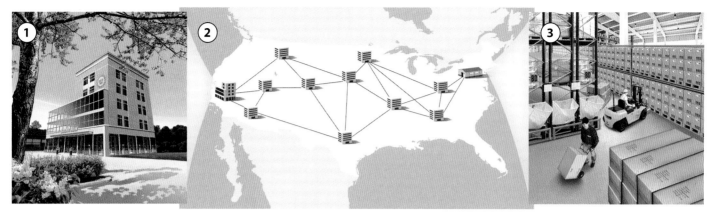

1. corporate offices / headquarters
مكاتب الشركة / المقر الرئيسي

2. branch locations
أماكن الفروع

3. warehouse
مخزن / مستودع

4. human resources
الموارد البشرية

5. research and development
البحث والتطوير

6. marketing
التسويق

Sales are up!

7. sales
المبيعات

8. logistics
اللوجستيات / السوقيات

9. accounting
الحسابات / المحاسبة

10. IT / information technology
تكنولوجيا المعلومات / IT (اي تي)

11. customer service
خدمة العملاء

12. building maintenance
صيانة المبنى

13. security
الأمن

Use the new words.

Look at pages 170–173. Find jobs for each department.

A: *Accountants* work in *accounting*.

B: *Security guards* work in *security*.

Survey your class. Record the responses.

Which department(s) would you like to work in?

Report: *Ten of us would like to work in logistics.*

Nobody wants to work in security.

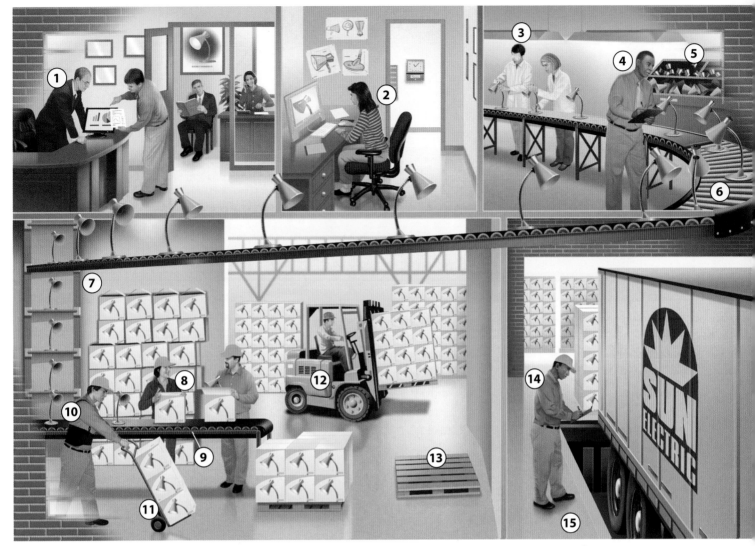

1. factory owner صاحب المصنع	**5. parts** قطع	**9. conveyer belt** سير ناقل	**13. pallet** منصة نقالة
2. designer مصمم	**6. assembly line** خط تجميع	**10. order puller** مسؤول إحضار الطلبات	**14. shipping clerk** موظف مسؤول عن الشحن
3. factory worker عامل بالمصنع	**7. warehouse** مستودع	**11. hand truck** عربة نقل يدوية	**15. loading dock** رصيف تحميل
4. line supervisor مشرف على خط التجميع	**8. packer** عامل تعبئة	**12. forklift** مرفاع شوكي	

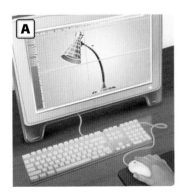

A. design
يصمم

B. manufacture
يصنع

C. assemble
يجمع

D. ship
يشحن

1. **gardening crew**
   طاقم البستنة

2. **leaf blower**
   نافخ أوراق الشجر

3. **wheelbarrow**
   عربة يد ذات عجلة واحدة

4. **gardening crew leader**
   ملاحظ طاقم البستنة

5. **landscape designer**
   مصممة تزيين الأراضي

6. **lawn mower**
   جزازة العشب

7. **shovel**
   جاروف

8. **rake**
   مدمّة / أداة لجمع العشب

9. **pruning shears**
   مجزة تشذيب

10. **trowel**
    مالج

11. **hedge clippers**
    مقلّمة الوشيع (الشجيرات)

12. **weed whacker / weed eater**
    قاطع العشب / أكل العشب

A. **mow** the lawn
يجز المرجة

B. **trim** the hedges
تقلّم الوشيع (الشجيرات)

C. **rake** the leaves
يجمع أوراق الشجر بالمدمّة

D. **fertilize / feed** the plants
يسمّد / يغذّي النباتات

E. **plant** a tree
تزرع شجرة

F. **water** the plants
تسقى الزرع

G. **weed** the flower beds
يقتلع العشب من أحواض الزهور

H. **install** a sprinkler system
يركّب نظاما لرش المياه

Use the new words.
Look at page 53. Name what you can do in the yard.

A: I can _mow the lawn_.
B: I can _weed the flower bed_.

Identify Inez's problem. Brainstorm solutions.

Inez works on a gardening crew. She wants to learn to install sprinklers. The crew leader has no time to teach her. What can she do?

Crops المحاصيل

1. rice
أرز

2. wheat
قمح

3. soybeans
فول الصويا

4. corn
ذُرة

5. alfalfa
فصفصة

6. cotton
قطن

7. field
حقْل

8. farmworker
عامل مزرعة

9. tractor
جَرّارة (تراكتور)

10. orchard
بستان فاكهة

11. barn
حظيرة

12. farm equipment
معدات مزرعة

13. farmer / grower
مزارع / فلاح

14. vegetable garden
حديقة خضروات

15. livestock
مواشي

16. vineyard
كرمة

17. corral
زريبة

18. hay
قش / برسيم

19. fence
سياج

20. hired hand
مستخدم مساعد

21. cattle
ماشية

22. rancher
مربي مواشي

A. plant
يزرع

B. harvest
يحصد

C. milk
يحلب

D. feed
يعلف / يقدم العلف

1. supply cabinet	**9.** desk
خزانة المؤن	مكتب
2. clerk	**10.** file clerk
موظف	موظف تنظيم الملفات
3. janitor	**11.** file cabinet
حاجب	خزانة ملفات
4. conference room	**12.** computer technician
غرفة مؤتمرات	فني كمبيوتر (حاسوب)
5. executive	**13.** PBX
مسؤولة تنفيذية	نظام تحويل هاتفي / تليفوني
6. presentation	**14.** receptionist
عرض	موظفة الاستقبال
7. cubicle	**15.** reception area
مقصورة	منطقة الاستقبال
8. office manager	**16.** waiting area
مدير مكتب	منطقة الانتظار

Ways to greet a receptionist

Good <u>morning</u>. I'm here for a <u>job interview</u>.
Hello. I have a <u>9 a.m.</u> appointment with <u>Mr. Lee</u>.
Hi. I'm here to see <u>Mr. Lee</u>. <u>He's</u> expecting me.

Role play. Talk to a receptionist.

A: *Hello. How can I help you?*
B: *<u>I'm here for a job interview with Mr. Lee</u>.*
A: *OK. What is your name?*

Office Equipment معدات المكتب

17. computer
كمبيوتر (حاسوب)

18. inkjet printer
طابعة نفاثة للحبر

19. laser printer
طابعة ليزر

20. scanner
ماسحة

21. fax machine
جهاز فاكس

22. paper cutter
قاطعة أوراق

23. photocopier
ماكينة تصوير مستندات

24. paper shredder
آلة تمزيق الورق

25. calculator
آلة حاسبة

26. electric pencil sharpener
مبراة أقلام كهربائية

27. postal scale
ميزان بريدي

Office Supplies مستلزمات المكتب

28. stapler
خرازة / دباسة

29. staples
خرزات / دبابيس من السلك

30. clear tape
شريط لاصق بدون لون

31. paper clip
مشبك ورق

32. packing tape
شريط حزم لاصق

33. glue
صمغ

34. rubber band
طوق (شريط) مطاطي

35. pushpin
دبوس كبسي

36. correction fluid
سائل تصحيح

37. correction tape
شريط تصحيح

38. legal pad
كراسة ورق طويل

39. sticky notes
مذكرات لاصقة

40. mailer
مغلف بريد

41. mailing label
بطاقة تعريف بريدية

42. letterhead / stationery
ورق طبع في رأسه اسم المؤسسة /
قرطاسية

43. envelope
ظرف / مغلف

44. rotary card file
ملف بطاقات دوار

45. ink cartridge
خرطوشة حبر

46. ink pad
لبادة تحبير / مختمة

47. stamp
ختم

48. appointment book
دفتر مواعيد

49. organizer
دفتر منظّم

50. file folder
حافظة ملفات / دوسيه

1. mainframe computer
كمبيوتر (حاسوب) رئيسي

2. computer operations specialist
اختصاصي العمليات الكمبيوترية (الحاسوبية)

3. data
بيانات

4. cybersecurity
الأمن الحاسوبي (أمن الإنترنت)

5. virus alert
إنذار بوجود فيروس

6. tablet
كمبيوتر (حاسوب) لوحي

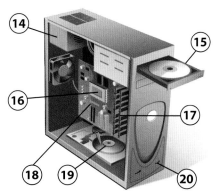

7. tower
برج

8. monitor
شاشة

9. desktop computer
كمبيوتر (حاسوب) مكتبي

10. power cord
سلك الكهرباء

11. surge protector
جهاز واق من اشتداد التيار

12. cable
كبل

13. mouse
فأرة (ماوس)

14. power supply unit
وحدة التزويد بالطاقة

15. DVD and CD-ROM drive
مسيّر قرص دي في دي DVD و سي دي روم CD-ROM

16. microprocessor / CPU
معالج صغير (ميكروبروسيسور) / وحدة المعالجة المركزية CPU

17. RAM (random access memory)
رام RAM (ذاكرة عشوائية الإتاحة)

18. motherboard
اللوحة الأم

19. hard drive
محرك القرص الصلب

20. USB port
منفذ الناقل التسلسلي العام USB (منفذ يو إس بي)

21. printer
طابعة

22. laptop computer
كمبيوتر (حاسوب) محمول

23. keyboard
لوحة المفاتيح

24. track pad
لوحة تحريك المؤشر باللمس

25. flash drive / thumb drive
محرك أقراص USB محمول (فلاش درايف) / محرك أقراص USB بحجم الإصبع

26. hub
موزع

27. external hard drive
قرص صلب خارجي

28. speaker
سماعة

Software / Applications التطبيقات / البرمجيات

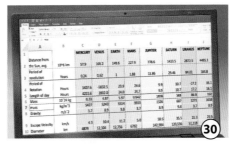

29. word processing program
برنامج معالجة النصوص

30. spreadsheet program
برنامج جداول البيانات

31. presentation program
برنامج عرض

Internet Connectivity التوصيل بالإنترنت

32. Wi-Fi connection
توصيلة واي فاي Wi-Fi

33. router
موجّه الإنترنت

34. modem
مودم (جهاز التوصيل بالإنترنت)

Web Conferencing عقد المؤتمرات عبر الإنترنت

35. headset
سماعة رأس

36. mic / microphone
ميك / ميكروفون

37. webcam
كاميرا مستخدمة
على الإنترنت

A. The computer **won't start**.
الكمبيوتر (الحاسوب) لا يعمل.

B. The screen **froze**.
الشاشة تجمدت.

C. I **can't install** the update.
أنا لا أستطيع تنصيب التحديث.

D. I **can't log on**.
أنا لا أستطيع تسجيل الدخول.

E. It **won't print**.
إنها لا تطبع.

F. I **can't stream** video.
أنا لا أستطيع تحميل بث مباشر للفيديو.

1. doorman بواب	**4. concierge** حاجب / ناطور	**7. bellhop** خادم فندق	**10. guest** نزيل
2. revolving door باب دوار	**5. gift shop** محل هدايا	**8. luggage cart** عربة لنقل الأمتعة	**11. desk clerk** موظف فندق
3. parking attendant خادم لإيقاف السيارات	**6. bell captain** رئيس مستخدمي حمل الأمتعة	**9. elevator** مصعد	**12. front desk** مكتب الاستقبال والتسجيل

13. guest room غرفة نزيل	**15. king-size bed** سرير واحد ضخم	**17. room service** خدمة غرف	**19. housekeeping cart** عربة تجهيز وتنظيف الغرف
14. double bed غرفة بسريرين	**16. suite** جناح	**18. hallway** رواق	**20. housekeeper** عاملة تجهيز وتنظيف الغرف

21. pool service خدمات المسبح (حمّام السباحة)	**23. maintenance** صيانة	**25. meeting room** قاعة اجتماعات
22. pool مسبح / حمّام سباحة	**24. gym** مركز جمباز (جمنازيوم)	**26. ballroom** قاعة حفلات

A Restaurant Kitchen المطبخ في مطعم

1. short-order cook
طباخ الطعام السريع

2. dishwasher
غاسل الصحون

3. walk-in freezer
مجمّد ضخم يمكن السير فيه

4. food preparation worker
عامل تحضير الطعام

5. storeroom
غرفة تخزين

6. sous-chef
نائب رئيس الطهاة (سو شيف)

7. head chef / executive chef
رئيس الطهاة (شيف)

Restaurant Dining تناول الطعام في مطعم

8. server
نادلة / جرسونة

9. diner
زبونة

10. buffet
بوفيه

11. maitre d'
مدير صالة الطعام

12. headwaiter
رئيس الجرسونات / رئيس النوادل

13. bus person
مساعدة النادل

14. banquet room
قاعة الولائم

15. runner
ساعي

16. caterer
مؤونة أطعمة

More vocabulary

line cook: short-order cook
wait staff: servers, headwaiters, and runners

Think about it. Discuss.

1. What is the hardest job in a hotel or restaurant? Explain.
   (*Being a _____ is hard because these workers have to _____.*)
2. Pick two jobs on these pages. Compare them.

HAND TOOLS

HARDWARE

POWER TOOLS

1. hammer مطرقة	**4. handsaw** منشار يدوي	**7. pliers** زردية	**10. jigsaw** منشار منحنيات
2. mallet مطرقة خشبية	**5. hacksaw** منشار معادن	**8. electric drill** مثقاب كهربائي	**11. power sander** ماكينة سنفرة للتنعيم
3. ax فأس	**6. C-clamp** قامطة تثبيت	**9. circular saw** منشار دائري	**12. router** مسحاج تخديد

26. vise منجلة / ملزمة	**30. screwdriver** مفك براغي	**34. nail** مسمار	**38. toggle bolt** مسمار العقدة
27. blade نصلة / شفرة	**31. Phillips screwdriver** مفك براغي مصلّب الرأس	**35. bolt** مسمار ملولب	**39. hook** خطّاف / كلاب
28. drill bit لقمة ثقب	**32. machine screw** برغي ربط ملولب	**36. nut** عزقة	**40. eye hook** خطاف عروة
29. level ميزان بنائين / شلقول	**33. wood screw** برغي خشب	**37. washer** فلكة	**41. chain** سلسلة

Use the new words.
Look at pages 62–63. Name the tools you see.

A: *There's a hammer.*
B: *There's a pipe wrench.*

Survey your class. Record the responses.
1. Are you good with tools?
2. Which tools do you have at home?
Report: *75% of us are… Most of us have…*

ELECTRICAL **PLUMBING** **LUMBER** **PAINT**

13. wire سلك	**16. yardstick** عصا الياردة	**19. 2 x 4 (two by four)** لوح خشبي مقاس ٢ بوصة × ٤ بوصة	**22. paintbrush** فرشاة طلاء	**25. paint** دهان / طلاء
14. extension cord سلك تمديد	**17. pipe** أنبوب / ماسورة	**20. particle board** لوح خشب حبيبي	**23. paint roller** فرشاة طلاء أسطوانية	
15. bungee cord حبل مطاطي	**18. fittings** تجهيزات	**21. spray gun** مرشة	**24. wood stain** صبغة للخشب	

42. wire stripper مقشرة أسلاك	**46. outlet cover** غطاء مأخذ التيار الكهربائي	**50. plunger** كباس	**54. drop cloth** قماش من القنب لوقاية الأثاث والأرضية
43. electrical tape شريط لاصق للأسلاك الكهربائية	**47. pipe wrench** مفتاح أنابيب	**51. paint pan** صينية طلاء	**55. chisel** إزميل
44. work light ضوء عمل (بلادوس)	**48. adjustable wrench** مفتاح ربط قابل للضبط	**52. scraper** مكشطة	**56. sandpaper** ورق سنفرة
45. tape measure شريط قياس	**49. duct tape** شريط شديد اللصق	**53. masking tape** شريط لاصق للتغطية	**57. plane** مسحاج / فأرة النجار

Role play. Find an item in a building supply store.

A: *Where can I find particle board?*
B: *It's on the back wall, in the lumber section.*
A: *Great. And where are the nails?*

Identify Jean's problem. Brainstorm solutions.

Jean borrowed Jody's drill last month. Now she can't find it. She doesn't know what to do!

1. construction worker
   عامل بناء

2. ladder
   سلم

3. I beam / girder
   عارضة

4. scaffolding
   سقالة

5. cherry picker
   رافعة ذات ذراع طويل

6. bulldozer
   جرافة لشق الطرق (بولدوزر)

7. crane
   مرفاع (ونش)

8. backhoe
   مجرفة خلفية

9. jackhammer / pneumatic drill
   ثقابة آلية / آلة حفر بالهواء المضغوط

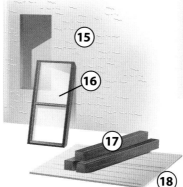
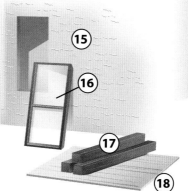
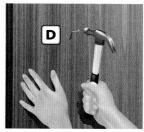

10. concrete
    خرسانة

11. tile
    بلاط

12. bricks
    قرميد / طوب

13. trowel
    مالج

14. insulation
    مواد عازلة

15. stucco
    جص

16. windowpane
    لوح زجاجي في نافذة

17. wood / lumber
    خشب

18. plywood
    خشب رقائقي

19. drywall
    جدار داخلي

20. shingles
    لويحات تسقيف

21. pickax
    معول

22. shovel
    جاروف

23. sledgehammer
    مطرقة ثقيلة / مرزبة

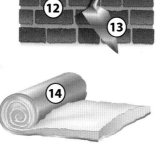
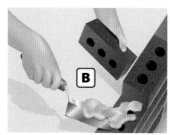

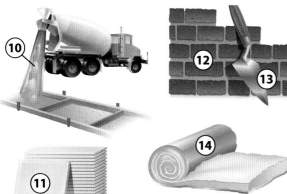

A. paint
   يطلي / يدهن

B. lay bricks
   يرصد القرميد (الطوب)

C. install tile
   يركّب البلاط

D. hammer
   يدق بالمطرقة

Safety Hazards and Hazardous Materials الأخطار على السلامة والمواد الخطرة

1. **careless worker**
عامل غير محترس

2. **careful worker**
عامل محترس

3. **poisonous fumes**
أبخرة سامة

4. **broken equipment**
معدات مكسورة

5. **frayed cord**
سلك تالف

6. **slippery floor**
أرضية زلقة

7. **radioactive materials**
مواد مشعة

8. **flammable liquids**
سوائل قابلة للاشتعال

Safety Equipment معدات السلامة

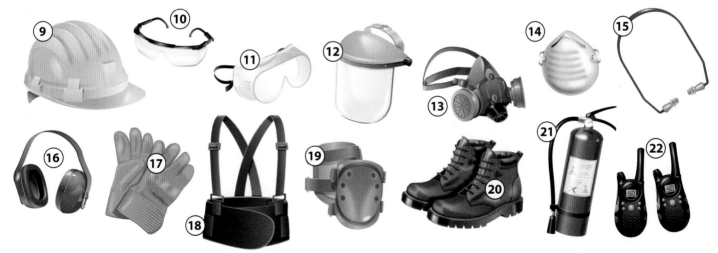

9. **hard hat**
قبعة صلبة

10. **safety glasses**
نظارات سلامة

11. **safety goggles**
منظار واقٍ

12. **safety visor**
قناع واقٍ

13. **respirator**
كمامة ضد الغازات السامة

14. **particle mask**
قناع واقٍ من الجسيمات

15. **earplugs**
سدادة أذن

16. **earmuffs**
واقية الأذان

17. **work gloves**
قفازات عمل

18. **back support belt**
حزام لدعم الظهر

19. **knee pads**
لبادات للركب

20. **safety boots**
حذاء وقاية

21. **fire extinguisher**
مطفئة حريق

22. **two-way radio**
جهاز لاسلكي مرسل ومستقبل

A Bad Day at Work

يوم سيء في العمل

1. dangerous
خطير

2. clinic
عيادة

3. budget
ميزانية

4. floor plan
مخطط (تصميم) طابق في مبنى

5. contractor
مقاول

6. electrical hazard
خطر كهربائي

7. wiring
ضفيرة أسلاك

8. bricklayer
راصد قرميد

A. **call in** sick
اتصل واطلب أجازة مرضية

What do you see in the pictures?

1. How many workers are there? How many are working?

2. Why did two workers call in sick?

3. What is dangerous at the construction site?

 Read the story.

A Bad Day at Work

Sam Lopez is the <u>contractor</u> for a new building. He makes the schedule and supervises the <u>budget</u>. He also solves problems. Today there are a lot of problems.

Two <u>bricklayers</u> <u>called in sick</u> this morning. So Sam has only one bricklayer at work. One hour later, a construction worker fell. He had to go to the <u>clinic</u>.

Construction work is <u>dangerous</u>. Sam always tells his workers to be careful. Yesterday he told them about the new <u>wiring</u> on the site. It's an <u>electrical hazard</u>.

Right now, the building owner is in Sam's office. Her new <u>floor plan</u> has 25 more offices. Sam has a headache. Maybe he needs to call in sick tomorrow.

Reread the story.

1. Make a timeline of the events in this story. What happened first? next? last?

2. Find the sentence "He had to go to the clinic" in paragraph 2. Is "he" the worker or Sam? How do you know?

What do you think?

3. Give examples of good reasons (or excuses) to give when you can't come in to work. Give an example of a bad excuse. Why is it bad?

4. Imagine you are Sam. What do you tell the building owner? Why?

Schools and Subjects

1. preschool /
   nursery school
   حضانة

2. elementary school
   مدرسة ابتدائية

3. middle school /
   junior high school
   مدرسة إعدادية

4. high school
   مدرسة ثانوية

5. career and technical
   school / vocational
   school
   المسار الوظيفي والمدرسة التقنية
   / المدرسة المهنية

6. community college
   كلية أهلية

7. college / university
   كلية / جامعة

8. adult school
   مدرسة للكبار

Listen and point. Take turns.

A: *Point to the* <u>preschool</u>.
B: *Point to the* <u>high school</u>.
A: *Point to the* <u>adult school</u>.

Dictate to your partner. Take turns.

A: *Write* <u>preschool</u>.
B: *Is that* <u>p-r-e-s-c-h-o-o-l</u>?
A: *Yes, that's right.*

9. language arts
فنون اللغات

10. math
رياضيات

11. science
علوم

12. history
تاريخ

13. world languages
لغات العالم

14. English language instruction
تعليم اللغة الإنجليزية

15. arts
فنون

16. music
موسيقى

17. physical education
تربية بدنية

More vocabulary

core course: a subject students have to take.
Math is a core course.

elective: a subject students choose to take. Art is an elective.

Pair practice. Make new conversations.

A: *I go to a community college.*
B: *What subjects are you taking?*
A: *I'm taking history and science.*

English Composition

الإنشاء باللغة الإنجليزية

1

factory

2

I worked in a factory.

3

Little by little, work and success came to me. My first job wasn't good. I worked in a small factory. Now, I help manage two factories.

4

1. **word**
   كلمة
2. **sentence**
   جملة
3. **paragraph**
   فقرة
4. **essay**
   مقال

Parts of an Essay
أجزاء المقال

5. **title**
   عنوان
6. **introduction**
   مقدمة
7. **evidence**
   دليل / حقيقة
8. **body**
   نص
9. **conclusion**
   ختام
10. **quotation**
    اقتباس
11. **citation**
    استشهاد / اقتباس
12. **footnote**
    تذييل
13. **source**
    مصدر / مرجع

Carlos Lopez
Eng. Comp.
10/03/16

5

Success in the U.S.

6   I came to Los Angeles from Mexico in 2006. I had no job, no friends, and no family here. I was homesick and scared, but I did not go home. I took English classes (always at night) and I studied hard. I believed in my future success!

7   According to the U.S. Census, more than 400,000 new immigrants come to the U.S. every year.[1] Most of us need to find work. During my first year here, my routine was the same: get up; look for work; go to class; go to bed. I had to take jobs with long hours and low pay. Often I had two or three jobs.

8   Little by little, work and success came to me. My first job wasn't good. I worked in a small factory. Now, I help manage two factories.

9   Hard work makes success possible, and **10** "men were born to succeed, not to fail" (Thoreau, 1853). My story demonstrates the truth of that statement. **11**

12 [1] U.S. Census, 2015

13

Punctuation
علامات الوقف والترقيم

14. · **period**
    نقطة
15. ? **question mark**
    علامة استفهام
16. ! **exclamation mark / exclamation point**
    علامة تعجب / حرف تعجب
17. , **comma**
    فاصلة
18. " " **quotation marks**
    علامات اقتباس
19. ' **apostrophe**
    فاصلة عليا
20. : **colon**
    نقطتان
21. ; **semicolon**
    فاصلة منقوطة
22. ( ) **parentheses**
    قوسان
23. – **hyphen**
    شرطة

Writing Rules قواعد الكتابة

A

Carlos

Mexico

Los Angeles

A. **Capitalize** names.
اكتب الأسماء بحروف كبيرة.

B

Hard work makes success possible.

B. **Capitalize** the first letter in a sentence.
اكتب الحرف الأول في الجملة بحرف كبير.

C

I was homesick and scared, but I did not go home.

C. **Use** punctuation.
استخدم علامة الوقف والترقيم.

D

   I came to Los Angeles from Mexico in 2006. I had no job, no friends, and no family here. I was homesick and scared, but I did not go home. I took English classes (always at night) and I studied hard. I believed in my future success!

D. **Indent** the first sentence in a paragraph.
اترك فراغا في سطر أول جملة في فقرة جديدة.

Ways to ask for suggestions on your compositions

What do you think of this title?

Is this paragraph OK? Is the punctuation correct?

Do you have any suggestions for the conclusion?

Pair practice. Make new conversations.

A: What do you think of this title?

B: *I think you need to revise it.*

A: *Thanks. How would you revise it?*

The Writing Process عملية الكتابة

---PREWRITING---

E Writing assignment - Due 10/3
Write an essay about
your first year in the U.S.

*my life… hmm…
what can I say…
I have one week…*

E. Think about the assignment.
فكَّر في المهمة.

G. Organize your ideas.
نظِّم أفكارك.

F. Brainstorm ideas.
اطرح لنفسك أفكارا وتمعن فيها.

---WRITING AND REVISING---

H

*I came to
Los Angeles
from Mexico
in 2006…*

H. Write a first draft.
اكتب مسودة أولى.

I. Edit. / Proofread.
نقِّح. / دقِّق.

J. Revise. / Rewrite.
راجع. / أعد الكتابة.

---SHARING AND RESPONDING---

OCTOBER 1

*I like the part
about your
daily routine.* **K**

K. Get feedback.
احصل على رأي شخص آخر.

L

L. Write a final draft.
اكتب مسودة نهائية.

OCTOBER 3

M

M. Turn in / Hand in your paper.
قدِّم / سلِّم ورقتك.

Survey your class. Record the responses.

1. Do you prefer to write essays or read them?
2. Which is more difficult: writing a first draft or revising?

Report: *Five* people I surveyed said ___.

Think about it. Discuss.

1. What are interesting topics for essays?
2. Do you like to read quotations? Why or why not?
3. In which jobs are writing skills important?

203

Mathematics الرياضيات

Integers الأعداد الصحيحة

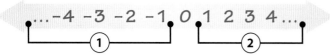

$$...-4 \ -3 \ -2 \ -1 \ 0 \ 1 \ 2 \ 3 \ 4 ...$$

1. negative integers
أعداد صحيحة سالبة

2. positive integers
أعداد صحيحة موجبة

Fractions الكسور

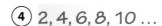

③ 1, 3, 5, 7, 9, 11 ...

④ 2, 4, 6, 8, 10 ...

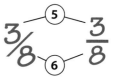

$\dfrac{3}{8}$ ⑤ ⑥ $\dfrac{3}{8}$

3. odd numbers
أرقام فردية

4. even numbers
أرقام زوجية

5. numerator
البسط

6. denominator
المقام

Math Operations عمليات رياضية

A. add
اجمع

B. subtract
اطرح

C. multiply
اضرب

D. divide
اقسم

$$8 + 4 = 12$$
$$8 - 4 = 4$$
$$8 \times 4 = 32$$
$$8 \div 4 = 2$$

7. sum
المجموع

8. difference
الفرق

9. product
الحاصل

10. quotient
خارج القسمة

A Math Problem مسألة رياضية

⑪ Tom is 10 years older than Kim. Next year he will be twice as old as Kim. How old is Tom this year?

⑫ — x = Kim's age now
$x + 10$ = Tom's age now
$x + 1$ = Kim's age next year
$2(x + 1)$ = Tom's age next year
$x + 10 + 1 = 2(x + 1)$
$x + 11 = 2x + 2$
$11 - 2 = 2x - x$ ⑬

$x = 9$, Kim is 9, Tom is 19 ⑭

⑮
horizontal axis
vertical axis

11. word problem
مسألة كلامية

12. variable
متغير

13. equation
معادلة

14. solution
حل

15. graph
مخطط بياني

Types of Math أنواع الرياضيات

⑯ How much are they?

$79 NOW 40% OFF!

x = the sale price
x = 79.00 - .40 (79.00)
x = $47.40

16. algebra
الجبر

⑰ How many do I need?

area of path = 24 square ft.
area of brick = 2 square ft.
24 / 2 = 12 bricks

17. geometry
الهندسة

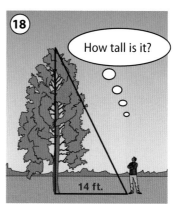

⑱ How tall is it?

14 ft.

tan 63° = height / 14 feet
height = 14 feet (tan 63°)
height ≃ 27.48 feet

18. trigonometry
حساب المثلثات

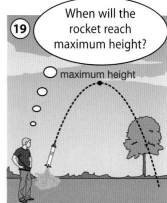

⑲ When will the rocket reach maximum height?

maximum height

$s(t) = -\frac{1}{2}gt^2 + V_0 t + h$
$s^I(t) = -gt + V_0 = 0$
$t = V_0 / g$

19. calculus
التفاضل والتكامل

Lines الخطوط

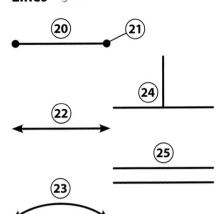

Angles الزوايا

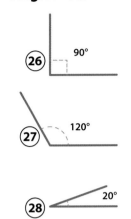

90°
120°
20°

Shapes الأشكال

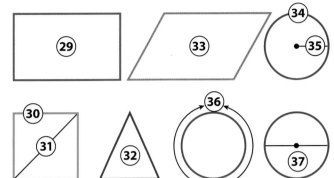

20. line segment
مقطع من خط

21. endpoint
نقطة نهاية

22. straight line
خط مستقيم

23. curved line
خط منحني

24. perpendicular lines
خطوط متعامدة

25. parallel lines
خطوط متوازية

26. right angle / 90° angle
زاوية مستقيمة / زاوية ٩٠°

27. obtuse angle
زاوية منفرجة

28. acute angle
زاوية حادة

29. rectangle
مستطيل

30. square
مربع

31. diagonal
منحرف

32. triangle
مثلث

33. parallelogram
متوازي أضلاع

34. circle
دائرة

35. radius
نصف قطر

36. circumference
محيط

37. diameter
قطر

Geometric Solids الأشكال الهندسية المجسمة

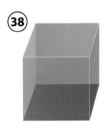

Measuring Area and Volume قياس المساحة والحجم

$\ell \times w = $ area

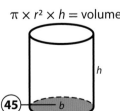

$6 \times f = $ surface area

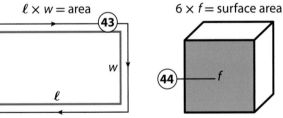

38. cube
مكعب

39. pyramid
هرم

40. cone
مخروط

43. perimeter
محيط خارجي

44. face
وجه

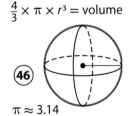

$\pi \times r^2 \times h = $ volume

$\frac{4}{3} \times \pi \times r^3 = $ volume

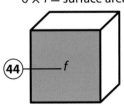

$\pi \approx 3.14$

41. cylinder
أسطوانة

42. sphere
كرة

45. base
قاعدة

46. pi
باي (الرمز الذي يمثل النسبة بين طول
محيط الدائرة وقطرها)

Survey your class. Record the responses.

1. Is division easy or difficult?
2. Is algebra easy or difficult?
Report: _50% of the class thinks ____ is difficult._

Think about it. Discuss.

1. What's the best way to learn mathematics?
2. How can you find the area of your classroom?
3. Which jobs use math? Which don't?

Biology علم الأحياء (بيولوجيا)

1. organisms
كائنات حية

2. biologist
أحيائي (عالم بيولوجيا)

3. slide
شريحة

4. cell
خلية

5. cell wall
جدار الخلية

6. cell membrane
غشاء الخلية

7. nucleus
نواة

8. chromosome
صبغي (كروموسوم)

9. cytoplasm
هيولى

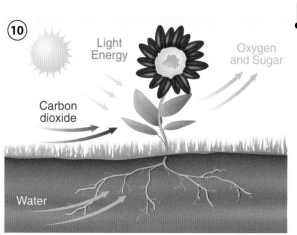

10. photosynthesis
تخليق ضوئي

11. habitat
موئل

12. vertebrates
فقاريات

13. invertebrates
لافقاريات

A Microscope مجهر (ميكروسكوب)

14. eyepiece
عينيّة المجهر

15. revolving nosepiece
أنفيّة المجهر الدوارة

16. objective
الشَّيئيّة (عدسة المجهر)

17. stage
رف في المجهر

18. diaphragm
الحجاب

19. light source
مصدر ضوئي

20. base
قاعدة

21. stage clips
مشبك الرف

22. fine adjustment knob
مقبض تعديل دقيق

23. arm
ذراع

24. coarse adjustment knob
مقبض تعديل تقريبي

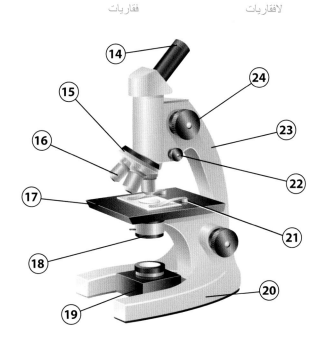

Chemistry الكيمياء

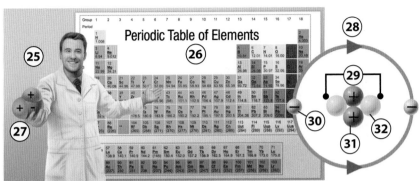

Periodic Table of Elements

25. **chemist**
كيميائي (عالم كيمياء)

26. **periodic table**
الجدول الدوري

27. **molecule**
جزيء

28. **atom**
ذَرَّة

29. **nucleus**
نواة

30. **electron**
إلكترون

31. **proton**
بروتون

32. **neutron**
نيوترون

33. **physicist**
فيزيائية (عالمة طبيعة)

Physics علم الطبيعة (الفيزياء)

$$C = f\lambda$$

f = frequency
λ = wavelength

34. **formula**
معادلة / صيغة

35. **prism**
موشور / منشور زجاجي

36. **magnet**
مغنطيس

A Science Lab مختبر العلوم

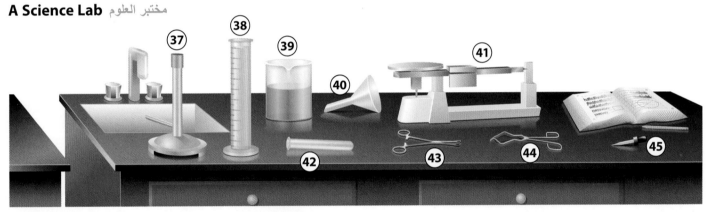

37. **Bunsen burner**
حاروق / ملهب بنزن

38. **graduated cylinder**
أنبوب مدرج

39. **beaker**
كوب صيدلي

40. **funnel**
قمع

41. **balance / scale**
ميزان

42. **test tube**
أنبوب اختبار

43. **forceps**
كَلّاب

44. **crucible tongs**
ملقط بوتقي

45. **dropper**
قطّارة

An Experiment تجربة

Salt and sugar crystals will grow the same way.

A

A. **State** a hypothesis.
تُبسط / تَطرح فرضية.

B

B. **Do** an experiment.
تقوم بإجراء تجربة.

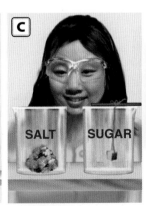

C

C. **Observe.**
تراقب.

D

D. **Record** the results.
تُسجل النتائج.

E

Salt crystals grow faster than sugar crystals.

E. **Draw** a conclusion.
تصل إلى خلاصة.

Colonial Period فترة الاستعمار

New Hampshire
Massachusetts
Connecticut
New York
Rhode Island
Pennsylvania
New Jersey
Delaware
Virginia
Maryland
North Carolina
South Carolina
Georgia

1. thirteen colonies
   ثلاث عشرة مستعمرة

2. colonists
   المستعمرون

3. Native American
   أمريكي أصلي

4. slaves
   عبيد

5. Declaration of Independence
   إعلان الاستقلال

6. First Continental Congress
   الكونجرس القاري الأول

7. founders
   الآباء المؤسسون

8. Revolutionary War
   الحرب الثورية / حرب الاستقلال

9. redcoat
   جندي بريطاني

10. minuteman
    جندي هوّاري على استعداد للحرب بإنذار دقيقة واحدة

11. first president
    أول رئيس

12. Constitution
    الدستور

13. Bill of Rights
    ميثاق الحقوق

World War I
1914–1918

Western Expansion
1803–1893

Civil War
1861–1865

Jazz Age
1920–1929

World War II
1941–1945

Civil Rights Movement
1954–1972

Information Age
1959–now

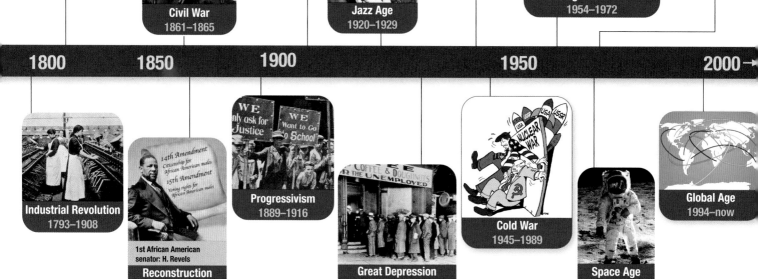

1800   1850   1900   1950   2000 →

Industrial Revolution
1793–1908

1st African American senator: H. Revels
Reconstruction
1865–1877

Progressivism
1889–1916

Great Depression
1929–1941

Cold War
1945–1989

Space Age
1958–now

Global Age
1994–now

Civilizations الحضارات

Pyramids | Parthenon
1

2

Times Square

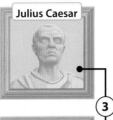

Julius Caesar

King Sobhuza II

3

4

Qin Shi Huang

Queen Elizabeth I

5

Benito Juárez

6

Benito Mussolini

7

Shinzo Abe

1. ancient
قديمة

2. modern
حديثة

3. emperor
إمبراطور

4. monarch
ملك

5. president
رئيس

6. dictator
دكتاتور

7. prime minister
رئيس وزراء

Historical Terms مصطلحات تاريخية

8

9

Vikings | Astronauts

10

11

12

13

8. exploration
استكشاف

9. explorer
مستكشف

10. war
حرب

11. army
جيش

12. immigration
هجرة

13. immigrant
مهاجر

14

15

Wolfgang Mozart | Duke Ellington

16

17

Susan B. Anthony | César Chávez

18

19

Thomas Edison | Guillermo Camarena

14. composer
مؤلف موسيقي / ملحّن

15. composition
تأليف موسيقي / مؤلّفة موسيقية

16. political movement
حركة سياسية

17. activist
ناشط سياسيا

18. inventor
مخترع

19. invention
اختراع

Creating a Document إنشاء وثيقة

A. **open** the program
افتح البرنامج

B. **create** a new document
قم بإنشاء وثيقة جديدة

C. **type**
اكتب باستخدام لوحة المفاتيح

D. **save** the document
احفظ الوثيقة

E. **close** the document
اغلق الوثيقة

F. **quit** the program
اغلق البرنامج

Selecting and Changing Text اختيار وتعديل النص

G. **click** on the screen
انقر على الشاشة

H. **double-click** to select a word
انقر مرتين سريعتين لاختيار كلمة

I. **delete** a word
احذف كلمة

J. **drag** to select text
اسحب بالفأرة لاختيار نص

K. **copy** text
انسخ نصا

L. **paste** text
الصق نصا

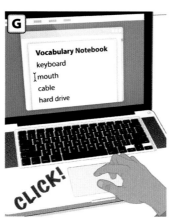

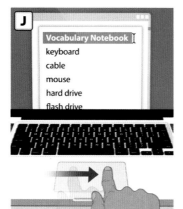

More vocabulary

keyboard shortcut: use of the keys on the keyboard to cut, copy, paste, etc. For example, press "control" on a PC ("command" on a Mac) and "C" to copy text.

Identify Diego's problem. Brainstorm solutions.

Diego is nervous around computers. He needs to complete an online job application. His brother, Luis, offers to apply for him. What could Diego do?

Moving around the Screen التحرك على الشاشة

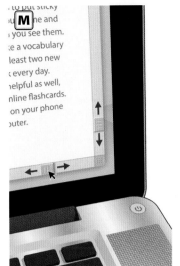

Registering an Account تسجيل حساب

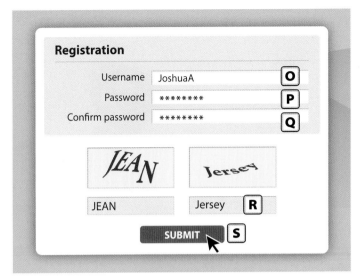

M. scroll
قم بالتمرير / التصفح

N. use the arrow keys
استخدم مفاتيح الأسهم

O. create a username
اخلق اسم مستخدم

P. create a password
اخلق كلمة سر

Q. reenter the password /
type the password again
أعد إدخال كلمة السر / اكتب كلمة السر مرة أخرى
باستخدام لوحة المفاتيح

R. type the verification code
اكتب الرقم الكودي للتحقق من هويتك

S. click submit
انقر زر التقديم

Sending Email إرسال بريد إلكتروني

T. log in to your account
قم بتسجيل **دخول** إلى حسابك

U. address the email
ادخل **عنوان** البريد الإلكتروني

V. type the subject
اكتب موضوع الرسالة **باستخدام لوحة المفاتيح**

W. compose / write the message
قم بإنشاء / كتابة الرسالة

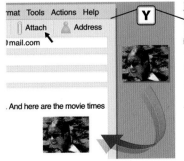

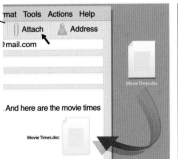

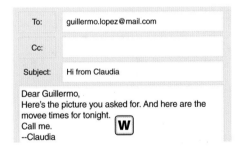

X. check your spelling
راجع هجاء كلماتك

Y. attach a file
أرفق ملفا

Z. send the email
ارسل البريد الإلكتروني

Internet Research البحث على الإنترنت

1. research question
سؤال البحث

2. search engine
محرك / آلية البحث

3. search box
مربع / خانة البحث

4. keywords
الكلمات الرئيسية

5. search results
نتائج البحث

6. links
روابط

Conducting Research إجراء بحث

A. **select** a search engine
اختر محرك / آلية بحث

B. **type** in a phrase
اكتب عبارة باستخدام لوحة المفاتيح

C. **type** in a question
اكتب سؤالا باستخدام لوحة المفاتيح

D. **click** the search icon / **search**
انقر على أيقونة البحث / ابحث

E. **look** at the results
انظر النتائج

F. **click** on a link
انقر على رابط

G. **bookmark** a site
احفظ عنوان الموقع بإضافته الى قائمة العلامات المرجعية

H. **keep** a record of sources
احتفظ بسجل للمصادر

I. **cite** sources
استشهد بالمصادر

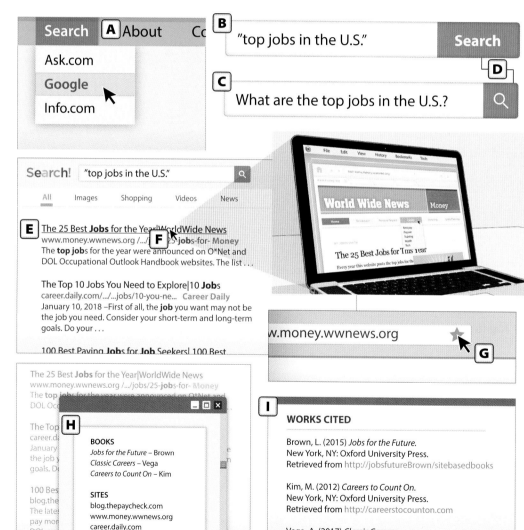

More vocabulary

research: to search for and record information that answers a question

investigate: to research a problem or situation

Ways to talk about your research

My research shows _____.

According to my research, _____.

These are the results of my research: _____.

7. menu bar
شريط القوائم

8. browser window
نافذة المتصفح

9. back button
زر الرجوع

10. URL / website address
يو آر إل URL / عنوان الموقع على الإنترنت

11. refresh button
زر تجديد الصفحة

12. web page
صفحة وب (صفحة على الإنترنت)

13. source
مصدر

14. tab
علامة تبويب

15. drop-down menu
قائمة منسدلة

16. content
المحتوى

17. pop-up ad
إعلان وثاب يظهر فجأة

18. video player
مشغّل الفيديو

19. social media links
روابط لمواقع تواصل اجتماعي

20. date
التاريخ

Internet Research: online practice

Type "practice" in the search bar. Add more keywords. ("ESL vocabulary," etc.)

Report: *I found vocabulary practice on a site called ____.*

Think about it. Discuss.

1. Which is better for Internet research: searching with a question, a phrase, or keywords? Explain.

2. Do you enjoy research? Why or why not?

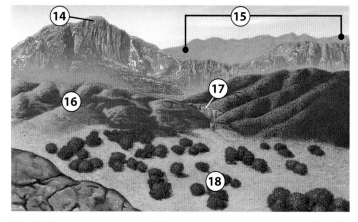

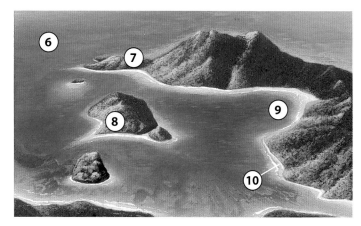

1. rain forest
   غابات المطر

6. ocean
   محيط

10. beach
    شاطئ رملي

14. mountain peak
    قمة جبل

18. valley
    وادي

2. waterfall
   شلال

7. peninsula
   شبه جزيرة

11. forest
    غابة

15. mountain range
    سلسلة جبال

19. plains
    سهول

3. river
   نهر

8. island
   جزيرة

12. shore
    ساحل

16. hills
    تلال

20. meadow
    مَرْج

4. desert
   صحراء

9. bay
   خور / شرم

13. lake
    بحيرة

17. canyon
    وادي ضيق

21. pond
    بركة

5. sand dune
   كثيب

More vocabulary

body of water: a river, a lake, or an ocean
stream / creek: a very small river
inhabitants: the people and animals living in a habitat

Survey your class. Record the responses.

1. Would you rather live by the ocean or a lake?
2. Would you rather live in a desert or a rainforest?
Report: *Fifteen of us would rather* ____ *than* ____.

The Solar System and the Planets النظام الشمسي والكواكب

Sun

1

2

3

4

5

asteroid belt

6

7

8

orbit

1. Mercury	3. Earth	5. Jupiter	7. Uranus
عطارد	الأرض	المشتري	أورانوس
2. Venus	4. Mars	6. Saturn	8. Neptune
فينوس	المريخ	زحل	نبتون

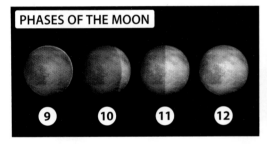

PHASES OF THE MOON

9   10   11   12

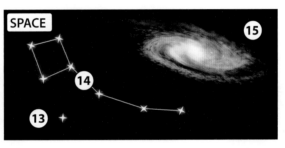

SPACE

15

14

13

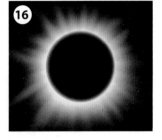

16

9. new moon	11. quarter moon	13. star	15. galaxy
هلال / قمر أول الشهر	ربع قمر	نجم	المجرّة
10. crescent moon	12. full moon	14. constellation	16. solar eclipse
هلال	بدر	مجموعة نجوم متألقة	كسوف الشمس

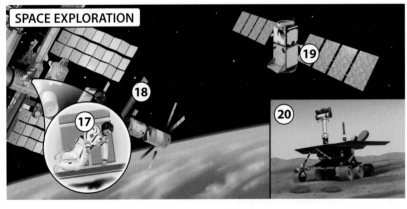

SPACE EXPLORATION

19

18

17

20

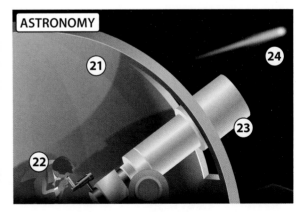

ASTRONOMY

21

24

23

22

17. astronaut	19. satellite	21. observatory	23. telescope
رائد فضاء	قمر صناعي / ساتل	مرصد	تلسكوب
18. space station	20. probe / rover	22. astronomer	24. comet
محطة فضاء	مسبار / روفر (مركبة استكشاف الفضاء)	فلكي / عالم فلكي	مذنّب

More vocabulary

lunar eclipse: when the moon is in the earth's shadow
Big Dipper: a famous part of the constellation Ursa Major
Sirius: the brightest star in the night sky

Think about it. Discuss.

1. Do you want to travel in space? Why or why not?
2. Who should pay for space exploration? Why?
3. What do you like best about the night sky?

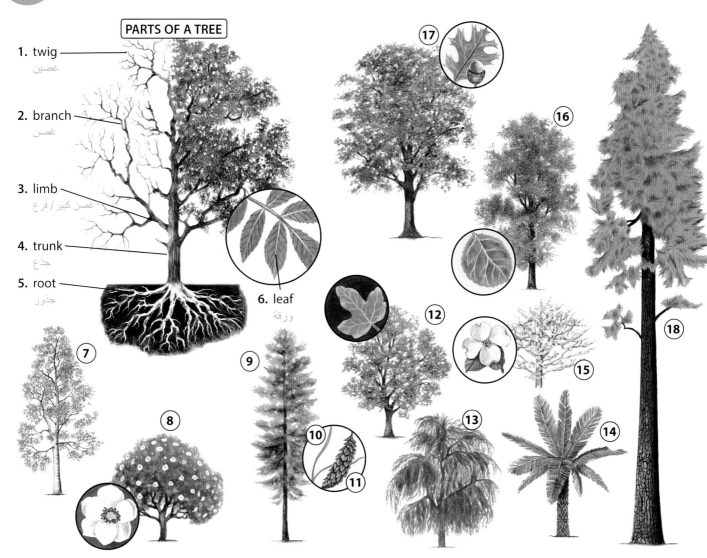

PARTS OF A TREE

1. twig
غصين

2. branch
غصن

3. limb
غصن كبير / فرع

4. trunk
جذع

5. root
جذور

6. leaf
ورقة

7. birch بتولا (شجر القضبان)	**10.** needle ورقة إبرية	**13.** willow صفصاف	**16.** elm دردار
8. magnolia مغنولية	**11.** pine cone كوز صنوبر	**14.** palm نخل	**17.** oak سنديان
9. pine شجر الصنوبر	**12.** maple قيقب	**15.** dogwood قرانيا	**18.** redwood الشجر الأحمر (صنوبر حرجي)

Plants نباتات

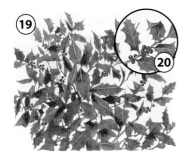

19. holly البهشية	**21.** cactus صبار	**23.** poison sumac سماق سام	**25.** poison ivy لبلاب سام
20. berries توت	**22.** vine كرمة	**24.** poison oak بلوط سام	

Parts of a Flower أجزاء الزهرة

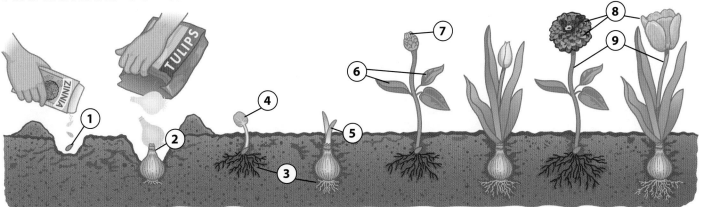

1. seed	**4.** seedling	**7.** bud
بذرة	نبتة صغيرة	برعم
2. bulb	**5.** shoot	**8.** petals
بصلة	نبتة / فرخ	بتلات (تويجات)
3. roots	**6.** leaves	**9.** stems
جذور	ورق	جذوع

10. sunflower	**15.** rose	**20.** carnation	**25.** daffodil
عباد الشمس	وردة	فُل	نرجس بري
11. tulip	**16.** iris	**21.** chrysanthemum	**26.** lily
زنبقة	سوسن	أقحوان	زنبق
12. hibiscus	**17.** crocus	**22.** jasmine	**27.** houseplant
خبيزة	زعفران	ياسمين	نبتة منزلية
13. marigold	**18.** gardenia	**23.** violet	**28.** bouquet
قطيفة	غردينيا	ليلك	باقة زهور
14. daisy	**19.** orchid	**24.** poinsettia	**29.** thorn
زهرة الربيع	سحلبية	بونسيتة	شوكة

Sea Animals الحيوانات البحرية

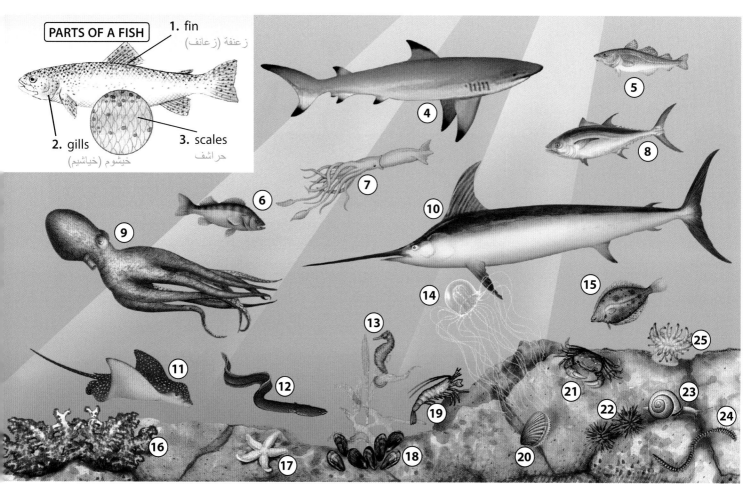

PARTS OF A FISH

1. fin
زعنفة (زعانف)

2. gills
خيشوم (خياشيم)

3. scales
حراشف

4. shark القرش	**9. octopus** أخطبوط	**14. jellyfish** السمك الهلالي (قنديل البحر)	**19. shrimp** الربيان / القريدس (الجمبري)	**24. worm** دودة
5. cod القد	**10. swordfish** أبو سيف	**15. flounder** السمك المفلطح	**20. scallop** الأسقلوب	**25. sea anemone** شقيق البحر
6. bass القاروس	**11. ray** شفنين بحري	**16. coral** مرجان	**21. crab** السلطعون (سرطان البحر)	
7. squid الحبار	**12. eel** الأنقليس (ثعبان بحري)	**17. starfish** نجم البحر	**22. sea urchin** قنفذ البحر	
8. tuna التونة (سمك التن)	**13. seahorse** فرس البحر	**18. mussel** بلح البحر	**23. snail** بزاقة	

Amphibians البرمائيات

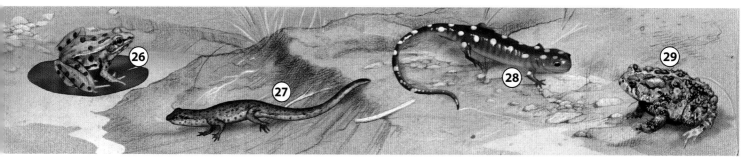

26. frog ضفدع	**27. newt** سمندل الماء	**28. salamander** سمندر	**29. toad** علجوم

Marine Life, Amphibians, and Reptiles

Sea Mammals الثدييات البحرية

30. water	32. porpoise	34. walrus	36. seal	38. rock
ماء / مياه	خنزير البحر	الفظ (فيل البحر)	فقمة	صخر
31. dolphin	33. whale	35. sea lion	37. sea otter	
دلفين	حوت	أسد البحر	قضاعة / قندس (كلب الماء)	

Reptiles الزواحف

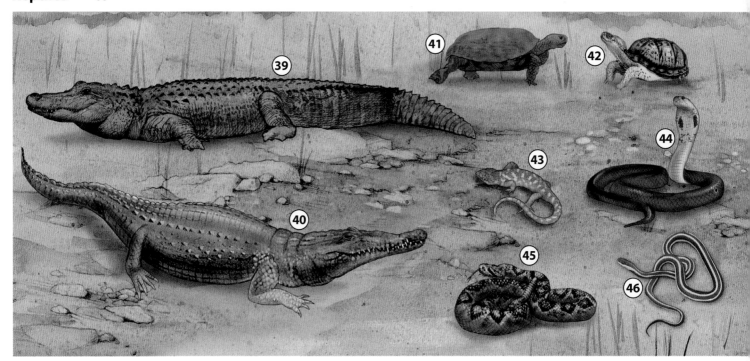

39. alligator	41. tortoise	43. lizard	45. rattlesnake
تمساح	رَق (سلحفاة)	سحلية	المجلجلة / ذات الأجراس
40. crocodile	42. turtle	44. cobra	46. garter snake
قاطور (تمساح أمريكي)	سلحفاة	الصل (كوبرا)	الغرطر

Birds, Insects, and Arachnids

الطيور والحشرات والعنكبوتيات

PARTS OF A BIRD

1. wing
جناح

2. claw
مخلب

3. beak / bill
منقار

4. feather
ريشة

5. nest
عش

6. owl
بوم

7. blue jay
القيق الأزرق / الزرياب

8. sparrow
عصفور / دُوري

9. woodpecker
نقار الخشب

10. eagle
صقر / نسر

11. hummingbird
الطنان

12. penguin
بطريق

13. duck
بط

14. goose
إوزَّة (إوزّ)

15. peacock
طاووس

16. pigeon
حمامة

17. robin
أبو الحناء

Insects and Arachnids الحشرات والعنكبوتيات

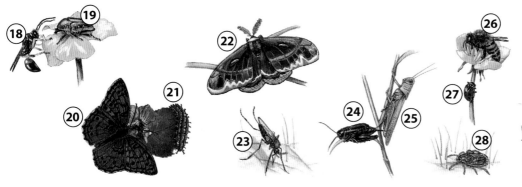
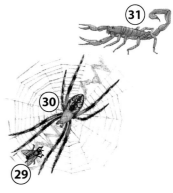

18. wasp
زنبور

19. beetle
خنفساء

20. butterfly
فراشة

21. caterpillar
يرقانة

22. moth
عثة

23. mosquito
بعوضة (ناموسة)

24. cricket
صرار الليل

25. grasshopper
جندب

26. honeybee
نحلة عسل

27. ladybug
دعسوقة

28. tick
قرادة

29. fly
ذبابة

30. spider
عنكبوت

31. scorpion
عقرب

الحيوانات الأليفة والقوارض

Farm Animals / Livestock حيوانات المزارع / المواشي

1. cow
بقرة

2. pig
خنزير

3. donkey
حمار

4. horse
حصان

5. goat
عنزة / ماعز

6. sheep
خروف

7. rooster
ديك

8. hen
دجاجة

Pets الحيوانات المنزلية

9. cat
هرة / قطة

10. kitten
هريرة (هرة صغيرة)

11. dog
كلب

12. puppy
جرو

13. rabbit
أرنب

14. guinea pig
خنزير هندي

15. parakeet
درة (ببغاء صغير)

16. goldfish
سمك ذهبي

Rodents القوارض

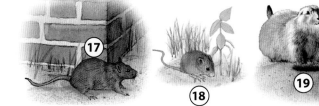

17. rat
جرذ

18. mouse
فأر

19. gopher
غوفر (سنجاب أمريكي)

20. chipmunk
صيدناني (سنجاب أمريكي صغير مخطط)

21. squirrel
سنجاب

22. prairie dog
كلب البراري

More vocabulary

Farm animals and pets are **domesticated**. They work for and/or live with people. Animals that are not domesticated are **wild**. Most rodents are wild.

Survey your class. Record the responses.

1. Have you worked with farm animals? Which ones?
2. Are you afraid of rodents? Which ones?

Report: _Lee_ has worked with _cows_. _He's_ afraid of _rats_.

221

1. moose موظ	**5.** wolf ذئب	**9.** beaver سَمُّور	**13.** raccoon راكون
2. mountain lion أسد الجبال (الكوغر)	**6.** buffalo / bison جاموس / بيسون	**10.** porcupine شيهم / نيص	**14.** deer غزال
3. coyote قيوط (ذئب أمريكي)	**7.** bat خفاش / وطواط	**11.** bear دب	**15.** fox ثعلب
4. opossum أبوسوم	**8.** armadillo المدرع	**12.** skunk ظربان	

 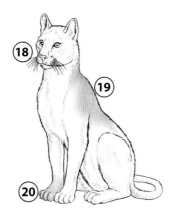  

16. antlers قرون الوعل	**18.** whiskers سبلات	**20.** paw كف الحيوان ذي البراثن	**22.** tail ذنب / ذيل
17. hooves حوافر	**19.** coat / fur فروة	**21.** horn قرن	**23.** quill أشواك القنفذ

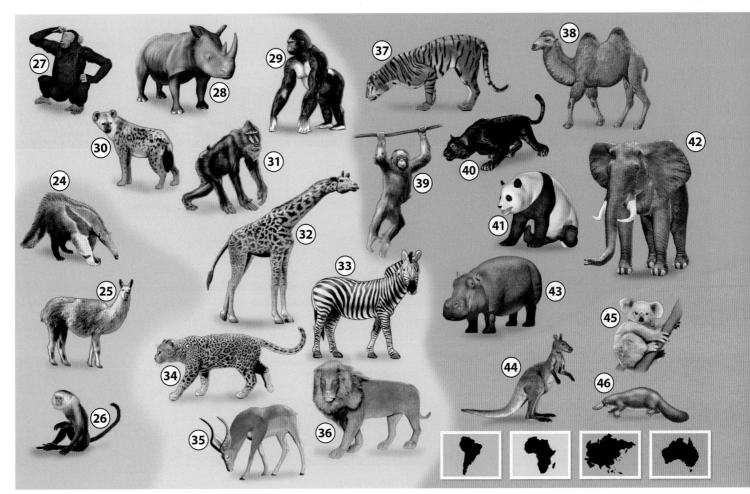

24. anteater آكل النمل	**29.** gorilla غوريلا	**34.** leopard فهد	**39.** orangutan إنسان الغاب	**44.** kangaroo كنغر
25. llama لاما	**30.** hyena ضبع	**35.** antelope ظبي	**40.** panther نمر أمريكي	**45.** koala كوال
26. monkey قرد	**31.** baboon سعدان إفريقي	**36.** lion أسد / سبع	**41.** panda بندة	**46.** platypus بلاتيوس
27. chimpanzee شمبانزي	**32.** giraffe زرافة	**37.** tiger نمر	**42.** elephant فيل	
28. rhinoceros كركَدَن (خرتيت)	**33.** zebra حمار وحشي	**38.** camel جمل	**43.** hippopotamus فرس النهر	

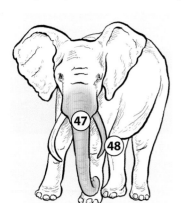   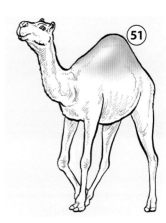

47. trunk خرطوم / زلومة	**48.** tusk ناب	**49.** mane عرف	**50.** pouch جيب	**51.** hump حدبة

223

Energy and the Environment الطاقة والبيئة

Energy Sources مصادر الطاقة

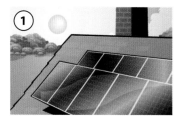

1. solar energy
الطاقة الشمسية

2. wind power
الطاقة الريحية

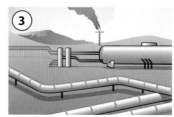

3. natural gas
الغاز الطبيعي

4. coal
فحم

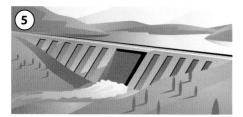

5. hydroelectric power
طاقة كهرمائية

6. oil / petroleum
النفط / البترول

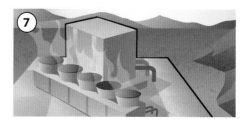

7. geothermal energy
طاقة حرارية أرضية

8. nuclear energy
طاقة نووية

9. biomass / bioenergy
طاقة الكتلة الإحيائية / الطاقة الإحيائية

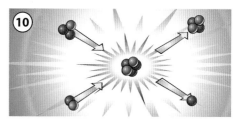

10. fusion
انصهار

Pollution التلوُّث

11. air pollution / smog
تلوث الهواء (الجو) / ضباب دخاني

12. hazardous waste
نفايات خطرة

13. acid rain
مطر حمضي

14. water pollution
تلوث المياه

15. radiation
إشعاع

16. pesticide poisoning
تسمم من مبيدات الحشرات

17. oil spill
انسكاب نفطي

More vocabulary

Environmental Protection Agency (EPA): the federal group that responds to pollution and environmental disasters

Internet Research: recycling

Type "recycle" and your city in the search bar. Look for information on local recycling centers.
Report: *You can recycle <u>cans</u> at ____.*

Ways to Conserve Energy and Resources وسائل للحفاظ على الطاقة والموارد الطبيعية

A. reduce trash
الحد من القمامة

B. reuse shopping bags
إعادة استعمال أكياس التسوق

C. recycle
إعادة التصنيع أو التدوير

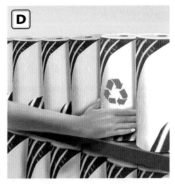

D. buy recycled products
شراء منتجات معاد تصنيعها

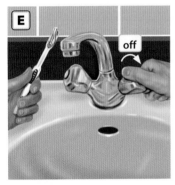

E. save water
التوفير في استهلاك الماء

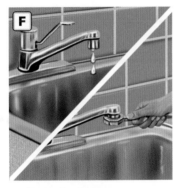

F. fix leaky faucets
إصلاح الحنفيات المتسربة

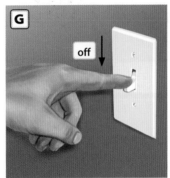

G. turn off lights
إطفاء الأنوار

H. use energy-efficient bulbs
استعمال لمبات كهربائية خفيضة الطاقة

I. carpool
المشاركة مع آخرين في ركوب سيارة واحدة

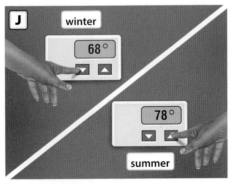

J. adjust the thermostat
ضبط منظّم الحرارة (الترموستات)

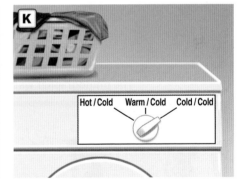

K. wash clothes in cold water
غَسل الملابس في ماء بارد

L. don't litter
عدم إلقء القمامة في الأماكن العامة

M. compost food scraps
حوّل بقايا الطعام إلى سماد

N. plant a tree
زرع شجرة

A Graduation حفلة التخرُّج

All Adelia's photos

I loved Art History.

My last economics lesson

Marching Band is great!

The photographer was upset.

We look good!

I get my diploma.

Dad and his digital camera

1. photographer مصور	3. serious photo صورة جادة	5. podium منصة	7. cap قبعة التخرج	A. **take** a picture يلتقط صورة فوتوغرافية	C. **celebrate** تحتفل
2. funny photo صورة مضحكة	4. guest speaker ضيفة الشرف	6. ceremony احتفال	8. gown رداء التخرج	B. **cry** تبكي	

People	Comments	
Sara	June 29th 8:19 p.m. Great pictures! What a day!	Delete
Zannie baby	June 30th 10 a.m. Love the funny photo.	Delete

I'm behind the mayor.

We're all very happy.

What do you see in the pictures?

1. Which classes are Adelia's favorites?
2. Do you prefer the funny or the serious graduation photo? Why?
3. Who is standing at the podium?
4. What are the graduates throwing in the air? Why?

Read the story.

A Graduation

Look at these great photos on my web page! The first three are from my favorite classes, but the other pictures are from graduation day.

There are two pictures of my classmates in <u>caps</u> and <u>gowns</u>. In the first picture, we're laughing and the <u>photographer</u> is upset. In the second photo, we're serious. I like the <u>serious photo</u>, but I love the <u>funny photo</u>!

There's also a picture of our <u>guest speaker</u>, the mayor. She is standing at the <u>podium</u>. Next, you can see me at the graduation <u>ceremony</u>. My dad wanted to <u>take a picture</u> of me with my diploma. That's my mom next to him. She <u>cries</u> when she's happy.

After the ceremony, everyone was happy, but no one cried. We wanted to <u>celebrate</u> and we did!

Reread the story.

1. Which events happened before the graduation? After?
2. Why does the author say, "but no one cried" in paragraph 4?

What do you think?

3. What kinds of ceremonies are important for children? for teens? for adults?

Places to Go

أماكن للزيارة

1. zoo
حديقة الحيوانات

2. movies
السينما

3. botanical garden
حديقة النباتات

4. bowling alley
مضمار البولينغ (لعبة الكرة الخشبية)

5. rock concert
حفلة موسيقى الروك اند رول

6. swap meet /
flea market
سوق المقايضة أو الخردوات

7. aquarium
معرض الأحياء المائية

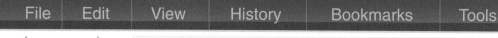

| File | Edit | View | History | Bookmarks | Tools |

Places to Go in Our City

Listen and point. Take turns.

A: Point to the <u>zoo</u>.
B: Point to the <u>flea market</u>.
A: Point to the <u>rock concert</u>.

Dictate to your partner. Take turns.

A: Write these words: <u>zoo, movies, aquarium</u>.
B: <u>Zoo, movies</u>, and what?
A: And <u>aquarium</u>.

 Search

8. play
مسرحية

9. art museum
متحف الفنون

10. amusement park
مدينة ملاهي

11. opera
الأوبرا

12. nightclub
نادي ليلي / ملهى ليلي

13. county fair
مهرجان ريفي

14. classical concert
حفلة موسيقى كلاسيكية

Ways to make plans using *Let's go*

Let's go to <u>the amusement park</u> tomorrow.

Let's go to <u>the opera</u> on Saturday.

Let's go to <u>the movies</u> tonight.

Pair practice. Make new conversations.

A: <u>*Let's go to the zoo this afternoon*</u>.

B: *OK. And let's go to <u>the movies tonight</u>*.

A: *That sounds like a good plan.*

229

1. ball field
ملعب كرة

2. cyclist
راكب دراجة

3. bike path
ممر دراجات

4. jump rope
حبل الوثب

5. fountain
فسقية

6. tennis court
ملعب كرة المضرب (تنس)

7. skateboard
مزلق ذو عجلات

8. picnic table
طاولة نزهة

9. water fountain
نافورة مياه للشرب

10. bench
دكة / مقعد طويل

11. swings
مراجيح

12. tricycle
دراجة ثلاثية العجلات

13. slide
زلاقة

14. climbing apparatus
قضبان تسلق

15. sandbox
صندوق رمل

16. outdoor grill
شواية خارجية

A. pull the wagon
تسحب العربة

B. push the swing
تدفع المرجيحة

C. climb the bars
يتسلقان القضبان

D. picnic / have a picnic
تنزه / يقوم (تقوم) بنزهة

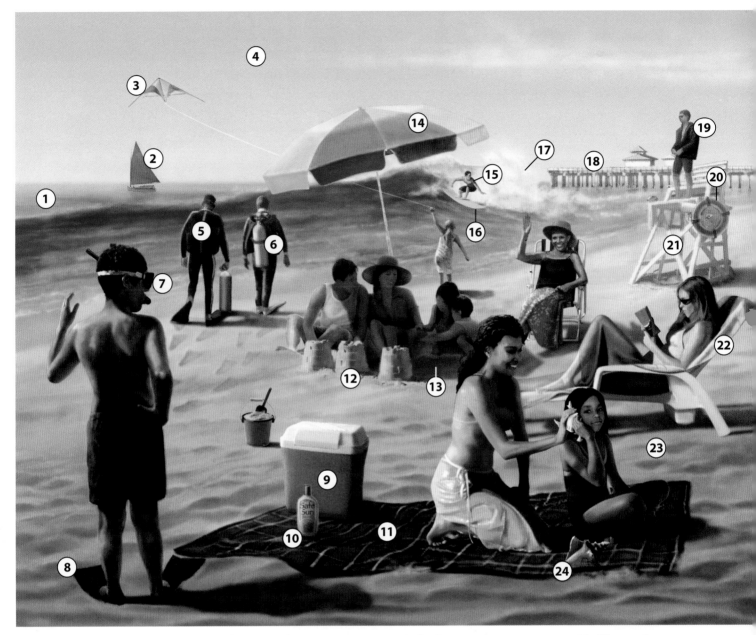

1. ocean / water المحيط / الماء	**7.** diving mask قناع الغطس	**13.** shade ظل	**19.** lifeguard منقذ / سباح الإنقاذ
2. sailboat زورق شراعي	**8.** fins زعانف	**14.** beach umbrella مظلة للشاطئ	**20.** lifesaving device أداة إنقاذ
3. kite طيارة من الورق والبوص	**9.** cooler صندوق تبريد	**15.** surfer راكب الأمواج المتكسرة	**21.** lifeguard station مقر سباح الإنقاذ
4. sky السماء	**10.** sunscreen / sunblock مرهم واقٍ من أشعة الشمس	**16.** surfboard لوح خشبي لركوب الأمواج المتكسرة	**22.** beach chair كرسي للشاطئ
5. wetsuit بدلة غوص	**11.** blanket بطّانية	**17.** wave موجة	**23.** sand رمل
6. scuba tank خزان أكسيجين للغوص	**12.** sandcastle قلعة من الرمل	**18.** pier رصيف ممتد داخل البحر	**24.** seashell صدفة بحرية

More vocabulary

seaweed: a plant that grows in the ocean
tide: the level of the ocean. The tide goes in and out every 12 hours.

Grammar Point: prepositions *in, on, under*

*Where are the little kids? They're **under** the umbrella.*
*Where's the cooler? It's **on** the blanket.*
*Where's the kite? It's **in** the sky.*

231

1. boating
ركوب الزوارق

2. rafting
رياضة ركوب الرمث

3. canoeing
ركوب الكانو (الصندل)

4. fishing
صيد الأسماك

5. camping
تخييم

6. backpacking
حمل الأمتعة على الظهر

7. hiking
التنزه سيرا على الأقدام

8. mountain biking
ركوب الدراجات على الجبال

9. horseback riding
ركوب الخيل

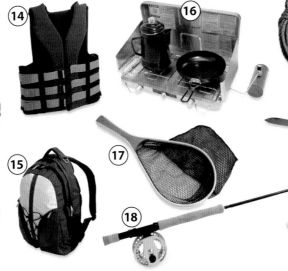

10. tent
خيمة

11. campfire
نار المخيم

12. sleeping bag
كيس للنوم

13. foam pad
فرشة من الإسفنج

14. life vest
صديرية النجاة

15. backpack
حقيبة تحمل على الظهر

16. camping stove
موقد تخييم

17. fishing net
شبكة صيد أسماك

18. fishing pole
صنارة صيد سمك

19. rope
حبل

20. multi-use knife
سكين متعدد الاستعمالات

21. matches
أعواد ثقاب / كبريت

22. lantern
فانوس

23. insect repellent
مادة طاردة للحشرات

24. canteen
مزادة (قربة ماء)

Winter and Water Sports

1. downhill skiing
التزلج على منحدر

2. snowboarding
التزلج على الثلج

3. cross-country skiing
التزلج في الضاحية

4. ice skating
التزلج على الجليد

5. figure skating
التزلج مع القيام بسلسلة من الحركات

6. sledding
ركوب المزلجة

7. waterskiing
التزلج على الماء

8. sailing
الإبحار بمركب شراعي

9. surfing
ركوب الأمواج المتكسرة

10. windsurfing
التزلج على الماء مع استعمال شراع

11. snorkeling
السباحة مع استعمال أنبوب التنفس

12. scuba diving
الغوص مع خزان التنفس

More vocabulary

speed skating: racing while ice skating
kitesurfing: surfing with a small surfboard and a kite

Internet Research: popular winter sports

Type "popular winter sports" in the search bar.
Compare the information on two sites.
Report: *Two sites said ____ is a popular winter sport.*

233

1. archery
رماية السهام

2. billiards / pool
بلياردو

3. bowling
بولينغ (لعبة الكرة الخشبية)

4. boxing
ملاكمة

5. cycling / biking
ركوب الدراجة

6. badminton
بادمنتون (لعبة تشبه كرة المضرب)

7. fencing
مبارزة بالسيف

8. golf
جولف

9. gymnastics
الرياضة الجمبازية

10. inline skating
التزلج بمزلج ذي خط دواليب

11. martial arts
الجودو

12. racquetball
راكتبول

13. skateboarding
التزلج على لوح بعجلات

14. table tennis
كرة الطاولة

15. tennis
كرة المضرب (تنس)

16. weightlifting
رفع الأثقال

17. wrestling
مصارعة

18. track and field
سباق المضمار والميدان

19. horse racing
سباق الخيول

Pair practice. Make new conversations.

A: *What sports do you like?*
B: *I like* <u>bowling</u>. *What do you like?*
A: *I like* <u>gymnastics</u>.

Internet Research: dangerous sports

Type "most dangerous sports" in the search bar.
Look for information on two or more sites.
Report: *According to my research, _____ is dangerous.*

1. score
نتيجة المباراة

2. coach
مدرب

3. team
فريق

4. fan
مشجّع

5. player
لاعب

6. official / referee
حَكَم

7. basketball court
ملعب كرة السلة

8. basketball hoop
حلقة السلة في لعبة كرة السلة

9. basketball
كرة السلة

10. baseball
بيسبول

11. softball
صوفتبول (لعبة شبيهة بالبيسبول)

12. football
كرة القدم الأمريكية (الفوتبول)

13. soccer
كرة القدم

14. ice hockey
هوكي الجليد

15. volleyball
الكرة الطائرة

16. water polo
كرة الماء

More vocabulary

win: to have the best score
lose: the opposite of win
tie: to have the same score

captain: the team leader
goalie: the team member who protects the goal in soccer, ice hockey, and water polo
umpire: the referee in baseball
Little League: a baseball and softball program for children

235

Sports Verbs
أفعال متعلقة بالرياضة

A. **pitch**
يرمي

B. **hit**
يضرب

C. **throw**
يلقي

D. **catch**
يلقف

E. **kick**
يركل

F. **tackle**
يمسك بالخصم لإيقافه

G. **pass**
يمرر

H. **shoot**
ترمي الكرة نحو السلة (تقذف الكرة)

I. **jump**
تقفز

J. **dribble**
تنطط الكرة

K. **dive**
يغطس

L. **swim**
يسبح

M. **stretch**
تتمدد

N. **exercise / work out**
تتمرن / تمارس تمرينات رياضية

O. **bend**
تنحني

P. **serve**
يستهل ضرب الكرة

Q. **swing**
توجّه / تصوّب

R. **start**
ينطلق

S. **race**
يسابق

T. **finish**
يصل لخط النهاية

U. **skate**
تتزلج

V. **ski**
يتزلج على الثلج

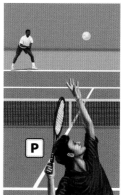

Use the new words.

Look at page 235. Name the actions you see.

A: He's <u>throwing</u>.

B: She's <u>jumping</u>.

Ways to talk about your sports skills

I can <u>throw</u>, but I can't <u>catch</u>.

I <u>swim</u> well, but I don't <u>dive</u> well.

I'm good at <u>skating</u>, but I'm terrible at <u>skiing</u>.

1. golf club هراوة / مضرب جولف	**8. arrows** سهام	**15. catcher's mask** قناع لاقف الكرة	**22. weights** أثقال
2. tennis racket مضرب تنس	**9. ice skates** مزلج جليد	**16. uniform** زي مُوَحَّد	**23. snowboard** لوحة للتزلج على الثلج
3. volleyball كرة الطائرة	**10. inline skates** مزلج بخط دواليب	**17. glove** قفاز	**24. skis** زلاجة
4. basketball كرة السلة	**11. hockey stick** عصا هوكي	**18. baseball** كرة بيسبول	**25. ski poles** عصا التزلج على الثلج
5. bowling ball كرة البولينغ	**12. soccer ball** كرة قدم	**19. football helmet** خوذة فوتبول (كرة قدم أمريكية)	**26. ski boots** حذاء التزلج على الثلج
6. bow قوس	**13. shin guards** واقيات قصبة الرجل	**20. shoulder pads** لبادة كتف	**27. flying disc*** قرص طائر
7. target هدف	**14. baseball bat** مضرب بيسبول	**21. football** كرة الفوتبول	*** Note:** one brand is Frisbee®, of Wham-O, Inc.

Use the new words.

Look at pages 234–235. Name the sports equipment you see.

A: *Those are ice skates.*

B: *That's a football.*

Survey your class. Record the responses.

1. What sports equipment do you own?
2. What sports stores do you recommend?

Report: *Sam* owns a ____ . *He* recommends ____ .

237

A. collect things
تجمع أشياءً

B. play games
تلعب ألعاباً

C. quilt
تمارس التضريب

D. do crafts
تمارس أشغالاً يدوية

Collectibles

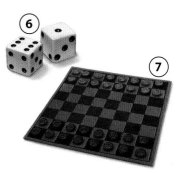

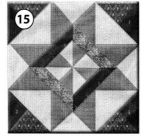

1. figurine
   تمثال صغير

2. baseball cards
   بطاقات بيسبول

3. video game console
   جهاز لألعاب الفيديو

4. video game controller
   أداة تحكم في ألعاب الفيديو

5. board game
   لعبة لوحية

6. dice
   زهر الطاولة / النرد

7. checkers
   رقعة الداما

8. chess
   شطرنج

9. model kit
   عدة لتركيب نماذج

10. acrylic paint
    دهان أكريليك

11. glue stick
    قلم صمغ

12. glue gun
    مسدس غراء

13. construction paper
    ورق إنشاء

14. woodworking kit
    عدة نجارة

15. quilt block
    كتلة تضريب

16. rotary cutter
    قاطع دوار

Grammar Point: *used to*

When I was a kid, I **used to** play cards every day.
Now, I don't play very often.

Pair practice. Make new conversations.

A: *What were your hobbies when you were a kid?*
B: *I used to <u>collect baseball cards</u>. And you?*
A: *I used to <u>play video games</u>.*

E. paint
ترسم بالألوان

F. knit
تحبك بالصنارة

G. pretend
تتظاهر

H. play cards
يلعبان الشدة

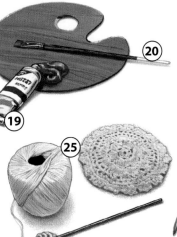

17. canvas
قماش قنب

18. easel
حامل لوحة

19. oil paint
دهان زيتي

20. paintbrush
فرشاة رسم

21. watercolors
لون مائي

22. yarn
لفيفة صوف أو قطن

23. knitting needles
مسلات حياكة

24. embroidery
تطريز

25. crochet
حبك بصنارة معقوفة (كروشيه)

26. action figure
تماثيل أبطال

27. model train
قطارات لعب نموذجية

28. dolls
دمى

29. diamonds
الديناري

30. spades
البستوني

31. hearts
الكوبة

32. clubs
الاسباتي

Ways to talk about hobbies and games

*This <u>board game</u> is **interesting**. It makes me think.*
*That <u>video game</u> is **boring**. Nothing happens.*
*I love to <u>play cards</u>. It's **fun** to play with my friends.*

Internet Research: popular hobbies

Type "most popular hobbies" in the search bar.
Look for information on one or more sites.
Report: *I read that _____ is a popular hobby.*

1. boom box
   جهاز إذاعة الموسيقى العالية

2. video MP3 player
   جهاز تشغيل الفيديو وملفات ام بي 3 (MP3) الموسيقية

3. dock / charging station
   قاعدة / محطة شحن

4. lightweight headphones
   سماعات رأس خفيفة الوزن

5. earbuds / in-ear headphones
   سماعات صغيرة داخل الأذن / سماعات رأس داخل الأذن

6. noise-canceling headphones
   سماعات رأس لاغية للضجيج

7. personal CD player
   جهاز تشغيل س دي شخصي

8. flat-screen TV / flat-panel TV
   تلفزيون ذو شاشة مسطحة

9. Blu-ray player
   مشغّل أقراص بلو راي (Blu-ray)

10. universal remote
    جهاز تحكم عن بعد (ريموت) شامل

11. DVD player
    جهاز تشغيل أقراص فيديو رقمية (دي في دي)

12. turntable
    جهاز تشغيل أسطوانات

13. tuner
    جهاز توليف (أمبليفاير)

14. speakers
    سماعات ستريو

15. portable charger
    شاحن نقال

16. microphone
    ميكروفون

17. digital camera
كاميرا رقمية (ديجيتال)

18. memory card
كارت ذاكرة

19. zoom lens
عدسة مقرّبة (زوم)

20. tripod
حامل ثلاثي القوائم

21. camcorder
آلة تصوير وفيديو

22. camera case / bag
علبة / حقيبة للكاميرا

23. battery pack
حزمة بطاريات

24. battery charger
شاحن البطارية

25. plug
قابس

26. international power adapter
مهايئ (ادابتور) طاقة دولي

27. LCD projector
آلة عرض على شاشة ببلور سائل (إل سي دي)

28. screen
شاشة

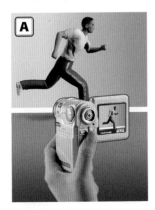

29. photo album
ألبوم صور

30. digital photo album
ألبوم صور رقمية (ديجيتال)

31. out of focus
صورة غير واضحة

32. overexposed
صورة زائدة التعريض للضوء

33. underexposed
صورة ناقصة التعريض للضوء

A. record
يسجّل

B. play
يشغّل / يذيع

C. rewind
ترجّع إلى الوراء

D. fast forward
تقدّم إلى الأمام بسرعة

E. pause
يوقف مؤقتا

Types of TV Programs   أنواع البرامج التليفزيونية

1. news program
برنامج إخباري

2. sitcom (situation comedy)
برنامج كوميدي

3. cartoon
أفلام كارتون (رسوم متحركة)

4. talk show
برنامج مقابلات

5. soap opera
مسلسل تلفزيوني

6. reality show
برنامج حياة واقعية

7. nature program
برنامج عن الطبيعة

8. game show
برنامج منافسات أو مسابقات

9. children's program
برنامج أطفال

10. shopping program
برنامج تسوّق

11. sports program
برنامج رياضي

12. drama
دراما

Types of Movies أنواع الأفلام

13. comedy
هزلي (كوميدي)

14. tragedy
مأسوي (تراجيديا)

15. western
رعاة البقر (كاوبوي)

16. romance
رواية حب (رومانسي)

17. horror story
رواية مرعبة (فيلم رعب)

18. science fiction story
رواية خيال علمي

19. action story / adventure story
رواية إثارة / رواية مغامرات

20. mystery / suspense
رواية بوليسية / تشويق

Types of Music أنواع الموسيقى

21. classical
كلاسيكية

22. blues
موسيقى الكآبة (بلوز)

23. rock
موسيقى صاخبة راقصة (روك أند رول)

24. jazz
جاز

25. pop
بوب (شعبية)

26. hip-hop
هيب هوب (راقصة)

27. country
ريفية

28. R&B / soul
إيقاعية حزينة (ريذم أند بلوز) / روحية (صول)

29. folk
شعبية فولكلورية

30. gospel
كنسية

31. reggae
موسيقى الرجي

32. world music
موسيقى عالمية

A. play an instrument
تعزف على آلة

B. sing a song
يغنّي أغنية

C. conduct an orchestra
يقود أوركسترا

D. be in a rock band
يلعب في فرقة روك أند رول

Woodwinds آلات النفخ الخشبية

1. flute
فلوت

2. clarinet
كلارينت

3. oboe
أوبو (مزمار)

4. bassoon
الزمخر (بسون)

5. saxophone
السكسبية (ساكسفون)

Strings الآلات الوترية

6. violin
كمان (كمنجة)

7. cello
فيولونسيل (كمنجة كبيرة)

8. bass
كمان أجهر (كونتراباص)

9. guitar
قيثار (جيتار)

Brass آلات النفخ النحاسية

10. trombone
المترددة (ترومبون)

11. trumpet / horn
بوق / نفير (ترومبت)

12. tuba
توبة

13. French horn
بوق فرنسي

Percussion الآلات الإيقاعية

14. piano
بيانو

15. xylophone
الخشبية (زيلوفون)

16. drums
طبل (طبول)

17. tambourine
رق / دف

Other Instruments آلات أخرى

18. electric keyboard
كيبورد (لوحة أصابع) كهربائي

19. accordion
أكورديون

20. organ
أرغن

21. harmonica
هرمونيكا

1. parade
موكب استعراضي

2. float
عربة ذات منصة

3. confetti
قصاصات النثار الورقية

4. couple
زوجان

5. card
كارت / بطاقة

6. heart
قلب

7. fireworks
ألعاب نارية

8. flag
راية / علم

9. mask
قناع

10. jack-o'-lantern
مصباح يصنع من قرعة

11. costume
لباس تنكري

12. candy
حلوى

13. feast
وليمة

14. turkey
ديك رومي

15. ornament
زينة

16. Christmas tree
شجرة أعياد الميلاد (الكريسماس)

17. candy cane
عصا الحلوى

18. string lights
أنوار عقدية (لتزيين الشجر)

*Thanksgiving is on the fourth Thursday in November.

1. decorations
زينة / زواق

2. deck
منصة جلوس خارجية

3. present / gift
هدية

A. videotape
تصوّر بكاميرا فيديو

B. make a wish
يتمنى

C. blow out
يطفئ الشمع

D. hide
يختبئ

E. bring
يحضر

F. wrap
تلف

Happy Birthday!

What do you see in the picture?

1. What kinds of decorations do you see?
2. What are people doing at this birthday party?
3. What wish did the teenager make?
4. How many presents did people bring?

 Read the story.

A Birthday Party

Today is Lou and Gani Bombata's birthday barbecue. There are <u>decorations</u> around the backyard, and food and drinks on the <u>deck</u>. There are also <u>presents</u>. Everyone in the Bombata family likes to <u>bring</u> presents.

Right now, it's time for cake. Gani <u>is blowing out</u> the candles, and Lou <u>is making a wish</u>. Lou's mom wants to <u>videotape</u> everyone, but she can't find Lou's brother, Todd. Todd hates to sing, so he always <u>hides</u> for the birthday song.

Lou's sister, Amaka, has to <u>wrap</u> some <u>gifts</u>. She doesn't want Lou to see. Amaka isn't worried. She knows her family loves to sing. She can put her gifts on the present table before they finish the first song.

Reread the story.

1. Which paragraph gives you the most information about the Bombata family? Explain why.
2. Tell the story in your own words.

What do you think?

3. What wish do you think Gani made? Give your reasons.
4. Imagine you are invited to this party. You want to get one special gift for Gani *and* Lou to share. What's one gift they could both enjoy?

Verb Guide

Verbs in English are either regular or irregular in the past tense and past participle forms.

Regular Verbs

The regular verbs below are marked 1, 2, 3, or 4 according to four different spelling patterns.
(See page 250 for the irregular verbs, which do not follow any of these patterns.)

Spelling Patterns for the Past and the Past Participle	Example	
1. Add -ed to the end of the verb.	**ASK**	**ASKED**
2. Add -d to the end of the verb.	**LIVE**	**LIVED**
3. Double the final consonant and add -ed to the end of the verb.	**DROP**	**DROPPED**
4. Drop the final y and add -ied to the end of the verb.	**CRY**	**CRIED**

The Oxford Picture Dictionary List of Regular Verbs

accept (1)
add (1)
address (1)
adjust (1)
agree (2)
answer (1)
apologize (2)
appear (1)
applaud (1)
apply (4)
arrange (2)
arrest (1)
arrive (2)
ask (1)
assemble (2)
assist (1)
attach (1)
attend (1)
bake (2)
bargain (1)
bathe (2)
block (1)
board (1)
boil (1)
bookmark (1)
borrow (1)
bow (1)
brainstorm (1)
breathe (2)
browse (2)
brush (1)
bubble (2)
buckle (2)
burn (1)
bus (1)
calculate (2)
call (1)

capitalize (2)
carpool (1)
carry (4)
cash (1)
celebrate (2)
change (2)
check (1)
chill (1)
choke (2)
chop (3)
circle (2)
cite (2)
claim (1)
clarify (4)
clean (1)
clear (1)
click (1)
climb (1)
close (2)
collate (2)
collect (1)
color (1)
comb (1)
comfort (1)
commit (3)
compare (2)
complain (1)
complete (2)
compliment (1)
compose (2)
compost (1)
conceal (1)
conduct (1)
consult (1)
contact (1)
convert (1)
convict (1)

cook (1)
cooperate (2)
copy (4)
correct (1)
cough (1)
count (1)
create (2)
cross (1)
cry (4)
dance (2)
debate (2)
decline (2)
delete (2)
deliver (1)
design (1)
dial (1)
dice (2)
dictate (2)
die (2)
direct (1)
disagree (2)
discipline (2)
discuss (1)
disinfect (1)
distribute (2)
dive (2)
divide (2)
double-click (1)
drag (3)
dress (1)
dribble (2)
drill (1)
drop (3)
drown (1)
dry (4)
dust (1)
dye (2)

earn (1)
edit (1)
empty (4)
end (1)
enter (1)
erase (2)
evacuate (2)
examine (2)
exchange (2)
exercise (2)
expire (2)
explain (1)
explore (2)
exterminate (2)
fast forward (1)
fasten (1)
fax (1)
fertilize (2)
fill (1)
finish (1)
fix (1)
floss (1)
fold (1)
follow (1)
garden (1)
gargle (2)
graduate (2)
grate (2)
grease (2)
greet (1)
hail (1)
hammer (1)
hand (1)
harvest (1)
help (1)
hire (2)
hug (3)

identify (4)
immigrate (2)
indent (1)
inquire (2)
insert (1)
inspect (1)
install (1)
introduce (2)
investigate (2)
invite (2)
iron (1)
jaywalk (1)
join (1)
jump (1)
kick (1)
kiss (1)
knit (3)
label (1)
land (1)
laugh (1)
learn (1)
lengthen (1)
lift (1)
list (1)
listen (1)
litter (1)
live (2)
load (1)
lock (1)
log (3)
look (1)
mail (1)
manufacture (2)
match (1)
measure (2)
microwave (2)
milk (1)
misbehave (2)
miss (1)
mix (1)
monitor (1)
mop (3)
move (2)
mow (1)
multiply (4)
negotiate (2)
network (1)
numb (1)
nurse (2)

obey (1)
observe (2)
offer (1)
open (1)
operate (2)
order (1)
organize (2)
overdose (2)
pack (1)
paint (1)
park (1)
participate (2)
pass (1)
paste (2)
pause (2)
peel (1)
perm (1)
pick (1)
pitch (1)
plan (3)
plant (1)
play (1)
polish (1)
pour (1)
praise (2)
preheat (1)
prepare (2)
prescribe (2)
press (1)
pretend (1)
print (1)
program (3)
protect (1)
pull (1)
purchase (2)
push (1)
quilt (1)
race (2)
raise (2)
rake (2)
receive (2)
record (1)
recycle (2)
redecorate (2)
reduce (2)
reenter (1)
refuse (2)
register (1)
relax (1)

remain (1)
remove (2)
renew (1)
repair (1)
replace (2)
report (1)
request (1)
research (1)
respond (1)
retire (2)
return (1)
reuse (2)
revise (2)
rinse (2)
rock (1)
sauté (1)
save (2)
scan (3)
schedule (2)
scroll (1)
scrub (3)
search (1)
seat (1)
select (1)
sentence (2)
separate (2)
serve (2)
share (2)
shave (2)
ship (3)
shop (3)
shorten (1)
shower (1)
sign (1)
simmer (1)
skate (2)
ski (1)
slice (2)
smell (1)
smile (2)
smoke (2)
solve (2)
sort (1)
spell (1)
spoon (1)
staple (2)
start (1)
state (2)
stay (1)

steam (1)
stir (3)
stop (3)
stow (1)
stretch (1)
study (4)
submit (3)
subtract (1)
supervise (2)
swallow (1)
tackle (2)
talk (1)
taste (2)
thank (1)
tie (2)
touch (1)
transcribe (2)
transfer (3)
translate (2)
travel (1)
trim (3)
try (4)
turn (1)
type (2)
underline (2)
undress (1)
unload (1)
unpack (1)
unscramble (2)
update (2)
use (2)
vacuum (1)
videotape (2)
visit (1)
volunteer (1)
vomit (1)
vote (2)
wait (1)
walk (1)
wash (1)
watch (1)
water (1)
wave (2)
weed (1)
weigh (1)
wipe (2)
work (1)
wrap (3)
yell (1)

Verb Guide

Irregular Verbs

These verbs have irregular endings in the past and/or the past participle.

The Oxford Picture Dictionary List of Irregular Verbs

simple	past	past participle	simple	past	past participle
be	was	been	make	made	made
beat	beat	beaten	meet	met	met
become	became	become	pay	paid	paid
bend	bent	bent	picnic	picnicked	picnicked
bleed	bled	bled	proofread	proofread	proofread
blow	blew	blown	put	put	put
break	broke	broken	quit	quit	quit
bring	brought	brought	read	read	read
buy	bought	bought	rewind	rewound	rewound
catch	caught	caught	rewrite	rewrote	rewritten
choose	chose	chosen	ride	rode	ridden
come	came	come	run	ran	run
cut	cut	cut	say	said	said
do	did	done	see	saw	seen
draw	drew	drawn	seek	sought	sought
drink	drank	drunk	sell	sold	sold
drive	drove	driven	send	sent	sent
eat	ate	eaten	set	set	set
fall	fell	fallen	sew	sewed	sewn
feed	fed	fed	shake	shook	shaken
feel	felt	felt	shoot	shot	shot
find	found	found	show	showed	shown
fly	flew	flown	sing	sang	sung
freeze	froze	frozen	sit	sat	sat
get	got	gotten	speak	spoke	spoken
give	gave	given	stand	stood	stood
go	went	gone	steal	stole	stolen
hang	hung	hung	sweep	swept	swept
have	had	had	swim	swam	swum
hear	heard	heard	swing	swung	swung
hide	hid	hidden	take	took	taken
hit	hit	hit	teach	taught	taught
hold	held	held	think	thought	thought
keep	kept	kept	throw	threw	thrown
lay	laid	laid	wake	woke	woken
leave	left	left	win	won	won
lend	lent	lent	withdraw	withdrew	withdrawn
let	let	let	write	wrote	written
lose	lost	lost			

Index

Index Key

Font

bold type = verbs or verb phrases (example: **catch**)

ordinary type = all other parts of speech (example: baseball)

ALL CAPS = unit titles (example: MATHEMATICS)

Initial caps = subunit titles (example: Equivalencies)

Numbers/Letters

first number in **bold** type = page on which word appears

second number, or letter, following number in **bold** type = item number on page

(examples: cool **13**–5 means that the word *cool* is item number 5 on page 13; across **157**–G means that the word *across* is item G on page 157).

Symbols

✦ = word found in exercise band at bottom of page

🔑 = The keywords of the **Oxford 3000™** have been carefully selected by a group of language experts and experienced teachers as the words which should receive priority in vocabulary study because of their importance and usefulness.

AWL = **The Academic Word List** is the most principled and widely accepted list of academic words. Averil Coxhead gathered information from academic materials across the academic disciplines to create this word list.

---

hard **23**–5, **23**–24 🔑
  external hard drive **190**–27 🔑
  hard drive **190**–19 🔑
  hard hat **92**–1, **197**–9 🔑
  hard-boiled eggs **76**–8 🔑
hardware store **152**–4
harmonica **244**–21
harvest 187–B
hash browns **80**–3
hatchback **160**–6
hats **90**–1, **95**–11 🔑
  chef's hat **93**–28
  cowboy hat **92**–18
  hard hat **92**–1, **197**–9 🔑
  ski hat **90**–11
  straw hat **90**–23
have 🔑
  have a baby **41**–L 🔑
  have a conversation **11**–L 🔑
  have a flat tire **166**–C 🔑
  have a heart attack **118**–D 🔑
  have a picnic **230**–D
  have an allergic reaction **118**–E 🔑 AWL
  have dinner **39**–S 🔑
  have regular checkups **116**–H
Hawaii-Aleutian time **19**–27
hay **187**–18
hazard **198**–6
  hazard lights **163**–36
Hazardous Materials **197**
hazardous waste **224**–12
Hazards **197**
head **104**–1 🔑
  Bluetooth headset **14**–14
  head chef **193**–7
  head of lettuce **69**–32
  headache **110**–1 🔑
  headband **90**–3
  headboard **58**–10
  headlight **162**–7
  headline **135**–7
  headphones **6**–8, **240**–4, **240**–5, **240**–6
  headset **14**–13, **191**–35
  headwaiter **193**–12
  headwrap **90**–7
  letterhead **189**–42
  overhead compartment **165**–13
headquarters / corporate offices **184**–1 🔑 AWL
health 🔑
  health history form **111**–4 🔑
  health insurance card **111**–3 🔑
HEALTH **116**–**117** 🔑
HEALTH FAIR **124**–**125** 🔑
HEALTH INSURANCE **121** 🔑
Health Problems **117** 🔑
hear 106–B 🔑
hearing 🔑
  hearing aid **117**–10 🔑 AWL
  hearing impaired **32**–12
  hearing loss **117**–2 🔑
heart **107**–38, **245**–6 🔑
  have a heart attack **118**–D 🔑
  heart disease **113**–28 🔑

hearts **239**–31 🔑
heat wave **13**–15 🔑
heating pad **115**–13
heavy **23**–13, **32**–7, **97**–27 🔑
hedge clippers **186**–11
heel **94**–22, **106**–24 🔑
  high heels **89**–21, **95**–25, **97**–32 🔑
  low heels **97**–31 🔑
height **17**–16, **32**–5 🔑
Height **32** 🔑
Heimlich maneuver **119**–19
helicopter **155**–9
helmet **93**–23, **237**–19
help 8–J, **151**–G 🔑
Help with Health Problems **117** 🔑
hem **100**–8
hen **221**–8
hepatitis **112**–9
herbal tea **81**–40 🔑
herbs **84**–9
hibiscus **217**–12
hide 246–D 🔑
high **97**–32 🔑
  high blood pressure **113**–24 🔑
  high chair **37**–6, **82**–3 🔑
  high heels **89**–21, **95**–25 🔑
  high school **200**–4 🔑
  high-rise **129**–13
  high visibility safety vest **92**–4 🔑 AWL
  junior high school **200**–3 🔑
  knee highs **91**–12 🔑
highlighter **7**–25
highway **159**–9 🔑
  highway marker **158**–17
hiking **232**–7
  hiking boots **95**–31 🔑
hills **214**–16 🔑
  downhill skiing **233**–1
hip **107**–27 🔑
hip-hop **243**–26
hippopotamus **223**–43
hire 144–B 🔑
hired hand **187**–20 🔑
Historical Terms **209** 🔑
history **111**–4, **201**–12 🔑
HISTORY **209** 🔑
hit 236–B 🔑
HIV / AIDS **113**–21
HOBBIES AND GAMES **238**–**239** 🔑
hockey **235**–14
  hockey stick **237**–11
hold 36–A 🔑
holder
  candle holder **56**–21
  policyholder **121**–5
  potholders **78**–29
  toothbrush holder **57**–24
holiday **22**–7, **22**–8 🔑
HOLIDAYS **245** 🔑
Holidays **22** 🔑
holly **216**–19
home **52**–7, **52**–12 🔑
  home healthcare aide **171**–32

home improvement store **129**–20 🔑
home phone **4**–12 🔑
homemaker **172**–33
homesick **43**–20
HOME **46**–**49** 🔑
honest **178**–4 🔑
honeybee **220**–26
hood **162**–4
Hood **162**
hoodie **89**–22
hoof / hooves **222**–17
hook **194**–39 🔑
  eye hook **194**–40 🔑
  hook and eye **99**–27 🔑
  hook and loop fastener **99**–29
horn **163**–32, **222**–21, **244**–11 🔑
  French horn **244**–13
horror story **243**–17 🔑
horse **221**–4 🔑
  horse racing **234**–19 🔑
  horseback riding **232**–9 🔑
  seahorse **218**–13
hose **53**–21
  pantyhose **91**–18
hospital **127**–9, **158**–18 🔑
  hospital bed **123**–22 🔑
  hospital gown **123**–19
HOSPITAL **122**–**123** 🔑
Hospital Room **123** 🔑
Hospital Staff **122** 🔑
hostess **82**–2
hot **13**–3, **42**–1 🔑
  hot cereal **80**–9
  hot dog **79**–6
  hot water **57**–9 🔑
  hot water bottle **115**–15 🔑
hotel **126**–3 🔑
A HOTEL **192** 🔑
hour **18**–1 🔑
house 🔑
  courthouse **127**–13
  dollhouse **59**–18
  House of Representatives **140**–3
  house painter **172**–46 🔑
  house salad **80**–15 🔑
  housekeeper **172**–34, **192**–20
  housekeeping cart **192**–19
  houseplant **56**–4, **217**–27
  townhouse **52**–6
  two-story house **52** ✦🔑
  warehouse **184**–3, **185**–7
  White House **140**–7
House **49** 🔑
HOUSE AND YARD **53** 🔑
HOUSEHOLD PROBLEMS AND REPAIRS
  62–**63** 🔑
HOUSEWORK **60**
housing **52**–11 🔑
hub **190**–26
hubcap **162**–9
hug 2–F
human resources **184**–4 🔑 AWL
humid **13**–17

272

produce section **72**–2
product **204**–9
Products **72, 73**
professional development **175**–7 AWL
program
  children's program **242**–9
  nature program **242**–7
  news program **242**–1
  open the program **210**–A
  presentation program **191**–31
  quit the program **210**–F
  shopping program **242**–10
  sports program **242**–11
  spreadsheet program **191**–30
  word processing program **191**–29
program 176–I
Programs **242**
projector **6**–5, **241**–27
promotion **175**–8 AWL
proof of insurance **138**–8
proofread 203–I
prosecuting attorney **144**–10
prospective tenant **51**–29 AWL
protect 146–D
Protect Children **147**
protector **190**–11
proton **207**–31
proud **43**–21
prunes **68**–26
pruning shears **186**–9
psychiatrist **122**–8
PUBLIC SAFETY **146**
public school 5 ◆
PUBLIC TRANSPORTATION **156** AWL
pull 120–F, **230**–A
puller **185**–10
pullover sweater **88**–3
pulse **124**–A
pumps **95**–26
Punctuation **202**
puppy **221**–12
purchase 94–A AWL
purifier **115**–14
purple **24**–6
purses **94**–2, **94**–14
push 230–B
pushpin **189**–35
put 9–X, **49**–O, **164**–I
  put away 9–Z, **60**–G
  put down 6–J
  put in 161–I
  put on 87–B, **108**–D, **109**–P, **137**–C,
    177–N
puzzle **59**–17
pyramid **205**–39

quad **5**–1
quart **75**–4
quarter
  quarter / 25 cents **26**–4
  quarter after one **18**–9
  1/4 cup **75**–8

quarter moon **215**–11
quarter to two **18**–13
3/4 sleeved **96**–13
question **212**–1, **212**–C
  question mark **202**–15
Quick and Easy Cake **77**
quiet **23**–12
quill **222**–23
quilt **58**–16
  quilt block **238**–15
quilt 238–C
quit the program **210**–F
quotation **202**–10
  quotation marks **202**–18
quotient **204**–10

rabbit **221**–13
raccoon **222**–13
race 236–S
racing **234**–19
rack **98**–16
  dish rack **54**–5
  roasting rack **78**–14
  towel rack **57**–15
racket **237**–2
racquetball **234**–12
radiation **224**–15
radiator **162**–19
radio **102**–6, **197**–22
radioactive materials **197**–7
radiologist **122**–6
radishes **69**–4
radius **205**–35
rafting **232**–2
rags **61**–9
rail **59**–10
railroad crossing **158**–14
rain **13**–11
  acid rain **224**–13
  rain boots **90**–20
  rain forest **214**–1
  raincoat **90**–18
raise 6–A
raisins **68**–25
rake **186**–8
rake 186–C
rally **143**–7
RAM (random access memory) **190**–17
ranch **52**–10
Ranch Hand **92**
rancher **187**–22
RANCHING **187**
R&B **243**–28
range **214**–15 AWL
ranger **166**–1
rash **113**–14
raspberries **68**–15
rat **63**–27, **221**–17
rattle **37**–27
  rattlesnake **219**–45
raw **70**–24
ray **218**–11

razor **109**–27
  razor blade **109**–28
reaction **118**–E AWL
read
  proofread **203**–I
  read the card **137**–G
  read the definition **8**–B AWL
  read the paper **39**–V
  read to **36**–N
Reading a Phone Bill **15**
reality show **242**–6
rearview mirror **163**–35
receipt **27**–6
receive 137–F
receiver **14**–4
reception area **188**–15 AWL
receptionist **111**–2, **173**–51, **182**–5,
  188–14
reclined seat **165**–27
record 207–D, **241**–A
records **172**–39
RECREATION **232**
Recreation Room **50**
recreational vehicle (RV) **160**–10
recruiter **174**–J
rectangle **205**–29
recycle 60–B, **225**–C
recycling bin **61**–2
red **24**–1
  red hair **33**–13
  redcoat **208**–9
  redwood **216**–18
redecorate 48 ◆
reduce 225–A
reenter 211–Q
referee **235**–6
reference librarian **135**–9
refresh button **213**–11
refrigerator **54**–9
refund 97 ◆
refuse 12–F
reggae **243**–31
register **27**–10, **73**–16 AWL
register 142–D, **161**–F AWL
registered nurse (RN) **122**–10
Registering an Account **211** AWL
registration AWL
  registration sticker **138**–13
  registration tag **138**–13
regular price **27**–2
regulations **182**–6 AWL
relatives **44**–6
relax 39–U AWL
relieved **42**–15
reliever **115**–26
religious holiday **22**–7
remain 151–E
remarried **35**–24
remote **240**–10
remove 109–Q, **134**–F AWL
remover **109**–42
renew a license **138** ◆

281

289

290

294

298

301

302

306

307

Research Bibliography

The authors and publisher wish to acknowledge the contribution of the following educators for their research on vocabulary development, which has helped inform the principles underlying *OPD*

Burt, M, J K Peyton, and R Adams *Reading and Adult English Language Learners: A Review of the Research* Washington, DC: Center for Applied Linguistics, 2003

Coady, J "Research on ESL/EFL Vocabulary Acquisition: Putting it in Context" In *Second Language Reading and Vocabulary Learning*, edited by T Huckin, M Haynes, and J Coady Norwood, NJ: Ablex, 1993

de la Fuente, M J "Negotiation and Oral Acquisition of L2 Vocabulary: The Roles of Input and Output in the Receptive and Productive Acquisition of Words" *Studies in Second Language Acquisition* 24 (2002): 81–112

DeCarrico, J "Vocabulary learning and teaching" In *Teaching English as a Second or Foreign Language,* edited by M Celcia-Murcia 3rd ed Boston: Heinle & Heinle, 2001

Ellis, R *The Study of Second Language Acquisition* Oxford: Oxford University Press, 1994

Folse, K *Vocabulary Myths: Applying Second Language Research to Classroom Teaching* Ann Arbor, MI: University of Michigan Press, 2004

Gairns, R and S Redman *Working with Words: A Guide to Teaching and Learning Vocabulary* Cambridge: Cambridge University Press, 1986

Gass, S M and M J A Torres "Attention When?: An Investigation of the Ordering Effect of Input and Interaction" *Studies in Second Language Acquisition* 27 (Mar 2005): 1–31

Henriksen, Birgit "Three Dimensions of Vocabulary Development" *Studies in Second Language Acquisition* 21 (1999): 303–317

Koprowski, Mark "Investigating the Usefulness of Lexical Phrases in Contemporary Coursebooks" *Oxford ELT Journal* 59(4) (2005): 322–332

McCrostie, James "Examining Learner Vocabulary Notebooks" *Oxford ELT Journal* 61 (July 2007): 246–255

Nation, P *Learning Vocabulary in Another Language* Cambridge: Cambridge University Press, 2001

National Center for ESL Literacy Education Staff *Adult English Language Instruction in the 21st Century* Washington, DC: Center for Applied Linguistics, 2003

National Reading Panel *Teaching Children to Read: An Evidenced-Based Assessment of the Scientific Research Literature on Reading and its Implications on Reading Instruction* 2000 https://wwwnichdnihgov/publications/pubs/nrp/documents/reportpdf

Newton, J "Options for Vocabulary Learning through Communication Tasks" *Oxford ELT Journal* 55(1) (2001): 30–37

Prince, P "Second Language Vocabulary Learning: The Role of Context Versus Translations as a Function of Proficiency" *Modern Language Journal* 80(4) (1996): 478–493

Savage, K L, ed *Teacher Training Through Video - ESL Techniques: Early Production* White Plains, NY: Longman Publishing Group, 1992

Schmitt, N *Vocabulary in Language Teaching* Cambridge: Cambridge University Press, 2000

Smith, C B *Vocabulary Instruction and Reading Comprehension* Bloomington, IN: ERIC Clearinghouse on Reading English and Communication, 1997

Wood, K and J Josefina Tinajero "Using Pictures to Teach Content to Second Language Learners" *Middle School Journal* 33 (2002): 47–51